Francis Younghusband
and
the Great Game

by the same author

THE ROAD TO ZIMBABWE 1890–1980
THROUGH THE LOOKING GLASS:
BRITISH FOREIGN POLICY IN THE AGE OF ILLUSIONS

Francis Younghusband
and
the Great Game

ANTHONY VERRIER

JONATHAN CAPE
LONDON

First published 1991
© Anthony Verrier 1991
Jonathan Cape, 20 Vauxhall Bridge Road, London SW1V 2SA

Anthony Verrier has asserted his right
under the Copyright, Designs and Patents Act, 1988
to be identified as the author of this work

A CIP catalogue record for this book
is available from the British Library

ISBN 0-224-02505-8

Printed in Great Britain by
Butler & Tanner Ltd, Frome and London

In affectionate memory
of
Frederick Warburg
who first interested me in
the Great Game

Contents

Illustrations

MAPS

The author and the publishers would like to thank the following for their kind permission to reproduce illustrations: the Royal Geographical Society: (nos. 1, 6, 7, 10, 11, 13, 15, 16, 17, 18, 19, 20, 21, 22, 23, 24); the British Library (nos. 2, 3, 4, 5, 8).

Acknowledgements

Two members of the Younghusband family gave support and encouragement. Younghusband's daughter Eileen provided a portrait, both deeply affectionate and astringent. Dame Eileen also loaned diaries and letters, which reveal her father's nature, reserved yet ardent, as no other source could possibly do. The late Elizabeth Younghusband – met through the kindness of Mrs Cecille Stampa – was a great niece of Sir Francis and provided important clues about a family never lacking in forceful opinions, forcefully expressed.

Mrs Christine Kelly, archivist of the Royal Geographical Society, encouraged and advised when spirits flagged. Indeed, to the whole staff of the Society, thanks are gratefully given.

I am grateful to the staff of the Royal Archives, the India Office Library and the London Library; the librarians of Christ Church, the Scottish Record Office, and the National Library of Ireland; the archivists of the Hereford and Hertford County Record Offices; the staff of the Ogilby Trust; the headmaster and his colleagues at Clifton College; Lady Alexandra Metcalfe; the Librarian and staff of the Royal Holloway College; my good friend Joan Barber, who as always produced an impeccable typescript from a manuscript which bore all the marks of much toil; and certainly not least Anthony Colwell and Sarah Wiesendanger at Cape, whose combination of patient exhortation and editorial skill improved the work to a marked degree. Thanks are also due to Marjorie Maclean and Evelyn Sobremonte, of the History Department, University of Calgary, for swift and efficient secretarial assistance.

I have to thank Isobel Maclean for compiling the index.

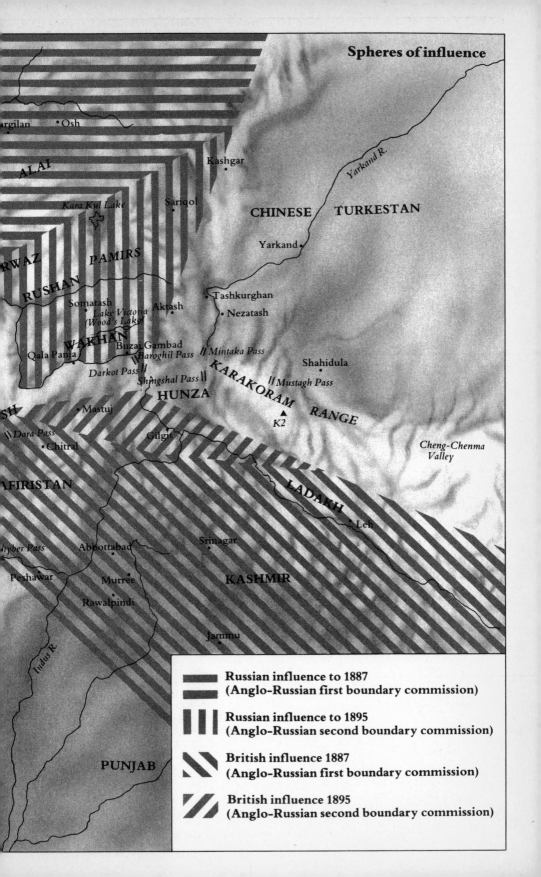

Spheres of influence

Bargilan   • Osh

ALAI

Kashgar

DARWAZ   Kara Kul Lake   Sariqol

RUSHAN   PAMIRS   **CHINESE   TURKESTAN**

Yarkand R.

Somatash   Aktash   Yarkand •

WAKHAN   Lake Victoria   Tashkurghan
(Wood's Lake)   • Nezatash

Qala Panja   Buzai Gambad   ‖ *Mintaka Pass*

Baroghil Pass   Shahidula

Darkot Pass ‖   KARAKORAM

Shingshal Pass ‖   ‖ *Mustagh Pass*

HUNZA   RANGE

KUSH   • Mastuj   K2 ▲

‖ *Dora Pass*   Gilgit
• Chitral   Cheng-Chenma
Valley

KAFIRISTAN   LADAKH

Khyber Pass   Abbottabad   Srinagar   • Leh

• Peshawar   Murree   **KASHMIR**
Rawalpindi

Indus R.   Jammu •

PUNJAB

▬	**Russian influence to 1887** (Anglo-Russian first boundary commission)
‖‖‖	**Russian influence to 1895** (Anglo-Russian second boundary commission)
╱╱╱	**British influence 1887** (Anglo-Russian first boundary commission)
╱╱	**British influence 1895** (Anglo-Russian second boundary commission)

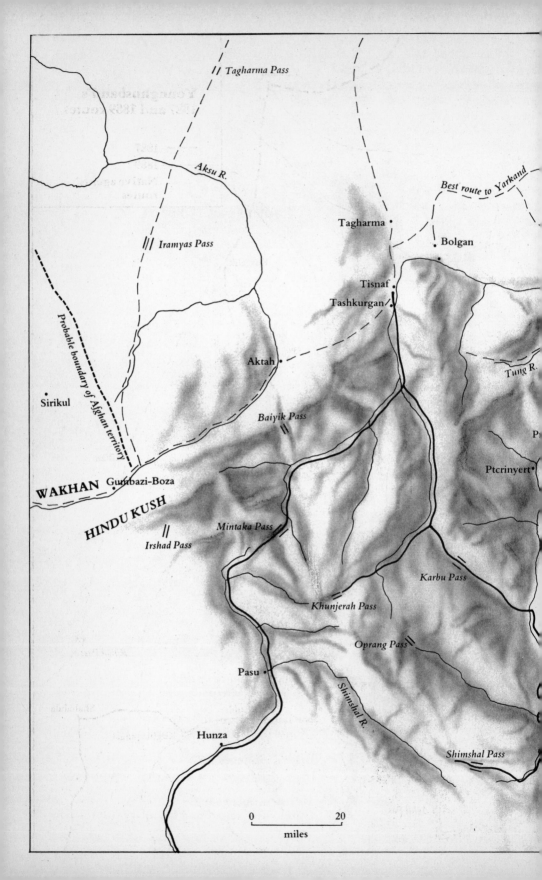

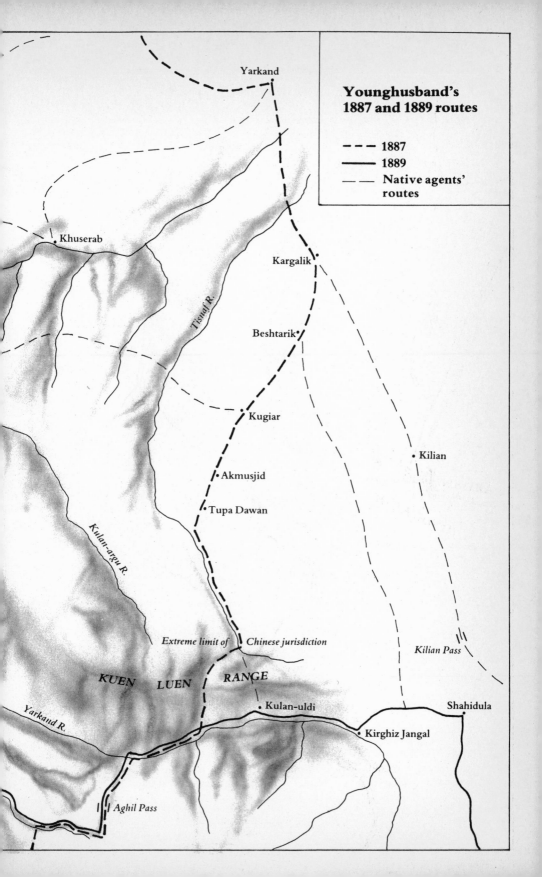

Younghusband's
1887 and 1889 routes

- - - 1887
——— 1889
- - - Native agents'
routes

Yarkand

Khuserab

Kargalik

Tisnaf R.

Beshtarik•

Kugiar

Kilian

Akmusjid

Tupa Dawan

Kulan-argu R.

Extreme limit of   Chinese jurisdiction

KUEN   LUEN   RANGE

Kilian Pass

Shahidula

Kulan-uldi

Kirghiz Jangal

Yarkand R.

Aghil Pass

Preface

This book is not a biography in the usual sense of the word but rather the evocation of a man's personality and the spirit of his times. Younghusband was born into the world of Kipling, where British officials and soldiers played the Great Game, a cold war of wits against the Russians and their inexorable advance south towards India from the wastes of Central Asia. Viceroys and agents presumed to alter the course of British Indian policies so as to realise their own ambitions; orders from the Home government were ignored, mistakes were made, wars fought and careers ruined; delusions of grandeur were commonplace. Only belatedly did the Home government intervene, calling viceroys and agents to order in pursuit of *rapprochement* with St Petersburg.

None carried his delusions further, or into more distant places, than Sir Francis Younghusband. He experienced a brief moment of triumph on entering Lhasa in August 1904 but, after that 'the bright day was done'; he became a scapegoat and suffered rejection by the men he had loyally served. His later years were, however, marked by esteem and modest distinction. Presidency of the Royal Geographical Society between 1919 and 1922 was a fitting honour, repaid by Younghusband's advocacy of the first Everest expeditions; founding and sustaining the World Council of Faiths – often in the face of ignorant hostility and prejudice – provided Younghusband with spiritual solace.

These achievements, though, do not form part of the book's story. *Younghusband and the Great Game* developed from speculation about a curious aspect of British imperialism in its Asiatic context: a consistent but quite irrational fear of Russian expansionism – in which Younghusband believed tenaciously. Some personal experience of

Britain's long 'retreat from Empire' in the post-war years focused attention on the legacy which nineteenth-century imperialists left for their heirs. Fred Warburg, prince of publishers, encouraged conjecture. Elizabeth Monroe who, with characteristic support, 'thought I might come in useful at St Antony's' provided an introduction to academic life not, then, available to many journalists. Fellowship of the Royal Geographical Society, and use of its library, further improved my education.

The book has had a long gestation but, with this century's cold war, one hopes, finally over, the time seems right for publication.

PART ONE

THE GREAT GAME

'The Black Sea and the Caucasas and these great Asiatic Empires inflame imaginations wonderfully.'

Lord Melbourne

'Turkestan, Afghanistan, Transcaspia, Persia – to many these words breathe only a sense of utter remoteness, or a memory of strange vicissitudes, and of moribund romance. To me, I confess, they are the pieces on a chess board upon which is being played out a game for the domination of the world.'

Lord Curzon

I

꧁꧂꧁꧂꧁꧂꧁꧂꧁꧂꧁꧂꧁꧂꧁꧂꧁꧂꧁꧂꧁꧂꧁꧂

Sir Francis Younghusband

Francis Edward Younghusband was born at Murree in the Punjab on 31 May 1863, the second son of John Younghusband a major-general in the Royal Artillery. Four of his brothers served in India, two becoming generals, two being killed in action. General John Younghusband served with Napier in Sind and with Nicholson in the Punjab. Francis Younghusband's brothers served with him in India; both became generals, the youngest brother concluding his service in Persia in the First World War. No more representative Anglo-Indian family can be found. With such a background a path in life is marked. The Younghusband who played and lost the Game went to Clifton, where he was a contemporary of Henry Newbolt, the laureate of imperial endeavour.

Failing twice for Woolwich, Younghusband passed into Sandhurst in 1881, being commissioned the following year into the King's Dragoon Guards, a fashionable and expensive regiment with no Indian connections, although stationed in Meerut. In 1884 he escaped from that world and was attached to the 'Intelligence Branch – Quartermaster-General's Office' for reconnaissance duties in Kohat and Kashmir. Younghusband secured 'General leave in India from 12 February 1886 to 30 November 1887', enabling him to explore in China, and return to Simla through Sinkiang, or what was officially called 'The Northern Frontier of Kashmir'.

After this adventurous journey, Younghusband became 'Political Assistant, 3rd Class (seconded), on special duty under the Government of India, Foreign Department', from October 1890 to April 1892; this is the period covered by his operations on the Pamirs which culminated in his explusion from the area by a Russian agent. Thereafter he was successively Political Officer in Hunza and, until the end of 1894, Political Agent in Chitral. From then until late in 1897 he took an extended leave – to observe the relief of Chitral and to witness comparable activities in South Africa, most notably the Jameson Raid. There followed one of those interludes, never easy to explain in a life of action lived mostly beyond the limelight. Between November 1897 and June 1903 Younghusband occupied a series of appointments in Rajputana, Haraoti, Tonk and Indore, states in central India, 'a gilded life of perfect security and much pomposity, about as different from the old frontier life as could well be imagined'.[1] Why Younghusband was thus immured has never been explained satisfactorily, but the Game had its penalties as well as its rewards.

In May 1903, however, Curzon picked Younghusband to join the Tibet frontier commission. 'It was like being awakened. I was suddenly myself again, and all that exotic life of Maharajas and Durbars and gold chairs and scarlet chuprassies a sickly dream.'[2] Fortune had other tricks in store, however. The Tibet frontier commission became an expedition, ending in the public repudiation by the British government of the terms of Tibetan subjection to Calcutta's *diktat* which Younghusband sought, demanded, and secured in Lhasa. The official machine, so apt at disguising Younghusband's part in the Great Game, pondered the repudiation and produced the appropriate answer: Younghusband became a Knight Commander of the Indian Empire, an order which Gladstone had always considered good enough for 'Indian clerks'. The scapegoat of a viceroy's adventure was then posted back to the Foreign Department, from April 1906 as 'Political Agent, 3rd Class reorganisation'.

Although Younghusband was immediately made Resident in Kashmir, holding that appointment until 1909, he was, in terms of a career, broken, not made by his Tibetan experience, and his treatment at the hands of Curzon and the government at home. Younghusband was finished in 1905, aged forty-two. Thereafter the active man turned to a kindly, cloudy philosophy of universal goodwill. A widespread impression of Younghusband as a dreamer would be wrong; whatever he did was done with all his might. The system had, however, dealt harshly with him. When Sir Francis Younghusband died in July 1942, after a life most honourably lived, the world of his youth had gone, and had been ebbing even as he was removed from the centre of its affairs.

This book is concerned with Younghusband's part in the Game. Since, however, Younghusband was the kind of man who is active by psychological necessity as well as inheritance, and because he was a victim of the cold war rather than a free agent in it, something of his inner nature and the mood of his times deserve appreciation and comment. The motive which animated Younghusband and the force which drove him were factors in his make-up which he was never able fully to realise or understand, much less articulate: similarly, he never seems to have grasped that he was used by others to serve their own purposes. Younghusband was not a complex man in that there were aspects of his nature which were diametrically opposed. Except in his latter years the reflective part of him was strictly subordinate to the active, and was employed to stimulate further endeavour. He was, both in in the conventional usage of his times and, in a more personal sense, a religious man. 'I have made my own religion for myself';[3] its purpose, in his years of playing the Great Game, was to sustain the conviction that 'through all my life I have had from time to time the feeling that I was born for some great thing'.[4]

What that was remained a mystery. It was not success in the obvious sense. Despite his intense, inner – and unrealised – compulsions, Younghusband was an unshakeably modest and self-effacing man. He had a strong sense of Victorian patriotism, and a conviction that Russia hungered for India, but he did not consciously see himself as a kind of imperial Roland of the Pamirs or one picked out by destiny to keep the Northern Frontier safe. Yet, in 1889 and 1891 this was precisely how Younghusband behaved. His strategic views lacked any originality whatsoever; the role of higher authority, embodied especially in the viceregal Curzon, was to put him on the road to the hills, where he could, alone, live an intense life of action and danger, with only his thoughts for company. He was willing to be used – 'for life is a battle', and 'the best should be sacrificied'[5] – and Curzon, in picking him for a task of peril when he was fearful that the future held nothing but 'Maharajas and Durbars', found him a perfect scapegoat. Younghusband was solitary even at the school; and disliked 'the system that boys should not have a moment to themselves'. He detested regimental life; without realising it he wanted his own way, not only in going where the spirit listed, but in the more mundane affairs of men. Cantonment life and taking young ladies down to dinner only hardened his heart against society;

his world had to be one where action and reflection could alternate without interruption even from his own kith and kin.[6]

There was, however, at the core of it all, a conflict. Younghusband's letters to his father and sisters from the time when he landed in India to the end of the Tibet expedition form, with his diaries and journals, a revealing picture of a man unable either to accept or even participate in a community. Whether that community lived pointless or purposeful lives was irrelevant. Younghusband's service in central India was not all durbars and maharajas; much of it was constructive work in the Guardian tradition. He held it of no account: 'How much more difficult it was to write reports than to tackle the Hunza Chief face to face.'[7] Only in solitude could Younghusband free himself from his endemic depression, from his 'unworthiness'; only in remote places could he write freely to his adored father and sister Emily of his longing for them. Only when alone could he write to her, 'for six years I can hardly even mention your name.'[8]

So great was his need to communicate with them, who made no demands on him, that he invariably described his intelligence operations in detail when writing. This compulsion proved stronger than the requirements of security. It is not surprising that marriage, with its relentless challenge to the ego, remained a mystery to Younghusband; it is typical of his scrupulous honesty that, in recalling his married life, he admitted his unsuitability. To the end he remained restless if confined. Had Younghusband not been jilted when still new to India, much might have been different. There is, arguably though, a fitness in these things.

Younghusband's nature did not, however, fulfil itself in abnegation of the kind comforting to higher authority when crises erupted. He was both stubborn and impetuous, never more so than in times of acute danger. These attributes, coupled with a great unawareness or innocence about the real nature and working of the imperial machine of his times as an agent, meant that Younghusband rarely grasped what was actually at stake.

In a clear and unambiguous assessment of the role of a frontier officer, whose life must always be lived at high tension, Younghusband unwittingly revealed that element in his character which lay just beneath the surface of an obedient imperial agent. 'A frontier officer should see to it, then, that he is as fit in nerve and temper and spirit as he is in body and mind. He should not be taken unawares by the most heartrending contentions. He must be capable of keeping his temper, maintaining his spirit, and pressing his opinion with equal equanimity and cheerfulness.'[9]

Younghusband, however, had an individual notion of how opinions should be pressed, and it was one which partly explains his fate.

> An agent must, too, learn the way of carrying the Government with him. He and they are both bent on the same object. There may be differences as to ways and means of carrying it out; but it is important that he should understand the Government's point of view and that they should understand his. He should soak himself in the Government policy till he is saturated with it. But when he has completely absorbed it he should present the local conditions clearly and convincingly to Government. He and he alone can do that, and he should learn to do it with effect . . . British Governments are excellent governments to serve. They are most reasonable and considerate and accommodating with their agents. And if a local case is put temperately before them, and backed by sound arguments, they are perfectly ready to accept the views of the man on the spot![10]

Only a man of singular innocence could have written these words; that Younghusband should go on to cite Cromer as 'a perfect example of the way in which an agent on the spot can carry Government with him' emphasises his isolation from the political facts of life. Agents and men on the spot had more independence under the British imperial system than any other. The Great Game was played by British agents revelling in their freedom; their opposite numbers were never so free. The British agent only had to make one serious slip, however, and he was finished, the more especially if he 'carried' his government with him by the simple expedient of acting first and asking for approval afterwards. It is doubtful whether Younghusband would have gone to Tibet after his experiences on the Pamirs if Curzon had not been Viceroy. It is not surprising that an agent who dictated terms to the Tibetans when his government was backing out of imperial adventures should be shunted off to a bureaucratic siding.

Cromer would never have stepped out of line; he was indeed an agent, but not in Younghusband's mould. The latter, to a far greater extent than Gordon or T. E. Lawrence, was born out of his time. He simply never grasped that being a British officer, as Gordon always felt himself to be, or king-making and breaking, as Lawrence described his agent's role, had very little to do with the politics of imperialism. Both Gordon and Lawrence understood the world of men, however much they professed to despise it; Younghusband never did. He regretted the days of the first Indian Governor-General, Warren Hastings when frontier policy was based on taking risks. Quite apart from the fact that in those distant, confident days frontiers were made, not fudged by buffer zones, Younghusband did not, in his self-absorption, perceive what Gordon and Lawrence – and Kipling – in their different ways knew very well: that the whole imperial impulse had become a business, a shabby one by Gordon's time, a failing one by Lawrence's. Nothing is more revealing than Younghusband's belief that India should not be independent because it would sunder two great cultures, and the assertions of men so comparatively liberal as Sir John Strachey and Lansdowne that India was not going to be independent, and that was that.[11]

With soldiers like Roberts, Brackenbury and Chapman, all of whom did much to push him, Younghusband was at home. With politicians like the Viceroy, Curzon and his colleagues and friends at Westminster Younghusband was nowhere. Such men were not 'bent on the same object'; they were bent on fame, or the continuation of their Party in office. These objectives could clash. For example, 'Balfour once said that Curzon as Viceroy claimed a predominance for his views on policy which, if granted, "would raise India to the position of an independent and not always friendly power".'[12] When such a clash did occur, and over the very issue which Balfour so neatly summarised, there had to be someone who could be sacrificed. Curzon lived to fight another day, although it was not until 1918 that he got his chance to play the Great Game again. By then Younghusband – in 1914 he had offered his services first to the India Office, then to the War Office; both were declined – was a mere spectator of events.

2

Rules of the Game

Younghusband, his achievements and failures, can only be understood if put in historical context. He was heir not only to a tradition
of imperial service in India, but also to the execution of strategies
based on a presumed Russian threat to the whole sub-continent and,
in consequence, to British imperial policy as a whole.

Muscovite Russia had been expanding south and east to the
Causcasus, Caspian and Turkestan throughout the later eighteenth
century without arousing undue alarm in either the Home or Indian
government. Two subsequent developments, however, established
a conviction in both London and Calcutta that Russia did have
designs on India.

These developments were intermittent Franco-Russian schemes,
during the Napoleonic Wars, for a joint invasion of India by way of
Persia and Turkestan respectively; and a growing appreciation in
London and Calcutta that neither Ottoman nor Persian rulers could
withstand seemingly inexorable Russian expansion. Later in the
century, and as Russian expansion gathered in momentum throughout Transcaucasia and Turkestan, a like apprehension was extended
to Afghanistan and China. The Franco-Russian invasion schemes
were ingenious, and detailed, on paper: Napoleon's temporary
conquest of Egypt and the Levant established, to French and Russian
military visionaries, a grand strategy capable of threatening India
from north and west. The schemes, however, remained on paper:
even the visionaries were daunted by the prospect of marching a
joint force across hundreds of miles of inhospitable terrain in order
to emulate the feats of Alexander the Great.

These schemes had their effect nonetheless, and from the brief
period of Franco-Russian amity which followed the Peace of Tilsit

in July 1807 we may discern the growth of a singular British imperial disease: Russophobia. The practical difficulties facing any Czar contemplating the invasion of India no more checked the growth of this disease than did the beliefs of Dalhousie (the last Governor-General of the East India Company) and others that Russian imperial expansion was based on the attainment of a different objective: the assertion and consolidation of power in Central Asia. Russophobia was not to be cured by the process of investigation and analysis; moreover, throughout the nineteenth century a spate of books and articles from the Russian press, in which Napoleonic and Czarist schemes were mischievously revived, ensured that the disease became a chronic element in British imperial policy. Whether or not Russia's prime objective in and beyond Central Asia was only assertion and consolidation of power – by means no different from those by which Britain conquered, and held, India – it cannot be denied that putting British governments in the vapours about threats to the sub-continent never failed to give pleasure to Anglophobes in St Petersburg.

Fears of Russian designs on India were not only inflamed by the failure of Persia, Afghanistan, and China to withstand what the traveller and historian Peter Fleming has aptly called 'the grey tide', but by the inherent problem of defending India in strategic terms from the threat or the fact of invasion. With every passing year the problem not only appeared to increase in scale and complexity, but actually did so in terms of Britain's disposable strategic assets.

Throughout the nineteenth century the grey tide certainly lapped forward: 'In the half century preceding 1880, Russia advanced some 1,200 miles towards India. In the four years ending in June 1884 [effectively, the final conquest of northern Persia] she advanced about 600 miles along the line based on the Caspian.'[1] Czarist and Napoleonic notions of invading India appeared, eighty years later, to be reaching fruition, in purely Russian terms. Whilst Russia's advance towards India so remorselessly continued, British imperial expansion in Egypt and Africa ensured that the forces readily available to defend the sub-continent against external attack decreased rather than otherwise.

Despite the growth of Russophobia in Calcutta and Simla, London and St Petersburg had no reason to quarrel, every reason to seek accommodation. This was the level where Anglo-Russian relations were finally arbitrated. The last quarter of the nineteenth century and, despite Curzon's ambition and Younghusband's folly, the early years of the twentieth, were to witness a patient search for accommodation, enshrined in the 1907 Anglo-Russian Convention. This defined respective spheres of influence, or provided for diplomatic and commercial compensation in lieu of them, in Persia, Afghanistan and Tibet.

British and Russian motives for seeking an *entente* were fundamentally different: Britain was concerned with its empire, Russia with the menace of Germany. But, the search in London and St Petersburg for accommodation notwithstanding, the British strategic problem remained constant and complex throughout the nineteenth century. Russophobia aside, numbers were simply insufficient to garrison India and establish a field army which could either defend the Northern Frontier in the event of outright Russian attack, or execute a pre-emptive operation into territory west of a line Herat-Kandahar-Quetta. Such an operation was intended, on paper, as preliminary to a major assault on Russia in Transcaspia, thence west to the Caspian, and Black Sea. No thought was ever given to marching through the northern passes, despite fears that a Russian army might attempt it. By a further paradox, little consideration was given to India's vulnerability to invasion from territories west of the Herat-Kandahar-Quetta line. One might suppose, therefore, that the distinct improbability of a direct Russian invasion of India would have lessened fears and put the man-power factor into some sort of perspective.

Yet the fact remains that Russia's seemingly inexorable advance towards India's northern frontiers not only sustained Russophobia in various quarters, but led to the concoction of schemes for the establishment of a field army in India which could meet either direct attack or engage in pre-emptive operations. Even today, and with the perspective of time, it is difficult to take such schemes seriously or to know whether their proponents did so. No British soldier in or concerned with India, and whether 'expert' or otherwise, denied that maintenance of internal security by the establishment of garrisons throughout India was the priority strategic requirement, absorbing much of the available strength of both the British and Indian armies.

A secondary requirement was to maintain the stability of the Northern and North-West Frontiers, not in terms of a Russian threat but in order that the Punjab might also remain peaceful. These requirements would obtain – and until Independence in 1947 did so – whether a Russian threat was taken seriously or not; whether a 'close frontier' – and demarcation of the territories of buffer states and satellites – was established, or a 'forward policy' based on opposition to definable borders, was pursued; and whether agents playing the Great Game succeeded or failed in sustaining that policy by subterfuge and bribe.[2]

The overriding internal security requirement should have scotched the idea of a field army. With an enormous effort, a *two-division* force was raised for the invasion of Afghanistan in November 1878. Most of this force was unavoidably committed to lines of communication tasks. In no sense was a credible field army established, even by Kitchener, twenty years later. Whether or not the Czar of the day 'mobilised the whole Turkestan army', no field army raised in India could match the numbers which the Russian Army as such could commit as required to Central Asia. Russia disposed of a standing army of over 1,000,000 men; Britain of under 200,000. The Indian or 'native' army consisted after the Mutiny of less than 300,000. When all the various factors of Russia's European priorities and Britain's world-wide commitments are taken into consideration, the fact remains that the latter, in India, was permanently on the defensive against the former.

By the 1880s, and in the aftermath of the Second Afghan War, fears of Russian pressure on India's Northern Frontier reached a climax. During this decade, Russian exploration of the Pamirs completed or appeared to complete, a process of territorial consolidation based on Tashkent and Osh. As a result, forward Russian posts, whether temporary or intended as permanent, were actually closer to the Hindu Kush than British garrisons at Peshawar, Murree and Rawalpindi. Distances, to men who looked so anxiously at the Northern Frontier, had shrunk to not more than 200 miles. The fears may seem as irrational as the phobias which nourished them, but there is a 'looking glass' factor which should be borne in mind. South of the Hindu Kush the terrain, although less precipitous than across the highest mountains, remains difficult for the passage of men and animals. North of the Hindu Kush, however, as the first British Agent at Gilgit, John Biddulph, reported in 1878, 'The Russians could not only advance on to the Pamirs by way of unclaimed territory but . . . an "excellent road" ran from the Russian military post at Osh across the Alai to Sariqol which was thought

"So good that only about twenty five miles . . . required any preparation for the passage of guns" [artillery].'

As if these revelations were not enough to flutter the dovecotes in Calcutta and Simla, a detailed exploration of the northern passes and the Pamirs undertaken in 1885 and completed before the decade was out, noted: 'The most curious and startling feature in this part of the world is that the mighty main range suddenly sinks down abruptly into absolute insignificance, and for a short distance low undulating hills take the place of lofty peaks.'³ As Biddulph put it, reversing the looking glass in order to impress his fears on the Viceroy, Lord Northbrook, 'You step in a day from India into Asia.' Biddulph, however, ignored more fundamental considerations.

The terrain south of the passes was an effective deterrent to the passage of men, artillery and animals – except in small and isolated parties. This fact was ignored. The viceroys of the period, Dufferin and Lansdowne, were proponents and exponents of the forward policy. Because facts were ignored, and because Dufferin and Lansdowne were strong and determined men, Calcutta and Simla collectively put the worst possible construction on the Russian advance from Osh, and paid the most serious attention to the descriptions just given of the ease with which the Pamirs could be traversed. No field army existed – except on paper. What then was to be done to deter Russian designs?

Only one decision was possible on the basis of such reasoning, or prejudice: the Great Game, which had been somewhat in abeyance during the viceroyalty of Lord Ripon – Gladstone's appointment – was to be resumed with full vigour, based on a policy of finally buying the allegiance of the petty states lying south of the passes. Ripon had been fully in agreement with Gladstone's dictum that Britain's representatives at 'a distant point' should do as they were told by higher authority. He was, moreover, opposed to a policy of buffers and bribes. Dufferin and Lansdowne disagreed – up to a point. The stage was thus set for Francis Younghusband to play the Game, unconscious of the perils of failure which befell an agent who interpreted orders wholly to suit his own compulsions.

3

The Nature of the Players

Those agents who played the Great Game shared many characteristics, but differed in background, upbringing, and temperament. Whether civilians or soldiers, they knew that Calcutta and Simla would give them a pretty free hand when the forward policy held sway. The real power, however, lay with the Home government, which would give short shrift to agents whose actions caused embarrassment in Britain's dealings with St Petersburg or in her conduct with foreign policy as a whole. This fact was not understood by Younghusband, or many others.

In the barren areas bordering the Northern Frontier, agents often suffered from a lack of information. London was not always prompt in transmitting to Calcutta intelligence received from St Petersburg. When such intelligence was passed on it was often dismissed due to Russophobia in the Indian civil and military establishments. Neither was it easy for the agents to gain information as to the motives and actions of the Shah in Tehran, the Amir in Kabul, the Chinese authorities and the host of petty rulers squabbling and feuding between the Hindu Kush and Jammu.

Several agents had been regular soldiers and, however much they became absorbed in the machinations of the viceroy's 'Foreign Office' – the Indian Political Department – remained convinced that they had a semi-independent and very active role in creating buffer states and satellites on the basis of a somewhat illusory military authority. Two of the more successful agents in terms of acquiring intelligence and surveying territory, Ney Elias and William McNair, were civilians, absolved from a psychological necessity or professional compulsion to order people about.

Younghusband had been trained as a soldier and, like others

before him, was never able to grasp that the Home government was always liable to decide at what point the Game had to be seen in the light of wider imperial considerations. He was equally unaware of the Viceroy's power to manipulate his agents for his own ends. He was not alone. There is a striking similarity between Younghusband's treatment in 1904 by the Viceroy, Lord Curzon, and that of two agents endowed with a similar temperament, Alexander Burnes and Louis Cavagnari, at the hands of Lords Auckland and Lytton – both extreme in their interpretation of responsibility – during the First and before the Second Afghan Wars. By the same token, the British government in every case was initially disposed to let 'the man on the spot and those who know the country', in Queen Victoria's revealing words, precipitate events by bold and forward actions. In every case, however, discovery in London that such actions had caused or compounded problems with Russia rather than solved them led to painful retribution visited on governor-generals, viceroys, and Younghusband.

4

First Afghan War
1830–1840

Alexander Burnes, 'Officiating Resident' in Afghanistan, wrote bitterly of Auckland two months before he was butchered by a Kabul mob on 2 November 1841: 'Alas! I did not believe my first interview with the long, tall, gaunt man on the couch at Bowood was to end thus.'[1] These words, written by a besieged, doomed agent at a distant point, were a fitting obituary for one who was as susceptible to the lure of fame as his successors Louis Cavagnari and Francis Younghusband. In all three cases – two concerning Afghanistan, the third Tibet – desire for name and fame outran the performance of tasks which were, in any case, dictated not only by the ambitions, or compulsions, of governor-generals and viceroys, but distorted by a false perspective on events.

The genesis of the First Afghan War was exactly the same as the Second: 'Afghan overtures to Russia automatically involved Afghan hostility to British India.'[2] This appreciation of Auckland's was based on a false premise: the truth was that successive amirs of Afghanistan throughout the nineteenth century insisted endlessly to British and Russian envoys alike that they simply wanted to be left alone. Any desire which they might have to recover territory, rather than enlarge their domains, was based on the search for an Afghan identity which would not only reassure their mighty neighbours about the stability of Kabul's rule, but disabuse them of the notion that interference in Afghan affairs would increase the stability of imperial power and authority. Abdur Rahman, Amir of Kabul and Afghanistan, with whom the British authorities in India experienced a testing relationship throughout the 1880s and 1890s, vividly described Calcutta's constant pressure on him to do what viceroys bid as 'driving an awl into his stomach'.

In October 1838 Auckland intended to drive an awl into the Amir Dost Mohammed's stomach. Auckland had succumbed to a dispatch from the East India Company Court of Directors dated 25 June 1836, of which the material passage runs: 'To judge as to what steps it may be proper and desirable for you to take to watch, more closely than has hitherto been attempted, the progress of events in Afghanistan, and to counteract the progress of Russian influence in a quarter which, from its proximity to our Indian possessions, could not fail, if it were once established, to act injuriously on the system of our Indian alliances, possibly to interfere even with the tranquility of our own territory.'[3] Auckland, lacking judgement, construed Dost Mohammed's refusal to accept a British envoy at Kabul as justification for invasion.

As with Disraeli's choice of Lytton in 1876, Melbourne's appointment of Auckland was both a belated and unfortunate recognition of the Company's desire for a pliant instrument to assert and extend imperial authority. Afghan overtures to Russian were non-existent in 1836, a fact of which Melbourne, so far as he cared about these things at all, was quite aware. Auckland, temperamentally all for a quiet life, and certainly averse to either an assertion or extension of imperial authority, nevertheless allowed himself to be persuaded that mutual Afghan-Russian overtures were in the wind. He let himself believe that an invasion of Afghanistan was both feasible and desirable in order to protect 'the system of our Indian alliances . . . [and] the tranquility of our own territory'.[4]

What has been well called 'the moral and political blindness which characterised the origins, progress, and fatal end of the British expedition in Afghanistan'[5] is interesting mainly because of the character of Burnes, Auckland's protégé and victim. A Scot, from Montrose, physically puny and insignificant, he embraced religion with the fervour of those incipiently evangelical times but, at the ripe age of nineteen, became convert to a more compelling vocation: the secret service. An appointment in Cutch as assistant to the Resident, Sir Henry Pottinger, inclined Burnes first to consider a Russian threat to India from the direction of the Mekran and Seistan. Burnes thus followed in Pottinger's footsteps, who for years had been 'methodically working to find out what would happen if a Russian army found a way into Persia.'[6]

In 1810 Pottinger had travelled through Baluchistan into Persian territory, thence by way of Isfahan to Herat. This bold and adventurous journey was, perhaps, rendered possible by Pottinger's disguise as a 'Mohammedan Saint . . . carrying a stout stick as a protection against dogs.' On his return, Pottinger concluded that the Helmand desert and the wastes of Mekran and Sind formed an impassable barrier to an invading army, but that from Herat and Kabul the case might be very different. Sixty years later Russophobes were to take the Helmand desert and Seistan seriously – passage, with careful planning, was proved to be relatively straightforward – but by the time Pottinger settled into his duties at Cutch, it was the northern passes which were beginning to arouse fears. Not surprisingly, therefore, they became the destination of Burnes' first major journey. In 1827, aged twenty-five, he was sent on his way; a quasi-diplomatic mission to present a gift of dray horses from Lord Ellenborough, President of the Company's Board of Control, to none other than Ranjit Singh, creator of a Sikh kingdom north of the Sutlej, and the most powerful native ruler between the Hindu Kush and British governed territory to the south.

There is much that was appropriate in all the elements governing this mission. Ellenborough, President of the Board of Control was, in truth, the force which impelled Auckland into courses he instinctively feared. He perceived that Ranjit Singh was, to a degree, courted by Dost Mohammed after his conquest of Kashmir – a situation which obtained until the former was defeated by a Company army in 1845, whereupon this much disputed territory became, in name, a feudatory of the British Crown. Burnes understood strategic and political reality well enough when not distracted by flattery and ambition. 'The Punjab commands Hindustan', he wrote after his mission, adding: 'the ruler of the Punjab will always be a desirable ally to Britain, for he may invite the disaffection of Kabul, and unsettle, if not harass, the British territory.'[7] These prescient words, taken so much to heart a generation later by proponents of a close frontier, would have saved Burnes – and his spiritual successors – much trouble if he had heeded them. If Burnes had cemented his relationship with Ranjit Singh he would have been a happier man. The history of the next fifteen years – and, indeed, of the British on and beyond India's northern frontiers – might have been very different.

It was not to be. Maybe Burnes enjoyed himself too much at Lahore. He resisted the blandishments of the dancing girls, dressed as boys, who performed what best may be described as a transvestite ballet on the theme of Cupid. Ranjit Singh referred jovially to these adornments as his troops, but Burnes was more interested in his French and Italian officered army, by all accounts as good a fighting force as anything which the Company could put into the field. Burnes spotted the Koh-i-noor diamond, later to form part of Queen Victoria's loot, but then flashing on Ranjit Singh's sleeve. He noted rather unkindly that Mr Leckie, one of his companions, was overcome by Sikh festivities, and although invited to collect presents scarcely less magnificent than those bestowed on Burnes himself 'was unable to attend from indisposition'.

All this was diverting, and Burnes had apparently not only impressed Ranjit Singh but, with Lieutenant Wood of the Bombay Marine, had seen the lower Indus territories properly surveyed. He was, however, set on greater things. 'I have hung the sword in the hall and entered the Cabinet as a civilian'[8] he had written to his friend and patron Joseph Hume before commencing his Lahore embassy and in 1832 he set out to prove it. Just a year after Lieutenant Arthur Conolly, an intense young officer of the Bengal Cavalry, had returned to India after travelling from England by way of Tabriz, Herat, Kandahar and the Bolan Pass, Burnes set off for Kabul, Balkh, Bokhara, Khiva, the Caspian, Bushire, home and fame. 'Furth, fortune,' as the old Scots saying has it, was rarely better exemplified than in this journey, which made 'Bokhara' Burnes the lion of the London drawing room, a wonderful man in the eyes of William IV, to whom his travel-struck subject responded by talking of 'the designs of Russia'.

This much we know of Burnes, and it is a matter of record that, in London 'Lord Holland was eager to catch him for Holland House. Lord Lansdowne was bent upon carrying him off to Bowood. Charles Grant, then President of the Board of Control, sent him to the Prime Minister, Lord Grey, who had long confidential conferences with him.'[9] Discussions with Grant and Grey might have seemed more flattering to Burnes – and more important for history – than the salons of Holland House or the glades of Bowood, but it was at the latter that he met the man who was to ruin him. There he met Lord Auckland, shortly to become Governor-General, 'a bachelor, forty-nine years old, "quiet and unobtrusive in his manners, of a somewhat cold and impassive temperament, and altogether of a reserved and retiring nature"'.[10] This was the man, not originally intended for the post, the beneficiary in 1836 of a Whig government replacing Wellington's short-lived ministry, ignorant, other than through family connections, of India, who was about to try a fall with Dost Mohammed, Amir of Afghanistan.

'It is a trick, in my opinion, unworthy of our Government, which cannot fail, when detected, as it most probably will be, to excite the jealousy and indignation of the powers on whom we play it.' Thus, in November 1830, did Sir John Malcom, a member of the Governor-General's Council and one of British India's most able soldier-administrators, denounce not only covert intelligence operations but the dangers posed by any tricks involved in the attempt at bringing an amir at Kabul under British authority. In 1830 the Governor-General was Lord William Bentinck who, despite sanctioning Burnes' mission to Ranjit Singh, was wholly opposed to a forward policy if it threatened Calcutta's relations with Kabul. Malcom and Bentinck were of one mind, not only in regard to Kabul, but in opposing diplomatic missions which in fact were little more than a masquerade for intelligence operations on the one hand and covertly executed policies on the other.[11]

It was, however, on just such an operation that Burnes embarked in November 1836; Auckland, with the Home government's tacit, or passive approval, and with Ellenborough's spur goading him forward, sent Burnes, a flattered subordinate, on a mission which, whilst professing amity with Dost Mohammed, was designed as a means whereby the latter's presumed partiality for Russian overtures would justify his removal and legitimise his replacement by Shah Shujah. This unlucky prince had been deposed by Dost Mohammed in 1815, since when the *de facto* Amir had given every sign not only of wanting to cement relations with Calcutta, but to adopt a conciliatory if hardly neutral attitude to Ranjit Singh. Blind to the fact that Shah Shujah was incapable either of diplomacy or compromise, Auckland insisted that Burnes issue a *démarche* to Dost Mohammed: desist from his alleged involvement with Russian agents, or take the consequences.

Burnes had the wit to see what the real consequence would be: humiliation for Auckland, because Dost Mohammed, having personal qualities and the protection of a mountain fortress, might be subdued but could not be destroyed. Burnes, moreover, had perceived that Russian overtures were cautious, Dost Mohammed's response frigid. Burnes was, however, almost fatalistically convinced that war was inevitable, and he returned from Kabul to India, ready if hardly willing to support an invading expeditionary force. Burnes' task was 'to smooth the way with the Amirs of Sind and the Khan of Khelat for the passage through their territories of a British army which was about to be despatched to Afghanistan to aid in the restoration of Sha Shujah'. Burnes' state of mind is best illustrated by his own grandiose words, written on New Year's Day, 1839: 'Treaty making on a great scale, and what is well, carrying all before me.'

Burnes accompanied the invading army to Kabul, was knighted for his services, and remained immured in the Bala Hissar 'with but little to do, and with no power of responsibility, offering advice which was seldom acted on, and thoroughly dissatisfied with the state of affairs'.[12] Dost Mohammed was easy to depose – although he later returned – but investment of Afghanistan proving imposs-ible, the invading army disintegrated. Burnes' murder was the onset of a series of disasters which concluded with one solitary British survivor, Surgeon Brydon, riding into the British cantonment at Jalalabad on 13 January 1842.

At no time had Palmerston, the Foreign Secretary, approved war with Dost Mohammed as a means of warning St Petersburg that 'thus far and no further' must define the limits of imperial Russia's Central Asian conquests. As with Salisbury forty years later, Pal-merston concentrated his energies on containing Russia in the eastern Mediterranean and the Black Sea. Auckland ignored this fact; he was too weak, too passive to oppose Ellenborough. Burnes was destroyed, in consequence, aged thirty-nine, because of Auckland's folly and his own ambition.

Eighteen months before the fatal march into Afghanistan, Burnes had written to Auckland: 'Dost Mohammed . . . is a man of undoubted ability; and if half you do for others was done for him . . . he would abandon Persia and Russia tomorrow.'[13] As we have seen, Burnes was unable to prevail with Auckland – who, quite simply, lacked capacity: 'He was not an ambitious man – quiet sensible, inclined towards peace, he would not have given himself up to the requirements of a greater game, if he had not been stimulated, past all hope of resistance, by evil advisers, who were continually pouring into his ears alarming stories of deep-laid plots and subtle intrigues emanating from the Cabinet of St Petersburg, and of the widespread corruption that was to be wrought by Russian gold.'[14]

There was a Russian agent in Kabul during Burnes' mission to Dost Mohammed in November 1836, a Lithuanian called Vitkievitch, who later committed suicide because his services to the Czar were disowned in St Petersburg. This persevering but unfortunate agent brought few offers and less gold to an amir who, as Burnes also reported, only wanted to be left alone. But whether in the 'Cabinet of St Petersburg' or nearer at home, Russian observers could not fail to be struck by the collapse of Auckland's adventure into Afghanistan.

What during the 1840s, then, restored some measure of British credit in Afghanistan and beyond its undemarcated northern and western frontiers? The answer lies in the names of five agents, who shared Burnes' preoccupation with a latent Russian threat to India from the north, but who managed to see it as one which should be put in the perspective of wider issues: British India's need for internal security, resting on a clearly defined limit to British rule; and Russia's interest in Central Asian conquest, based on a like commitment to rule which, whether direct or exercised through control of native rulers, should be unequivocal and unambiguous.

The agents in question were James Abbott, Eldred Pottinger, Henry Rawlinson, Richmond Shakespear and D'Arcy Todd. Their largely self-appointed task can be stated simply: to preserve some semblance of a balance between Persia, Afghanistan and the Punjab by persuading Dost Mohammed that he was more likely to keep his throne through consolidation of rule than engagement in intrigue. Concomitant to this policy was an attempt, ultimately futile, to stiffen Persian resistance against Russian pressure; and an expedient, ultimately successful, whereby the Shah in Tehran was persuaded to acknowledge Kabul's authority in Herat. The overriding object of these exercises was to secure British India's Northern Frontier by defining the limits of Dost Mohammed's authority. If London and St Petersburg could not so define – and indeed, neither definition of authority not demarcation of territory was possible at that level for another thirty years and more – agents must do their best to encourage an amir of Kabul in ways of moderation and restraint.

That Dost Mohammed was so restrained is demonstrated by the fact that he only seized Herat outright just before his death in 1863.

By then British agents had established a certain influence in Kabul –
some compensation for the virtual extinction of a British role at
Tehran. The consolidation of Dost Mohammed's rule had assuaged
many fears in Calcutta. The post-Mutiny strategy of concentrating
the bulk of British and native forces in the north and north-west not
only defined the Punjab's role in the maintenance of India's internal
security, but tacitly served notice on any ruler of Kashmir that he
kept his throne by compliance with the viceroy's dictates. Tolerable
relations between Calcutta and Kabul, together with a sound
appreciation of the importance of the Punjab and Kashmir, should
have disposed of Russophobia. Four years after Herat was secured,
however, and despite Lawrence's objections and injunctions, the
Great Game was being played again.

5

⨯⨯⨯⨯⨯⨯⨯⨯⨯⨯⨯⨯⨯⨯⨯⨯⨯⨯⨯⨯⨯⨯⨯⨯⨯⨯⨯⨯⨯⨯⨯

The Cold War,
1860s and 1870s

Paradoxically, the Great Game was resumed because of a revived interest in Kashgaria as an area whereby Russian armies might reach the Hindu Kush, not because of the continued progress of Russia into the Khanates of Bokhara, Khiva and Kokand. The march in question was, even so, both remorseless and alarming. 'In June 1865 the great commercial city of Tashkent . . . was captured; in 1866 the Russians annexed the city and pushed their frontier still further across the Syr [Daria]; in 1867 the new territories were formally absorbed; and in 1868 Samarqand fell.' Such expansion demanded sacrifice. An expedition to Khiva in 1839 was defeated by factors which British strategists, well aware of the facts, should have, but did not, consider: 'A large number of the unfortunate troops was sent back mutilated by the cold; some had lost their hands, others their feet, others the whole cheek, the ears, nose, lips and even the tongue.'[1]

A glance at the map shows increased, if only prospective threats to India's Northern Frontier caused by conquest on this scale. It was from Kashgar and points south-west that players of the Game from the late 1860s onwards saw a direct, not a potential Russian threat to India's security. These fears led to an increase of Russophobia, and set in train defensive, and pre-emptive, measures which culminated in the Second Afghan War. In the 1830s Russophobia was prevalent among the Court of Directors in London; in the 1860s the disease had become established in Calcutta.

The Crimean War (1853–1856) had little or nothing to do with Russophobia in London. Indeed, the war's outcome temporarily decreased British governments' fears of a Russian threat to the Black Sea and the Mediterranean. More to the point, perhaps, even

Palmerston was reassured by a 'Circular to the Great Powers' issued on 21 November 1864 by the Russian Chancellor, Prince Gorchakov, which blandly announced that the progress of Russia in Central Asia need not lead to apprehension elsewhere of endless imperial conquest. The powers should grasp and accept one simple principle, one common to all 'civilised states which come into contact with half-savage wandering tribes possessing no fixed social organization'. Gorchakov stated that Russia was only securing its frontiers against such wanderers by subduing and bringing them within the pale. Gorchakov adroitly – and accurately – compared this form of imperialism with British rule in India.[2]

Gorchakov's circular had its desired effect – in London – because he was careful to describe what would happen in the process of establishing Russian imperial rule in Central Asia: the Syr Daria would form the southern frontier of conquest. This declaration was belied four years later with the capture of Samarqand, but Gorchakov gained a breathing space: British governments had not turned their backs on Europe after the Crimean War, but had not yet fixed their sights wholly on India and a prospective Russian threat to its security from Central Asia. Not until 1868 did a picture emerge in London of what appeared to be a Russian determination to march on India by way of the Khanates and the Pamirs. Even then the government remained sceptical of a threat from Kashgaria. Revived Russophobia and a renewal of the Great Game had their genesis in and beyond India.

Those responsible reported in the 1860s that growing Russian pressure on Chinese Sinkiang – or Kashgaria – posed a direct threat to India. There was no warrant for this assertion; that it was made at all, by the two agents Robert Shaw and George Hayward, is explicable only if the characteristics and ambitions of these hardy travellers are considered. They were both experienced explorers, but they preferred wild speculation about possible threats to Britain's imperial interests to objective analysis. Shaw was Younghusband's uncle, and oracle, hence later, by his excursions and alarms, a potent influence. Hayward was a somewhat moody, discontented soldier, whose ultimate fate – murder in circumstances even less explicable than Arthur Connolly's, although by a tribal ruler no less savage than Nasrullah – was caused by a dangerous blend of frustration and foolhardiness.

It was a paradox that revival of the Great Game in the later 1860s owed much to the ambiguous, not to say anomalous position which Kashmir occupied in the scheme of things once the Punjab was brought totally within the British sway. Although the Rajah in Jammu, Gulab Singh, was nominally feudatory to Calcutta, he was a ruler with ambitions of his own. These ambitions extended north, towards territory which might, or might not be within Chinese dominion – or eventual Russian influence. In 1834 Gulab Singh seized Ladakh; in doing so he posed a challenge not only to British authority but to all who chose to see a prospective Russian presence in Sinkiang as a direct threat to British India. The response from Calcutta to Gulab Singh's aggression – consideration of a possible commercial connection with Kashgar – was not entirely disingenuous, but it masked nonetheless a determination to establish a British presence of sorts in Ladakh and, by extension, Sinkiang. In the process, Calcutta both tacitly approved and explicitly endorsed travel, exploration, overt missions, and covert intelligence operations which, during the following thirty years not only revived the Great Game but brought Francis Younghusband, another brave but unlucky player, plaudits from Simla and rebuffs from Downing Street.

The notion of trade with Kashgar was not entirely new. Nor was fear of a Russian presence in Kashgaria based only on Gulab Singh's ambitions. Between 1812 and 1823, William Moorcroft, Superintendent of John Company's stud, travelled throughout Western Tibet, Eastern Afghanistan, and much of Sinkiang. Moorcroft, an agreeable character, 'whose chief preoccupations were horse coping and making love', hardly needed cover for his operations: buying horses gave him entrée to otherwise inaccessible places. But Moorcroft's real preoccupation was a real, or alleged, Russian threat. Four years before his death 'of fever, or poison, on 27 August 1825 in the north of Afghanistan', Moorcroft argued 'Had not trade moved between Leh and Kashgar at all seasons of the year for centuries? What then was to prevent a Russian army following the same route? Once established in Kashmir, a natural fortress easily defended against attack from the plains, a Russian force in co-operation with Ranjit Singh could then re-equip itself at leisure for a further move.'[3]

Much was faulty in this argument, above all the unwarranted assertion that passage between Kashgar and Ladakh was possible at all seasons. Nor, despite the activities in Ladakh and the Punjab of 'a shadowy but fascinating' Russian agent, Aga Mehdi, could

Moorcroft quite bring himself to believe in a definable Russian threat. This was 'a speculation "so degrading, so monstrous" that he was only able to describe it with difficulty'. Quite: later players of the Great Game might well have taken Moorcroft's words to heart, and borne them in mind. Calcutta, indeed, not only rejected Moorcroft's arguments but dismissed him as Superintendent. Higher authority's habit of punishing agents who went too far, geographically and figuratively, may be said to have its genesis in Moorcroft's rejection, and fate.

Nevertheless, Moorcroft sowed a seed which, despite – or because of – British conquest of the Punjab, flowered five years later in the appointment of a trade agent at Leh. Henry Cayley, the agent in question, was a doctor: Lawrence, reluctantly agreeing to the appointment, thought 'that a British medical man at Leh would be an easier pill to swallow than a purely political officer'. The pill in question was swallowed by Lawrence, not by Gulab Singh's successor, Ranbir Singh. By the time of Cayley's appointment in June 1867 – described, in Mandarin as 'permanent, at all events for some time to come' – Maharajahs in Jammu were asserting their authority to the north-west rather than the north-east; however much these renewed Kashmiri ambitions alarmed the Amir in Kabul and put a rod in pickle for those in Calcutta charged with defining the limits of British influence south of the Hindu Kush, there was little that Lawrence or anybody else could do. It was all very well for Lawrence to say 'We are not in India for territorial gain; the Indus is our frontier, not the mountains': the times were against him.

So much for the establishment of a revived forward policy, opposed by Lawrence but justified, in his colleagues' and subordinates' eyes by the progress of Russia in Central Asia. But the re-establishment of a forward policy actually derived from a revival of the Great Game. Cayley was essentially an official in the 'Guardian' mould, able, conscientious, content to stay within his orbit, ostensibly committed to trade, in practice concerned with the relief of suffering. Shaw and Hayward were of a different stamp entirely; morever they were supported in their conclusions by the operations of an organisation within Calcutta's bureaucracy which carried out intelligence operations beyond India's Northern Frontier, employing methods which, whilst verging at times on the bizarre, resulted in sufficient geographical knowledge for all that Shaw and Hayward wrote, and was said to be given an official imprimatur. The Great Trigono-metrical Survey of India was an admirable organisation in the Guardian tradition; it was also a secret service employing native agents on hazardous missions to unknown places. Despite bizarre methods, the reports of these agents confirmed in every particular the findings of Shaw and Hayward.

In October 1869 Robert Shaw, newly returned from Kashgar to India, stated in a memorandum which was immediately, and officially, transmitted from Calcutta to London: 'Artillery could be brought I believe, the whole way without being dismounted . . . Here, a Russian army would have to fulfil the same conditions of success as they have already been accustomed to in the passage of the enormous deserts of the Khirghis . . . the difference caused by the Tibetan desert being at an enormous elevation, and exposed to the extremes of cold instead of heat, may be dismissed as immaterial . . . It has lately been argued that although barbarous hordes traverse these regions, armies with civilised appliances of war cannot do so . . . but where the road itself, as in Tibet, poses no obstacle, scarcity of supplies forms no greater obstacle to civilised armies than to barbarous hordes.'

Shaw and Hayward had traversed Kashgaria separately and reached their conclusions without any attempt at collusion. Both travellers overstated their case regarding a prospective Russian threat to India because they believed that exaggeration was a necessary ingredient in persuasion. Maybe for this reason the historian Dr Alder has stated unequivocally that 'the views of Shaw and Hayward were never entertained seriously in high places'.[4] Neither traveller possessed overt official status at the time: Shaw travelled for his own pleasure; Hayward had left the British Army in 1867, and not until 1870 was he to be officially and covertly tasked by Calcutta for intelligence duties in Gilgit and Chitral. It was then hoped that, contrary to Dr Alder's belief, his recommendations would put into perspective current arguments about a revived Russian threat to the Northern Frontier. What Hayward actually did was to revive British interest in the hill states north of Kashmir and, prospectively persuade Younghusband that he had a vital role to play there.

Shaw's influence was not direct. In London, somewhat given to exploiting his travels, Shaw was 'the hero of the hour'. But of the hour only, and although Shaw's arguments about a Russian capacity

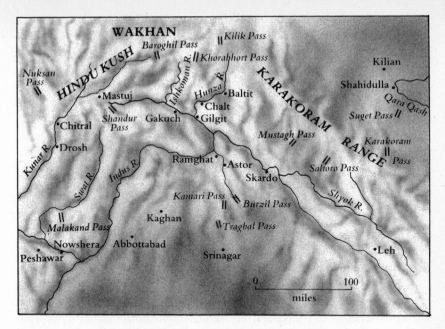

Showing Gilgit's central strategic importance

to traverse Kashgaria were officially noted, and distributed – to his satisfaction – he took more pleasure in seeing himself as an English-man who would be received with respect in distant places than in getting up a scare in Calcutta or London. Shaw gives a lively account of his adventures, rather in the manner of an earlier age, of 'being received in the most handsome manner' by notables in Kashgaria, and how 'A swell Moghul' greeted and entertained him.[5] Twenty-five years later, Younghusband was similarly to delude himself that an Englishman at a distant point automatically acquired status and prestige with petty notables. Indeed, in Kashgar, as later on the Pamirs and in Tibet, such a delusion blinded Younghusband to the realities of his situation, and was a direct, not a contributory cause of his progressive downfall.

Paradoxically, Hayward, far closer to Younghusband in intensity of temperament and introspection, not only sticks closely to strategic and topographical argument, but succeeded, by obtaining official employment after his travels in Kashgaria, in concentrating Calcut-ta's mind on Russian threats from Chinese territory, via the hill states south of the Hindu Kush. The two official missions of Thomas

29

Forsyth to Kashgar in 1870 and 1873 and, in particular, the extensive intelligence operations which followed the latter, owe much to the fact that Hayward was officially tasked in 1869 to assess Gilgit, Chitral and Yasin as centres of possible disaffection from Jammu's rule – and hence areas of possible Russian penetration. The establishment in 1877 of a British Political Agency at Gilgit followed logically from these assorted intelligence operations, and from the manner of their inception.

Hayward's operations in Gilgit and Chitral during 1870 were given a cover which revealed just how seriously some informed opinion in London was beginning to take continued Russian expansion in Central Asia and the concomitant revival of a forward policy by the Viceroy, Lord Mayo. Gladstone and Argyll, Secretary of State for India, were no friends to a forward policy; in 1869 the War Office scouted the feasibility of an army dependent on limited logistic support marching through wastes which 'Khirghiz horsemen . . . with nothing but what can be carried at the saddle bow' might cross with relative ease. Hayward riposted by arguing that 'The analogy cannot be maintained between a host of wild Tartars and what would be a disciplined European force equipped with every material and appliance of the art of war.'[6] Scepticism was not thereby set aside, but Mayo's increasing fears concerning Ranbir Singh and the hill states nevertheless began to produce an identical point of view between certain quarters in London and Calcutta – thus the highly secret decision to employ Hayward officially. He was provided with a cover by the Viceroy and also the Royal Geographical Society, the practice of which was to exercise an increasing influence on the framing and execution of Indian policy in the coming years.

The Royal Geographical Society did not indulge in Russophobia, but in 1869 the President, Sir Roderick Murchison, made his position clear nonetheless: 'Mr Hayward's travels [in Kashgaria] afforded another proof that geographical discovery was not a mere dilettante amusement, but was intimately connected with the public interest.' Murchison was careful to cover his tracks. He said, in commenting on Hayward's first journey: 'All this enterprise is undertaken at his own risk . . . he does not go as an accredited agent of the Government but simply as one of those adventurous explorers.'

This was nonsense, and Murchison knew it to be so. In October 1868 he had written a long memorandum for, and a longer letter to, Mayo who was about to take up his appointment as Viceroy. The core of Murchison's argument, as given in these papers, is that the Royal Geographical Society had a duty to carry out geographical exploration for political purposes; Murchison was specific: 'The country lying between the Upper Indus from Attock northwards, and the great centres of population in eastern Turkistan, namely Kashgar and Yarkand, but more especially the elevated district situated to the west of those cities'.

Murchison stressed the necessity to carry out such exploration in order to protect India's frontiers and to have a full picture of those regions 'to which Russians have of late years advanced'.[7] He also argued that 'it is especially necessary to obtain geographical knowledge of the unknown region which lies between the Punjab and Kashmir and the last advances of the Russians'. Murchison then stated that 'My society [has] despatched a very able young India officer, Lieutenant Hayward'.[8] So much for the idea that Hayward was a private person, travelling where the spirit listed.

The Royal Geographical Society was also Hayward's nominal sponsor for his travels in Gilgit and Chitral; moreover, the Mayo Papers show quite clearly that Hayward was operating at the Viceroy's behest. Hayward's death on 18 July 1870 at the hands of Mir Wali, ruler, by favour of his Uncle Aman-ul-Mulk, master of Chitral, and much else besides, has never been satisfactorily explained. Hayward once said that he had an 'insane desire to try the effect of cold steel across my throat'. His wish was, literally, granted by Mir Wali – but why? All we know is that Hayward's murder was hushed up by higher authority; that his few effects were sold at auction; and his sister, in want, was denied succour. Unlucky players of the Game, however brave, could only expect their masters to disown them.

Nor were Hayward's implied recommendations to Mayo of May 1870 given sufficient attention. Hayward was strongly critical of Ranbir Singh's attempts to impose his authority on the hill states, although he did not explicitly state that Calcutta should curb Ranbir Singh and impose its own authority. Hayward was in no position to make such specific recommendations and even if Hayward had been given, or had acquired, the authority not even a proponent of the forward policy would have accepted them. The hill states were left to nature, pawns on the chessboard, problems in store for later players of the Game – again, and not least, Francis Younghusband.

★

The native agents who were recruited and tasked by the Survey of India were luckier than Hayward: they survived and were, to a degree, rewarded. The value of such agents' intelligence was, however, hard to assess in the 1860s, and later: the passage of time has not eased the task. The intelligence not only contributed to Russophobia in Calcutta, but also justified a policy; in terms of an acceleration of the forward policy, the agent's intelligence is relevant because operations following the second Forsyth mission were based on examining it, in some detail and with reasonable professional skill.

The agents' travels were kept within the area of investigation laid down by Mayo, and cited on p. 30: Herat, Balkh, Kashgar, and Leh. Agents also undertook impressively arduous journeys among the hill states and in the Afghan panhandle. It was the latter area, and that to the east, namely the Great and the Little Pamirs, which the British officers and native agents of Forsyth's second mission explored in the middle 1870s. Such explorations, by the time of the Second Afghan War, had completed a series of reports and a collection of maps which Younghusband was to study, both diligently and credulously, when he embarked on his career in intelligence all but ten years later.

Diligence and credulity were, it must be said, the outstanding characteristics of the agents, and possibly also of that reflective, consumptive sapper T. G. Montgomerie who had recruited them. Montgomerie had something more than a point when he argued in 1861 from his headquarters at Dehra Dun that 'Asiatics, the subjects of the British Government, are known to travel freely without molestation in countries far beyond the British frontier; they constantly pass too between India and Central Asia, and also between India and Tibet, for trading and other purposes, without exciting any suspicion.' This argument proved persuasive: 'it was consequently proposed to take advantage of this facility possessed by Asiatics, and to employ them on explorations beyond the frontier. The Government of India approved of the project and agreed to support it liberally.' The economy of a plan in which agents would cost little when alive and would arouse no concern if dead must have been a strong contributing factor in Calcutta's approval for Montgomerie's scheme, being given moreover when the close frontier policy was still stamped with Lawrence's authority.[9]

Unfortunately, the agents selected were trained neither in intelligence nor survey. British intelligence officers who were immune from both the lure of the Great Game and Russophobia discounted Montgomerie's operations. 'The information derived from these Native Agents is often misleading, and a tendency to exaggerate was found in them all . . . even when dealing with intelligent natives [native surveyors] it is always difficult to make them understand what we want to know, especially concerning roads, passes and the approaches thereto . . . Where the latter are tolerably easy it is not unusual for them to be described as "a plain as flat as my open hand", while a mile or two of roadway in the immediate vicinity of the pass, utterly impracticable for any large number of laden men or package animals, is entirely ignored.'[10]

Thus Colonels Lockhart and Woodthorpe in 1885 – a time of relative objectivity in playing the Game. Whatever their shortcomings as political analysts – revealed in their faulty forecasts about Chitral and Gilgit – Lockhart and Woodthorpe knew how to observe and survey. Montgomerie's agents did not. Montgomerie, however, had argued that his agents would produce intelligence of a kind; he implied that until British agents could travel with some chance of survival, his method was better than none. He had a point: Conolly and Stoddart were something more than memories; two Company officers, Adolphe Schlagintweit and Lieutenant Wyburd had vanished between Leh and Kashgar in the 1850s; Hayward's murder was to reinforce Montgomerie's argument even as British agents embarked on another round of the Game.

When all is said and done, however, not much credence can be given to agents, however committed, whose cover of pundit, or seeker after spiritual truth, was barely sufficient for the tasks of intelligence gathering and survey. Too much time had to be spent in meditation, not enough in trigonometry. The ingenious device of adapting the Buddhist prayer wheel and rosary to the purposes of measuring distance, and of sticking messages in metal cylinders which were dropped in the Brahmaputra in the hopes of being picked up by some watcher on Bengal's shore suggest a certain indulgence in games for their own sake.

Maybe, 'with his prayer wheel and rosary, the pundit always managed in one way or another to take his bearings and count his paces', perhaps quicksilver could be carried in a cowrie shell, possibly 'a common bulls-eye lantern answered capitally' for making observations secretly at night, but, to read the pundits' reports is to be torn between incredulity and admiration. There was plenty of resource in the field if not much sagacity back at Dehra Dun, yet perhaps the best contribution which the pundits made was not geographical but descriptive. The picture of the dispatch riders of Cathay 'riding along as hard as they could go . . . haggard and worn . . . their faces cracked, their eyes blood-shot' is not one easily forgotten.

By 1868 the intelligence picture as seen from Dehra Dun basically came to this: two journeys made by native agents – the Munshi from Jammu to Kashgar, and pundit Munphool from Peshawar to Badakshan – had revealed that along some routes men and animals could travel with relative ease at certain periods of the year. The Munshi's march route through Kashmir was north-north-east, and he must therefore have reached the Pamirs through or near the Mustagh Pass, although this point was never made clear in the narrative of the journey which Montgomerie presented to the Royal Geographical Society. To Montgomerie and to others concerned with 'the debatable ground between India and Russia' there was no doubt of a direct route from Kashmir to Kashgar. The Munshi estimated that crossing the Pamirs alone took him fifty-five days, that 'the road for twenty-five days was over country never lower than 15,000 feet, and for forty-five days not lower than 9,000'. The Munshi further estimated that 'The distance, in a straight line from Jammu to Yarkand, is 430 miles, so that the mountains are at least 400 miles across at their smallest breadth'.

This last observation was pretty wide of the mark, but the Munshi did make several other points which were not only shrewd but attracted greater attention. The Munshi reported that Yarkand's altitude was no more than 4,000 feet, and that although the winter there was 'very severe, the thermometer, early in January, falling nearly to zero', the weather was bearable, movement was possible – and pasture was available. A picture was forming of a sloping tableland rather than a plateau, and one whose incline was gradual enough for men and animals to march. It was, in fact, a picture which was remarkably accurate on the Yarkand side. Where it fell short was that it lacked any real description of the going through the passes.

In May 1868, however, the report of pundit Munphool's journey from Peshawar to Badakshan passed into official circulation, a copy being sent in that month to Sir Stafford Northcote, the Secretary of State. To those Anglo-Indians who were making new maps of Asia, pundit Munphool's report provided more evidence of an interesting fact. Once you were across the Karakoram and well into Kashgaria or Kokand, you were on a high steppe where rapid movement was possible. The same point, for that matter, was believed to obtain with the country north of the Hindu Kush. The area of steppe whose western end may be indicated by Hissar (now Stalinabad) and its eastern by Kashgar, is in fact much more rugged than British geographers of the 1860s supposed; the plateau, a tableland which divides the desert and oases of Samarkand, Bokhara and Tashkent from the Hindu Kush and the Karakoram is a harsh terrain indeed.

The area marked on some modern maps as 'Badakshan within Russian territory' is, moreover, far more mountainous and has far less of the steppe about it than the geo-political Anglo-Indians believed. This western buffer area is one which only a foolhardy Russian column commander would have attempted to cross without the most meticulous preparation. There was a way across it, however, as one native agent was later to discover. A presumption was beginning to develop that even the highest ranges had passes; it was not yet known that there were passes which were literally a walkover – once you got to them; when, between 1873 and 1875 this curious physical feature was appreciated, a fluttering in the dovecotes was indeed caused, a reaction to be intensified in the late 1880s, when Lockhart and Woodthorpe provided further evidence of this geographical quirk. In 1868 there was already enough information to believe and to fear that the 'shortest invasion route' as Burnes had called it, and what Lawrence called 'this most dangerous of all the routes' might allow a Russian party to get on the south side of the Pamirs.

What would the Russians find when they crossed through the looking glass? Possibly a ruler in Jammu willing to trade one master for another – circumstantial evidence of Ranbir Singh's contact with Tashkent was not wanting. Such possibilities aside, pundit Munphool's report fuelled fresh fears. He returned to Dehra Dun with a picture of the hill states lying athwart the upper reaches of the Indus, feuding and fighting among each other, and only giving the barest acknowledgement to any higher authority – namely the Maharajah in Jammu. Pundit Munphool not only reported this disquieting political factor – one which was to bedevil and nearly to wreck the entire frontier defensive concept over the next forty years – but he suggested another possibility, and one which was not calculated to raise British spirits. Pundit Munphool did not in fact get over the Hindu Kush, but he did suggest that investigation east of the passes of which he had made report would repay. In particular he referred to the Dora Pass which, he believed, could be crossed with relative ease. Suddenly the great protective barriers of the Hindu Kush and the Karakoram were seen to be riddled with passes. This was not a reassuring prospect for men who knew that their security of tenure in India was a thing so finely balanced that rumours could tilt it.

Pundit Munphool's geographical sense was not quite so accurate as his political judgement. East of the Dora pass or rather north-east and then east of it, were other sally ports. The officers attached to Forsyth's second mission were to spend much time looking for them. Over the years these passes were to grow in number on the map and to keep apprehension alive; the Darkot, the Baroghil, the Ishkoman and many others acquired a status and importance which an objective examination of them shows to be somewhat exaggerated. Year after year the patient exploration of the southern face of the ranges continued. When, in 1889, Younghusband made an extensive survey of the passes at the eastern end of the Karakoram, the picture was more or less complete, and to men determined to believe that the bear desired to spread political havoc in the Indian plains, let alone to march through the Afghan defiles, it was not a pretty one.

Faraway to the south and south west stretched the high peaks and glaciers of the Karakoram and Mustagh range, some of whose loftiest summits attain to the height of from 25,000 to 28,000 feet above the sea. One peak, situated to the east of the Mustagh Pass, reaches the stupendous elevation 28,278 feet above sea level, and is one of the highest mountains in the world. [Godwin-Austen or K2]. Beyond where the river [Murghab] sweeps out west the snowy peaks above the Kunjut country were in sight towards Sarikol. East and west extended the whole chain of the Kuen Luen and the Kilian mountains, the last range to be crossed before the steppes and plains of Turkistan are reached, while immediately below lay the confined ravine up which the road ascends to the

Yangi Pass, now full in sight beneath me. The extent of view of the main Karakoram or Mustagh chain comprised a length of 200 miles, stretching from near the Karakoram Pass to the head of the Tashkurgan territory north of Hunza and Nagar.

The cold at this elevated station, nearly 19,000 feet above the sea, so late in the year, was very severe, the thermometer sinking to 5° Fahrenheit in the shade, notwithstanding it was midday and a bright sun was shining. I had reached many higher altitudes, but never any commanding so extensive a view of such a stupendous mass of mountains; and it was with a feeling of regret that one turned to leave a spot from which the peaks and glaciers could be so well seen, stretching far away on every side in their solemn grandeur.[11]

Thus Hayward's account of his traverse of Kashgaria, describing what he saw once north of Leh, beyond the Chang-Chenmo valley and the Kuen Luen range. Yet despite such clear evidence of an impassable barrier for all except the hardy mountain traveller, on foot – evidence which Younghusband was to reproduce exactly twenty years later – Hayward, in this account, repeats his assertion about the relative ease of movement once the barrier described above had been breached by one pass or another. 'The natural advantages are so great, [to Yarkand] and the road perfectly practicable for laden horses and camels, and might be made so for two-wheeled carts and conveyances, as well as for the passage of guns.'

Hayward was carried away by these strategic notions, losing his geographer's sense of proportion in the process. He was not alone. As the forward policy revived, not only from Calcutta's response to the progress of Russia in Central Asia but tacitly encouraged by the Home government's strengthened post-Mutiny concern for India, others appeared on the scene whose energies were concentrated on making a name for themselves in almost pro-consular terms. The realities of geography and climate were ignored in pursuit of ambition.

Foremost among this new breed was Thomas Douglas Forsyth, notable not so much for what he achieved as the legacy which he left in terms of the Great Game. The all but immediate bequest was the Gilgit Agency, expressing a concern about assumed Russian pressure due south from Tashkent rather than south-west from

Kashgar. The long term legacy was the implementation and progress of a policy whereby British and native trans-frontier agents would no longer play the Game for its own sake, but became representatives of the Raj in their own right. For all practical – or impractical – purposes, this policy was designed to establish a British presence, directly and at one or several removes, athwart any route whereby a Russian invasion of India might take place.

From 1870 onwards until the 1907 Anglo-Russian Convention, these agents of the Raj exercised a major influence on Indian Northern Frontier policy. (Younghusband was a throwback to Conolly, Stoddart and Hayward, in that he did play the Game mainly for his own sake.) Forsyth marched his missions to Kashgar in 1870 and 1873 very much in the well regulated manner of an official on tour. He was not a frontiersman by temperament – neither a lone wolf, nor a solitary adventurer among the Karakoram and Kuen Luen. Forsyth was essentially a bureaucrat – Commissioner at Jullundur, in the Punjab – but with ideas. In that easier age he was able to push them; when one foundered, another was revived with greater energy.

One idea was that Yaqub Beg, *de facto* ruler of eastern Kashgaria, could be the faithful ally whom men in Calcutta had searched for so long. Forsyth was chosen to approach Yaqub Beg. The object of this mission, or 'fishing expedition' in Forsyth's words, was to see whether Yaqub Beg would be able, and willing, to act as Calcutta's satellite in the debatable land which lay west of Kashgar and Yarkand. Belief in the value of satellites as substitutes for explicit power was a prevailing, and damaging, element in Calcutta's and London's policies for the defence of India. Amirs in Kabul and maharajahs in Jammu are the cases in point. They did represent authority, however arbitrarily expressed. To entertain hopes about Yaqub Beg as a puppet, though, distant as he was from any definite British presence, and liable at any time to be overthrown by rivals or a positive Manchu riposte, reveals all too clearly that objective appreciations formed no part in decision-making once the forward policy was resumed.

There was some justification for Forsyth's mission: Yaqub Beg had sent an emissary to Mayo on his own fishing expedition early in 1870, although with no more discernible reason than an upstart's desire for recognition. Returning the compliment raised no ante. The mission was, however, a complete failure. Accompanied only by Shaw and guides, Forsyth reached Kashgar to find the door shut in his face. Yaqub Beg refused even to see Forsyth. The official excuse given was what we might call pressure of business; the real reason for Yaqub Beg's refusal was the old and basic one which imperial agents treating with local rulers so frequently forgot. The 'orientals' were renowned for their love of diplomatic games. Hidden behind the verbal fencing, however, was a desire for specific proposals backed by clearly defined and realistic pledges of support.

Despite these unpalatable facts, and Forsyth's rebuff, another mission was set in train three years later. Northbrook, succeeding Mayo in 1872, agreed with Forsyth that another attempt must be made to establish genuine relations with Yaqub Beg or that his overthrow must be sought. This time there was little talk of trade. The dispatches, conferences, and plans in which Forsyth was prime mover during 1873 – the year Khiva fell to Russian arms – were devoted to strategic considerations; Kashgaria flanked the neutral zone of the Pamirs; would Kashgaria, through which horse, foot and artillery could march to the Pamirs, remain neutral? Was Yaqub Beg an ally of Britain or a creature of Russia? In June 1873 Forsyth prepared for a mission to Kashgar – a different affair from the trial run of three years before – which was designed to seek an answer to these questions, and to find the missing pieces in the strategic map drawn by the native agents, Shaw and Hayward.

Forsyth failed in the realisation of his objectives, but the men he took with him to Yarkand and Kashgar in the winter of 1873/1874 were not disappointed. Their playing of the Game, and the discovery that passes south of the Pamirs were extraordinarily easy to traverse in some seasons of the year, afford direct clues to the revival of Calcutta's doubts about Afghanistan as a reliable satellite which characterised Lytton's viceroyalty, and which led to the Second Afghan War.

The additional evidence about the Pamirs and hill states south of the Hindu Kush which began to appear in intelligence reports in the aftermath of Forsyth's second mission were based on journeys made by two *trained* Native Agents – the Mirza and the Havildar. Between 1868 and 1870 these agents had made route surveys, taken heights and collected geographical information which provided two more pieces for the strategic map detailing the land beyond the Northern Frontier. The Mirza marched from Peshawar to Faizabad, crossed the Oxus and then turned east-north-east for Kashgar. He thus confirmed that what he called the Kirghiz Steppe or the Little Pamir, afforded excellent going for men and beasts.

Marching across the steppe in the depths of winter was, however, exceptionally demanding. According to the Mirza, 'the intensity of cold was extreme whenever the wind blew. They then felt as if they were going to lose their extremities; the glare from the snow was very trying to the eyes, all suffering from snow-blindness; their breath froze on their moustaches; and every one, moreover, had to walk in order to keep some warmth in the body.' Nobody fell out, however, and the Mirza implied, although he did not categorically state, that men and horses could march across the Little Pamir, which for endless miles was a dead flat plain. The watershed of Central Asia was the most desolate scene which the Mirza had ever experienced: 'Not a sign of man, beast or bird, the whole country being covered with a mantle of snow'. Despite this, he insisted that Russian posts were being established in the Sarikol area.

The Havildar's report was, in the long term, of greater importance than the Mirza's. The former was a sapper, whose careful, thorough exploration and survey of the hill states, Chitral especially, should have been considered in all its implications by Viceroy and Commander-in-Chief. The Havildar reported that Chitral and its neighbours formed a fertile staging post, at no more than 7,000 feet. Invading or defending forces who had traversed the passes of the Hindu Kush or who had marched north from the Punjab, would be able to recruit their strength and replenish supplies in an area remote from effective authority, ruled by men prepared to deal, on several issues, with the highest bidder. Chief amongst those prepared to negotiate, with Russian agents, was Ranbir Singh.

If still alive, George Hayward could have confirmed all that the Havildar reported. Despite the establishment of the Gilgit Agency in 1877, another decade was to pass before the intrinsic importance of the hill states to the defence of the Northern Frontier was to be fully considered – and misunderstood, by Lockhart and Woodthorpe, and by Francis Younghusband. In the immediate aftermath of the second Forsyth mission, and at a time when Kashgaria and the Pamirs dominated the assumptions of those who favoured a forward policy, the Havildar and Hayward were ignored. To the soldiers who accompanied Forsyth to Kashgar in 1873 wide open spaces posed a more stimulating challenge than the feuds of petty rulers nominally feudatory to Ranbir Singh.[12]

These soldiers represented the second phase of the Great Game. This was now the taciturn age; trans-frontier agents no longer wrote or spoke of achieving fame. Even making a mark was hinted at in only a phrase or two. Such agents were no disguise on the high passes or the steppe. If not in uniform, Norfolk jackets and knicker-bockers were the mode. The agents smoked pipes, were good shots, accurate surveyors, and physically tough. Few dreamed dreams or indulged in notions. Their Russophobia, however, was consistent, professional and rational up to a point, but marred on the whole by a refusal, or an inability, to consider the objectives governing Russia's conquest of Central Asia and the methods used to consoli-date it. Such agents were Younghusband's progenitors in all but the compulsion to fulfil themselves spiritually.

As with Younghusband, the men of the Forsyth mission felt that they were free to do pretty much as they liked in the land west of Yarkand and Kashgar. They certainly interpreted their instructions liberally, and were only prevented by the Yaqub Beg's direct orders from reconnoitering north-east of Kashgar, and south-west from Yarkand. There were five soldiers in Forsyth's party, and they gave to his mission much more of a military character than was good for it. They were: Captain John Biddulph, 19th Hussars, one of North-brook's ADCs; Surgeon Major H. W. Bellew; Major T. E. Gordon, an experienced infantry soldier and frontier officer, who was second in command of the mission – and, at forty-one, the second oldest agent on it; Captain Henry Trotter, a sapper and a colleague of Montgomerie's; Captain E. F. Chapman, a gunner. Also included in the party was Ibrahim Khan – IK to Montgomerie – an exception-ally resourceful policeman, whose journeys in northern Afghanistan later confirmed in every important respect the findings of the Mirza and the Havildar.[13].

Not only was a substantial mission escort furnished by the Guides, but four of the five officers were men who were deter-mined to make their mark in the Great Game or the wider intelli-gence field. Two of them in particular, Biddulph and Gordon, grasped the opportunities afforded by the Forsyth mission to estab-lish themselves at an early stage in their careers. Biddulph became the first agent in Gilgit – and in consequence a *bête noire* of the Foreign Office. Gordon rose to be a full General, and in the course of a long career in intelligence had a good deal of influence on the issues of Indian defence. Trotter, the ablest surveyor of the party, filled in many blanks on the geographical map, and together with Dr Stoliczka, the mission geologist (who died from sheer exhaustion on the homeward march) provided the first detailed analysis of the Oxus region. Chapman, twenty years later, was Director of Military Intelligence at the War Office, and throughout this appointment a convinced, though reasoned proponent of the defence of the Northern and North-West Frontier as Britain's first strategic commitment. All five soldiers were closely in touch with informed opinion in India and London, as the detailed unofficial account of the mission – published in the Royal Geographical Society's *Proceedings* for 1873–74 – makes abundantly clear.

For all the second Forsyth mission's essentially military character, the five soldiers failed to put strategic issues in perspective. With the partial exception of Bellew, none of them grasped that Russia's objective in Central Asia was conquest and consolidation. All concluded that every year which passed increased the direct Russian threat to India. The mission's reports, individually and collectively, 'caused a considerable stir in Government circles', mainly because they seemed to presage danger everywhere. Gordon argued that Kashgar in Russian hands would provide a second flank to any advance on India from further west. Gordon, seizing on the reports of 'IK' and other native agents, then pushed home the assertion that a Russian advance south from Osh was quite feasible.

Gordon concluded by suggesting there was a positive threat to India's Northern Frontier: Russian forces could advance on the Frontier via Hunza – nominally feudatory to China, or through what was arguably Afghan territory to Sarhad, in Wakhan. From there, according to Gordon's sources, there were 'two easy roads' to the hill states – by the Ishkoman Pass into Yasin, or via Gilgit and Chitral. Biddulph, who was sent by Northbrook in 1874 to examine these alleged routes from north of the Hindu Kush accentuated fears by some startling observations: 'By the Chitral or Gilgit routes . . . and crossing either the Baroghil or Ishkoman Passes the traveller goes through a gate by which without for one day being away from human habitations, he is practically landed in Asia in a single march.'[14]

Although Biddulph's statement was based largely on assumption – he made no extensive survey, and misleadingly described terrain north and south of the passes as if it was uniform – there was a note of such confidence in what he asserted for 'Government circles' to experience further shocks. Biddulph then pushed his opinion home: '[From Osh] there is nothing to prevent the rapid advance of an army fully equipped to within a few miles of Sarhad. Not only is no road-making for the passage of field artillery necessary, but along the whole distance there is an unlimited quantity of the finest pasture in the world.'

In fact, and as Biddulph later reported, the approach marches to the passes from the south were a tougher proposition than from the north, despite the potential value of the hill states as staging posts. If this had been fully appreciated in the mid-1870s, it is just possible that a decision might have been made in Calcutta – and approved by London – that the security of India's Northern Frontier depended on a choice being made between holding the Punjab or seizing Kashmir and the hill states. But, by the 1870s the choice was fudged. The Punjab was so securely held that the hill states were allowed to remain as buffers or, in Lytton's view, as pawns on his particular chessboard. Lytton's advent as Viceroy in 1876, however, coupled with news of Russia's final conquest of Kokand precluded rational strategic – and political – assessments by either Calcutta or Simla.

A policy of bluff, threats, and coercion was more acceptable to excitable temperaments and players of the Game than level-headed strategic planning. Gordon had marched right across the Great Pamir on his return from Kashgar, and, from a local base which he established in Wakhan, had sent Trotter and Stoliczka to make a thorough survey of the area north of Wood's lake. Rissaldar Mohammed Afzal Khan, a native officer serving with the mission, and a Guides NCO acted as a communications link with Forsyth in Yarkand. The Rissaldar also made forays to Faizabad and back (on one occasion riding 280 miles in eight days), in order to assess the attitude of the local Afghan authorities to Gordon's party. It was hostile, but Gordon was undeterred: from Osh, a Russian force could march to the Pamirs and be amongst the hill states before the nearest British garrison at Abbottabad could prevent them. The inference was inescapable: the Amir in Kabul must be made either to enforce his unequivocal control of Wakhan or to accept a quasi-British presence there.

The five Russophobe soldiers in Forsyth's second mission had succeeded in attaining what one must suppose was their main objective: to contain further Russian advance by a combination of threats and persuasion to the Amir in Kabul, the rulers of the hill states, and the Maharajah in Jammu. Being soldiers, such a political objective was nowhere stated, or even implied, but there is no doubt that Lytton construed the reports of Gordon and Biddulph in terms of a forward policy which would depend on the assertion of imperial mystique, not the presence of imperial forces. By 1880, Lytton was to become the victim of his own folly; a decade later, Younghusband became as much the victim of an ill-conceived forward policy for the entire Northern Frontier as of his own virtues and failings.[15]

6

Second Afghan War
1878–1880

The prime cause of the Second Afghan War was surely the unstable character and neurotic impulses of the Viceroy, Lord Lytton, as fatal a choice by Disraeli for the most demanding imperial appointment in the Prime Minister's gift as had been Auckland by Melbourne forty years before. Whereas Melbourne had merely approved Ellenborough's selection of Auckland as a pliable instrument for executing a forward policy, Disraeli had, however, personally and deliberately picked Lytton to implement a version of that policy, aptly described by Salisbury as one of 'noise and splash'.

The middle years of Gladstone's first government had witnessed a revived concern in London for the security of India's Northern Frontier, and the role which the Foreign Office should play in seeking accommodation with St Petersburg. Disraeli bedecked in his 'suit of imperial spangles' – another Salisbury barb – turned fears into actions, of which sending Lytton to Calcutta was the most notorious. Unable to be more than a jingo in his dealings with Russia, Disraeli allowed Lytton to carry Russophobia to the point of war. Disraeli told the sceptical Salisbury 'We wanted a man of ambition, imagination, some vanity and much will – and we have got him'.[1] What Disraeli got was 'a diseased personality', as Lytton said of himself, although Salisbury, charitable for once, left it at 'a gaudy and theatrical ambition'.[2]

The Second Afghan War's genesis, course and consequences repeated that of the First, save that courage and imagination prevented comparable military disasters, whilst sense and skill, exercised by officials whom Lytton resisted and rejected, ensured a degree of co-operation at its close with the vicious ruffian and able tyrant who finally asserted authority in Kabul, Abdur Rahman.

There is another element in the circumstances preceding and following the war which marked change. Whether active or inept, Foreign Secretaries and Secretaries of State for India from the early 1870s onwards did not allow Calcutta or Simla wholly to decide the course of events regarding India's external security, however much the Home government collectively remained reluctant to shape policy or intervene unambiguously until a crisis erupted. Salisbury, who was successively Disraeli's Secretary of State and Foreign Secretary between 1874 and 1880, made his influence felt both by comment and action. Lytton was destroyed by his own folly rather than by a refusal to heed Salisbury's warnings, but Francis Younghusband, a decade later, was to feel the effect of Salisbury, as Prime Minister and Foreign Secretary, when exerting his authority on imperial issues.

The Second Afghan War's origins cannot be wholly divorced from events and policies which occurred and developed as the forward policy gathered momentum. To checkmate Russia's advance in Central Asia and towards India's Northern Frontier by enlisting Yaqub Beg as Calcutta's satellite had proved a waste of time and effort. Kashmir and the hill states remained largely unknown quantities; sending Biddulph to Gilgit in 1877 was hardly even a holding operation: Ranbir Singh could be bribed – and was; his ineffectual levies could be stiffened with an infusion of reliable troops. Biddulph remained nevertheless as nothing more than an expression of concern for the Northern Frontier: his presence in no way contributed to its security.

It was inevitable, then, that Lytton should turn to the Amir of Kabul, his policies being governed by phobias and assumptions and not by constructive thought. Lytton ignored Northbrook's strong recommendation on retiring as Viceroy that Kashmir's control should be extended over Chitral and Yasin right up to the southern side of the passes.[3] Even this advice did not lack for ambiguity; how was such control to be exercised if not by the presence of reliable garrisons? In apparently simple contrast, putting pressure on Sher Ali, the Amir in Kabul when Lytton assumed the viceroyalty in April 1876, implied an overall British capacity to operate in, and north of, Afghanistan. This would, it was supposed, deter Russia from extending its Central Asian territories south of the Oxus to the presumed Northern Frontier of Afghanistan.

Lytton made one basic mistake, however, which rendered his

46

1 The First Afghan War:
the invading army marches through the passes

2 'Bokhara' Burnes seeks fame and
fortune

3 Arthur Conolly, 'an intense young
officer of the Bengal Cavalry'

4 Temporary kings: Amir Yakub Khan with entourage
contemplates a bearded Louis Cavagnari

Northern Frontier policy suspect from the outset. He assumed that by threatening Sher Ali with retribution if he did not cease intrigues amongst the hill states (an endemic practice, based on some justified territorial claims), the latter could be persuaded into accepting a British political presence on and beyond Afghanistan's northern frontier. Lytton correctly perceived that the area between the Oxus and this frontier should be of far greater concern to Calcutta and Simla than any other – *if* a forward policy was to be pursued – but failed to grasp that Sher Ali would not be browbeaten, and that there was no effective coercion which viceroy or commander-in-chief could apply to compel his submission.

Lytton called Sher Ali 'a savage with a touch of insanity'. The description, although wide of the mark, reveals the truth: Lytton was reduced to insults because coercion failed. Many years later Roberts, the 'Sepoy General' noted privately: 'As in Dost Mohammed's case, we wanted Sher Ali to agree to a one-sided treaty [which would have brought Kabul, theoretically, within the British sway, denying any amir there the right to negotiate with Tashkent, on any issue]. This disgusted him, as it disgusted his father in 1842, and he turned to the Russians.'[4]

Sher Ali did not, in fact, 'turn to the Russians' in 1876 or 1878, any more than did his father in 1838. Dost Mohammed received a Russian agent, briefly and inconclusively; Sher Ali received a full-blown Russian mission in August 1878, cautiously and non-committally. The mission left Kabul in late 1878 with nothing more than a piece of paper, having spent three weeks kicking its heels in the boredom inseparable from an Oriental court. One member of the mission noted in his diary: 'This place gives me the blues', a remark which puts Lytton's suspicions of Russian intrigues at Kabul into the category of those conspiracy theories which his restless imagination was forever hatching. The one plausible element in these theories came to no more than an assumption that Gorchakov's so-called Agreement with Granville (Gladstone's Foreign Secretary) in 1873, whereby Afghanistan was recognized as having claims to territory between Faizabad and the Oxus, and possibly beyond, precluded any intervention by Tashkent in the affairs of Afghanistan.

The theory was plausible, but no more. The Agreement stipulated that Afghanistan 'is to remain outside the sphere of Russian action'. This was too vague a formula for any British Minister, diplomat, or pro-consul to argue convincingly that Russia was precluded from, say, the dispatch of a diplomatic mission to Kabul – the ostensible *casus belli* for Lytton's invasion of Afghanistan in November 1878.

Lytton would have had a point if he had complained to Disraeli and Salisbury about the frightful ambiguity of this Agreement; no frontiers were clearly defined, and as a result no limit was actually placed on either Afghanistan or Russia consolidating claims or seizing territory by force of arms. This positively encouraged Gorchakov and General Kaufmann, the Governor-General of Turkestan, to interfere in Afghanistan's affairs. The origin of the Agreement was Northbrook's unprecedented attempt to ginger up the Home government so that it took an active interest in Indian and Central Asian affairs. This was laudable, but in Granville's languid, not to say nerveless hands, all that resulted was exactly what Gorchakov and Kaufmann wanted: a situation where each Afghan frontier established by diplomatic negotiation would lack clear definition – let alone demarcation – and, sooner or later, become an embarrassment to London and Calcutta in its dealings with Kabul.

In exchange for accepting that the Oxus would not be construed as necessarily forming Afghanistan's northern frontier, Gorchakov asked Granville to accept the principle that all territory north of the Pamirs lay within the Russian sphere of interest. Just what constituted the Pamirs was a nice point, which was not established until Francis Younghusband endeavoured, between 1888 and 1891, to bring the area within the British orbit. In 1873, lack of definition, due to little reliable intelligence, was immensely useful to Gorchakov. As Bismarck said, 'Prince Gorchakov was not a statesman to give without requiring a quid pro quo'. What Gorchakov and Kaufmann ultimately wanted was demarcation, but their strategy was to achieve this by guile. The day would come when Anglo-Russian Boundary Commissions confined the forward policy to suppositions about possible future action. In 1873 that day had not yet come. Three years later Lytton was not only encouraged by Disraeli to believe in the forward policy, but deluded himself that this could best be achieved if Sher Ali was told that he must accept Calcutta's dictates and utterly repudiate any overtures from Tashkent.

For two years, and with increasingly shrill rhetoric, strikingly similar to Curzon's concerning Tibet nearly thirty years later, Lytton strove to get up what Owen Burne, his India Office mouthpiece in London called 'a Kabul scare'. It was based exclusively on Lytton's reports of Russian pressure against Sher Ali. Largely unsuccessful in London, Lytton did acquire a following in India. His main disciple was Louis Cavagnari, Deputy Commissioner of the Punjab, whose fate was to mirror Alexander Burnes', and whose temperament, plus his susceptibility to flattery, compared with Younghusband's. Lytton, unable to persuade, resorted to the kind of flattery which deluded some subordinates, otherwise level-headed enough, that they were major pieces on the strategic chess board. A revealing example is provided by this extract from a letter which Lytton wrote in September 1876 to Robert Sandemann, the Agent in Baluchistan: 'Potentates such as the Khan of Rhelat, or the Amir of Kabul, are mere dominoes, or counters which could be of no importance to us, were it not for the costly stakes we put upon them in the great game for empire which we are playing with Russia.'[5] The inference is clear: agents like Sandemann were neither mere dominoes nor counters, but pieces on the board which, directed by the viceregal hand, could sweep khans and amirs away.

Flattery takes various forms. Lytton was too much the egoist for his flattery to include praise for his subordinates; he reserved praise for Disraeli – 'My dear and great Chief' – and in writing to the Queen. In the latter case Lytton exceeded Disraeli's injunction to apply flattery with a trowel; Lytton laid it on with a shovel. In bamboozling his subordinates, Lytton not only implied that they could play their part in great events, but that the latter were rendered momentous by the Russian government's habitual deceit. He had a point, although he grossly overplayed his hand in responding to it. As so often on other occasions, London and Calcutta saw issues from very different perspectives, and failed to agree on a consistent policy of checking the Russian advance in Central Asia by a clear statement of where this must stop.

Russian ministers habitually lied to Loftus, the British Ambassador, specifically and repeatedly over the mission to Kabul which Kaufmann dispatched in May 1878. Before the 1873 Agreement was partly abrogated by mutual consent in February 1876 (or, to put it in contemporary terms, collapsed because it had become an absurdity), the British government had the right to question – *not* to prevent – Russian diplomatic activity in Afghanistan. After the Agreement had been dissolved, the British government certainly still had a diplomatic right to ask what the Russians were doing in Afghanistan. Most of the time Gorchakov, the Foreign Minister,

Giers, and their subordinates denied anything was being done at all, and continued to do so even when examples of the correspondence between Kaufmann and Sher Ali came to light in London.

The cumulative effect of such deceit had different effects on different people; it maddened Lytton, and gave him a stronger sense of being in the right; it irritated Salisbury, but it primarily confirmed him in his belief that the Russians were tricky customers. Absorbed in the Congress of Berlin, where, moreover, trickiness was not especially apparent but Russian diplomatic sophistication was, Salisbury overlooked the fact that lesser mortals might have, or needed to have, more primitive reactions. There was a further point, which Lytton conveniently ignored: when the 1873 Agreement lapsed, the British government declared that 'Badakshan and Wakhan [were] within the limits of Afghanistan'. This declaration, designed to do little more than impose a diplomatic check on Tashkent, was bound to produce a Russian riposte.

Neither territory had been delimited; Bokhara had claimed them: Sher Ali claimed them – even receiving congratulations from Lytton when he seized Maimana in May 1876. In reality, the two territories, like the Pamirs to the east, were neutral territory, Tom Tiddler's ground, or whatever an assertive ruler (or imperial power) chose to call them. The Russian riposte was swift: Osh was an outpost for further probes by the time Lytton embarked on his campaign of pressure against Sher Ali.[6]

Lytton coupled his inflation and distortion of the issues with a vendetta rather than a political campaign against Sher Ali. Lytton's pride was at stake within a month of his becoming Viceroy. He wrote to Sher Ali on 17 May 1876, requesting the presence of a British envoy in Kabul. On 1 June Sher Ali refused the request. He had two good grounds for doing so: his father's experience at Auckland's hands, and the fact that Mayo, who had certainly endeavoured to exert a friendly influence, had never sought for British representation at Kabul. Mayo had the wit to see that such a British presence would, in the Amir's eyes, mean either undue influence *or* a British pledge to defend his territories – particularly Badakshan and Wakhan. If the British Raj could not, or would not do this Sher Ali preferred to go his own way.

Mayo wisely avoided these pitfalls, Lytton did not. He continued to browbeat Sher Ali, and to demand that he cease corresponding with Kaufmann. Lytton refused to commit himself to Sher Ali's defence: he merely hinted at it, but compounded his lack of finesse by demanding that a British envoy should have the right to reside at Herat if appropriate for imperial purposes. Sher Ali was peremptory in refusing this demand. Lytton was quite right to be cautious over commitments because no strategic resources for defending Afghanistan existed in India or anywhere else within British control. It is, however, just because Lytton's policy was based on bluster and bluff, and because Sher Ali refused to be coerced, that a second, and equally pointless Afghan War occurred.

The tone of Lytton's approaches to Sher Ali is revealed in a letter of 27 August 1876 to the British Resident in Kathmandu. Lytton proceeded to define how Afghanistan's independence should be 'placed above all question' – namely by the Amir accepting 'the *sole* condition that his loyal friendship, and that of his people, for the British Government, be equally indubitable'. Lytton then explained that Sher Ali's independence not only demanded such unswerving loyalty, but total abstinence from any entangling alliance elsewhere. Not pausing to explain how 'a *sole* condition' could be thus given more than one element of compliance, Lytton stressed: '. . . we cannot allow him to fall under the influence of any Power whose interests are antagonistic to our own, and thereby become a tool of ambitions to which the whole energy of the British Government will, in case of need, be resolutely opposed'.

Lytton opined that Sher Ali, though more sinned against than sinning, appeared to be tumbling into a trap laid by the cunning Russians 'under the ludicrous illusion that he is strong enough, or crafty enough, to play off Russia against England' (another contradiction which is nowhere admitted). Lytton decided it was necessary to speak sharply and carry a big stick: 'But one lesson he will have to learn; and that is, that if he does not promptly prove himself our loyal friend, I shall be obliged to regard him as our enemy, and treat him accordingly. A tool in the hands of Russia I will never allow him to become. Such a tool it would be my duty to break before it could be used.'[7]

Lytton, of course, wanted to turn Afghanistan into a buffer state. As early as May 1876, Lytton revealed to the Queen the concept underlying his scheme: it was not necessary for Britain to rule everywhere in or beyond India's boundaries for the sway of the Queen-Empress to be apparent. 'Relations with great Native States feudatory to your Majesty, may be so remodelled and improved, as to render those states a great and durable source of strength and security to your Majesty's Indian Empire.'[8] The whole point of the September Delhi Durbar – celebrating the Queen's progression to Queen-Empress – was to demonstrate the idea in terms of pomp and ceremony. The whole point of the restless zeal which Lytton displayed throughout 1876 was to make Sher Ali a feudatory also, not an ally, a sovereign with whom one co-operated in terms of mutual national interest, but a buffer against Russian pressure.

Louis Cavagnari was to meet his fate in Kabul on 3 September 1879, the victim of Lytton's vanity and his own folly, yet the role in life of this successor to Burnes and predecessor of Younghusband seemed initially to be a happy combination of soldier, administrator and frontier agent. The son of one of Louis Napoleon's officers, who married into the militarily notable Ulster family of Montgomery, he was thirty-five in 1876, had served during the later stages of the Mutiny in a European Company regiment and then fought through several frontier campaigns. In 1861 he was seconded to the Punjab government via the Indian Staff Corps, that considerable nursery of 'politicals'. He had been Assistant Commissioner in charge of the Kohat district for ten years when Lytton's shadow fell across his path.

There is no record of Cavagnari's first meeting with Lytton, to match Alexander Burnes' account of his fated encounter with Auckland twenty-eight years before. In any event Cavagnari, despite his foreign blood, was of the Victorian English breed, except in favouring notions of fate and destiny. Christ's Hospital had schooled him and the Indian service had disciplined him. 'Possessed of remarkable energy, indomitable courage, and a genial character' Cavagnari conformed in personality to an earlier, a more serious age. A contemporary account gives a pretty good picture of the old style frontier agent before the lamp lit by Lawrence flickered and died.

> Let me describe to you Major Cavagnari, who has already played a prominent part, and will play a still more prominent part in our frontier policy. He is about five feet nine inches in height, and slimly but powerfully built. Broad shoulders set on a powerful chest, small and well-knit limbs, and an elastic buoyant step

betoken the utmost strength united with intense activity and powers of endurance.

At first sight Major Cavagnari might be thought to be a learned professor; his countenance wears a thoughtful and abstracted expression, which is intensified by the use of spectacles. But the placidity of expression on a closer scrutiny is lost in the resolute firmness of the lower face. He has a singularly pleasing and mild tone of address and conversation, and is a most agreeable host. Major Cavagnari is one of that school of Frontier Warriors and administrators of whom Nicholson and Edward[e]s were the grand representatives in a past generation.

The sensitive man was, however, also at home in the world of men.

Cavagnari, although he never loses his temper, can on occasion hit wonderfully straight from the shoulder – I remember once riding with him to an appointment he had with some Afridis to settle some vexed land question. I remained on the road, while he alone, in the centre of about a dozen stalwart ruffians, armed to the eyebrows, walked round the field. Presently the loud angry accents of a dispute reached my ears. The Afridis were surrounding Cavagnari, gesticulating with passionate vehemence, some with hands on their daggers. Cavagnari stood quiet, perfectly fearless, utterly impassive. Suddenly I saw the biggest of the Afridis go down like a bullock, and Cavagnari, with unruffled composure, returning his hand into his pocket. He had knocked the ruffian down, and the swift thoroughness of the act cowed the fierce hillmen. About halfway on the return journey, Cavagnari remarked apologetically, 'It was absolutely necessary. Please don't think I lost my temper. I was perfectly cool, but I was forced to maintain my ascendancy' and then he added meditatively, 'and I wanted to save my life.'[9]

This story would not have appealed to Lytton. He did approve of Cavagnari, however, despite his dislike of the Punjab government as a whole. 'Cavagnari is one of the very few Indian officials who have a really political head: a possession which he probably owes to his Genoese parentage.'[10] Lytton's predilection for such an ancestry in fact misled him: Cavagnari was the exact antithesis of all that Lytton stood for, as the above quotations show. But, although Cavagnari was an old style frontier officer in many ways, he is representative nonetheless of the transition from the Lawrence era to that wherein the frontier was as big a buffer area as could be devised and maintained.

Unlike Younghusband, who played the Great Game all too enthusiastically, Cavagnari was first and foremost an administrator, rather than a political officer or frontier agent. If Lytton had left him alone, Cavagnari might have died full of years and honour. Lytton tempted him, however, with ideas of playing a greater game than that of an 'anti-Afghan Confederacy'. He persuaded Cavagnari that Sher Ali could be brought down. Yet unlike Younghusband, who never administered a square foot of territory in his life – and who would have been bored to death doing so – Cavagnari drew on his experience in the Punjab to appreciate that buffer states, large and small, posed more problems than they solved, or even seemed to alleviate. From Peshawar to the Hindu Kush ran more states, so-called, than even a Cavagnari could easily describe or define, let alone bring successfully within the ambit of imperial authority. None of these states acknowledged an overlord; little more was known about them.

Cavagnari had a somewhat ill-defined responsibility for the congeries of states north of Peshawar. These were inhabited by chiefs and tribesmen who so prized their independence from British, Afghan or Kashmiri rule that one state, Buner, was not even entered by imperial troops until 1898. Both northern and southern states were alike in this fierce independence – one reason why neither Sher Ali nor Ranbir Singh did more than hint at conquest, then back off. A native agent had noted of one village near Chilas: 'The people are perfectly independent, not acknowledging even a nominal sovereignity.' Of Chaprot, another source warned that the chiefs guarded their rights as jealously 'as the strings of their wives' pyjamas'.

Shortly before succeeding Derby as Foreign Secretary in March 1878, Salisbury wrote to Lytton: 'Opinion here has been quite incapacitated . . . by the violent controversies which have taken place on the Eastern Question. You must be in one camp or the other; you must either disbelieve altogether in the existence of the Russians or you must believe that they will be at Kandahar next year. Public opinion recognises no middle holding ground.'[11]

Salisbury rather qualified this typically dispassionate comment with a tacit invitation to Lytton that he occupy Kandahar in the event of further Russian pressure on Afghanistan's northern frontier. The invitation was tacit, however, and it is clear from all the evidence that Salisbury, well aware that the real Eastern Question – who should control Constantinople and the Straits – would absorb all his energies for months to come, was averse to Lytton initiating an Afghan War off his own bat, or at all. Lytton's war was no mere sequel to the British government's passive acceptance of Russian demands for Turkish territory in Asia – and elsewhere – at the Congress of Berlin. Disraeli and Salisbury claimed to have brought 'peace with honour' back from the German capital, but although they had in reality done nothing of the kind, no attempt was made by them to communicate the nature of Russian success to Lytton, nor was he urged to counter it by the investment of Afghanistan and a thrust in Central Asia.

Lytton, however, believed he was following a strategy agreed with Disraeli from the moment of his becoming Viceroy; as Argyll, a Gladstone adherent as well as one of his former Ministers, piously remarked: 'there is no natural connection between conservatism and a low morality in politics', but the charges of 'mendacity, systematic fraud and a deliberate desire to shed blood'[12], however satisfyingly indicative of a politically more permissive age than ours and somewhat beyond the mark. Lytton was, then, the victim of his own weaknesses and Disraeli's idea of politics. It was Hartington, later to be Secretary of State for India under Gladstone, who summed up the matter justly and accurately: '(Lytton) was the incarnation and embodiment of an Indian policy which was everything that an Indian policy ought not to be'.[13] Not even Curzon, over Tibet in 1904, behaved with such a cavalier disregard for political and strategic realities as did Lytton in 1878, when the requirement was for a cool look at India's security and imperial assets, and their relationship to Britain's foreign policy.

In Lytton's defence it could be said that Kaufmann pursued a forward policy which, on the face of it, even cool heads in Calcutta, Simla and Peshawar might have construed as a direct threat to India's Northern Frontier. The critical factor here is reaction to events. Lytton made 'the worst case' assessment of Kaufmann's moves; Salisbury the best. But, with Salisbury preoccupied at Berlin, Lytton was given virtually a free hand throughout 1878 – until he marched into Afghanistan on 21 November. Lytton not only made the worst of the situation, but drew the wrong inference in terms of a riposte to Kaufmann. Salisbury did not show the insight needed to keep Lytton fully in the picture.

Lytton claimed his own intelligence picture of Kaufmann's moves was detailed and accurate: '[I have] a very complete system . . . of secret intelligence from all parts of the frontier [giving] us five secret agents at Kabul, two at Tashkent, one at Balkh, one at Maimana'. In reality, the source of Lytton's intelligence was news vendors, on whom Cavagnari also relied to a dangerous extent. The only reliable source of military intelligence was the British Embassy at St Petersburg. Salisbury had his hands full, but in distant retrospect, we could say that a clear warning from London to Lytton that he take seriously the reports of the St Petersburg Embassy as a reliable source might have prevented war with Sher Ali. Giers lied to Loftus over Russia's possible intentions regarding Afghanistan; no lies were told about Kaufmann's concentration and deployment of troops. The distinction is important, but was made neither in London nor Calcutta.

Kaufmann's ultimate task was to establish a frontier. In that context, virtual abrogation of the 1873 Agreement provided him with a legitimate reason for a forward policy. In particular, Badakshan was not just a Tom Tiddler's ground in Kaufmann's eyes; it could be traversed not only by small parties, but by formed bodies of troops. Early in 1878, two of Kaufmann's staff, Maiev and Bykov, operating with one Colonel Matvaiev, the astronomer Schwarz and assorted 'military topographers', confirmed what Forsyth's native agents had indicated in 1873 and 1874, and what Biddulph and Gordon had described so forcefully in their appreciations of the latter year: from Osh to Faizabad the country was wide open for the movement of troops.

Kaufmann, deploying parties for the immediate purpose of military survey, succeeded early in 1878 in hitting on two truths of great significance: he could march a force, whenever it suited him, into what both the British government and Sher Ali claimed as northern Afghan territory; Badakshan and its neighbours had no identity, no political reality in relation to each other, to Kabul or, for that matter, to Bokhara. Whether Kaufmann knew that Calcutta had been perfectly well aware of these awkward political and geographical facts since 1874 must be a matter of conjecture, despite Lytton's rather public congratulations to Sher Ali for his recovery of part of this disputed territory – Maimana – in 1876. This did not mean that the Viceroy was convinced of Sher Ali's jurisdiction in Badakshan and the neighbouring area. This uncertainty allowed Kaufmann to mount exploratory operations in these territories, demonstrating Russia's growing power north of the Oxus.

In May 1878 Kaufmann ordered General Abramov to march a column of 1,400 men 'from Margilan across the Alai, through Karategin down the Surkahab to Faizabad, and then south-eastward towards Qala Panja into Wakhan and the Chitral passes'. Two other columns were formed and concentrated in Fergana. These movements were known to the War Office in London within a matter of weeks, but no plan was concerted, let alone discussed, with General Haines, Commander-in-Chief at Simla, to counter them. British and native troops in the Punjab remained at their usual stations, and were neither reinforced nor exercised for operations in Afghanistan. What was not known in May, by Loftus, Salisbury or Lytton, was that a month before Abramov set off south, Kaufmann had been ordered by Giers to send General Stolietiev on a mission – to Sher Ali, at Kabul. Not until the following December was any Russian source publicly prepared to admit that the Stolietiev mission was a subordinate element in a campaign of opposition against British foreign policy, and was specifically seen as a 'diversion intended against India'.

What Alexander and his Ministers primarily wanted was a consolidation of Russia's European role, not a major expansion of its Asiatic one. The progress in Central Asia would continue until insurmountable barriers, physical, strategic or political, were met. Once met, the progress would stop. This point was well taken by Disraeli and Salisbury; unfortunately for Lytton, they did not bother to tell him that they had done so. Cranbrook at the India Office ensured that neither the Cabinet nor the War Office reminded Lytton and Haines that Kaufmann's regular forces in Turkestan totalled 25,000, or 30,000 on a war establishment. Cossack and locally enlisted units brought the total to 60,000, but the demands of internal security in a territory the size of northern and central India demanded the commitment of virtually all this force.

The War Office knew that the prime task of Russia's armies was 'the defence of home territory and to check revolt'. Lytton deluded himself that by invading Afghanistan he could prevent Kaufmann seizing the initiative along the entire length of the Karakoram and the Hindu Kush. Kaufmann had neither the means nor the intention to do anything of the kind. Abramov's force for the flag march throughout Fergana in the spring of 1878 comprised 15,000 regular and Cossack troops, all that could be spared from tasks which were a mirror image of those imposed on British and native forces in India: keeping the country quiet.[14]

British and native armies in India were no more able to furnish a permanent field army than Kaufmann's forces, nor could Haines draw on larger manpower resources than Kaufmann if outright war between England and Russia in Central Asia occurred. Not even Lytton seriously contemplated this possibility, despite rhetoric about thwarting Russia's European designs by a master stroke against its Asiatic Empire. The Queen may have desired to give the Russians 'such a beating' but had no belief in Lytton's capacity to do so. Disraeli and Salisbury became similarly convinced between February and July 1878 that turning to Bismarck so that Russia was checked at the Straits reinforced the dangers of Britain unilaterally going to war, at any point, distant or otherwise. The drift towards a Second Afghan War continued nonetheless.

By the time Salisbury had played his part at Berlin, Lytton was bent on war with Afghanistan. Just as Disraeli began to orchestrate a pre-election campaign based on 'peace with honour' (but four clear months after the Congress ended), Lytton went to war. Eighteen months later, in March 1880, Disraeli and the Party he had led so exotically were defeated by Gladstone, the 'Russian Agent'; Lytton resigned, to be succeeded by Lord Ripon; Abdur Rahman, the Amir for Afghanistan approved by Kaufmann and his masters, became the preferred choice of Ripon and his agent in Kabul, Leppel Griffin. On Lytton's return home all but Queen Victoria cold shouldered him; a couple of speeches in the House of Lords wherein he defended his Afghan policy with more eloquence than conviction, and the Paris Embassy appointment aside, Lytton suffered virtual extinction from public affairs and a sad retreat into his private world.

The genesis of Lytton's rise and fall can be found in his actions during Salisbury's defence of British interests during and following the Congress of Berlin. In the months before his brief triumph over Sher Ali, Lytton used all his considerable powers of flattery to seduce not only Cavagnari but others who should have known better from common sense policies and balanced decisions. By April Cavagnari believed himself in Lytton's confidence. The Viceroy encouraged this illusion. Cavagnari, relying on indirect information, and buying it moreover on his own admission at 'high prices', said that Sher Ali was faced with mounting opposition; that a Russian agent was already in Kabul; that the mother of the Amir's favourite son, Abdulla Jan, was opposed to the former and was willing to co-operate in 'disposing' of him. Cavagnari opined that 'threats' – to Sher Ali – might be used with a fair prospect of success if it became necessary to utilize Afghanistan in the endeavour to strike a blow at Russia in Central Asia.

All this was, to put it mildly, wide of the mark, both in terms of raw intelligence and assessment of the situation. Cavagnari had begun to succumb to the lure of Lytton's Great Game. In the process, and lacking reliable intelligence of Kaufmann's military dispositions or diplomatic activities, Cavagnari and others similarly inclined to play the Game, jumped to conclusions. The worst supposition prevailed: Lytton's sole source of intelligence was Cavagnari's agents, mere news vendors, of proven unreliability.[15] The 'intelligence' these agents bought and sold, dating in this instance from mid-June to the end of July, when Lytton asked the India Office for confirmation of the news he had received from the Foreign Office regarding Abramov's march and the Russian mission to Kabul, came to this: a large Russian mission had been sent to Kabul and had met with an 'enthusiastic reception'; Russian troops in Turkestan had been 'mobilised'. On receiving this so-called intelligence, Lytton and Cavagnari proceeded to concoct a Russophobic conspiracy theory.

Thus Lytton, at this period, might well have seen a connection of the gravest import between a mission to Kabul and the 'mobilisation' of troops – and have done so because of his own preparations for war. He assumed, moreover, that Abramov was marching to Kabul, and assumed further that it would be he who would conclude a treaty with Sher Ali. Lytton assumed the worst – that a senior officer on Kaufmann's staff was in Kabul in midsummer, 'alienating' Sher Ali from Britain, and paving the way for the inclusion of his territories in the Russian sphere. This was not the case, despite Lytton's fears – or hopes. By the time he did hear confirmation of Kaufmann's operations from London, however, any hope of assessing them at their true value had vanished.

Lytton can certainly be forgiven for not knowing that Stolietiev was stopped for five days in August by Afghan officials before crossing the Oxus, and that, although he was honourably received on his delayed entry in Kabul (hardly surprising, given oriental etiquette, and that he was a serving Major-General) he and his party were thereafter incommunicado until they left in mid-December. Nor would Lytton know that shortly before he arrived in Kabul, Stolietiev received an urgent message from Kaufmann, telling him to exercise the utmost caution and in no sense to commit himself to a binding treaty.

The three months between August and November remain, however, to point the finger at Lytton, months during which both London and Calcutta were in a position to have concerted a reaction to Kaufmann had they chosen to do so. Loftus made quite plain that Abramov's flag march had been concluded at the latest by the end of July. Loftus also received the first indication of Stolietiev's mission on 4 September. By mid-September at the outside, therefore, Lytton knew that whatever the objective of the mission, it was not going to be supported by troops, 'mobilised' or otherwise. Lytton would have been right, however, to have demanded an explanation from Sher Ali as to why he was prepared to receive a Russian mission in Kabul but determined to refuse a British agent. The answer would have included three factors: Sher Ali's suspicions of viceregal policies; the difference between a mission and an agent, the one itinerant, the other permanent; Lytton's tone in his earlier communications with Sher Ali, 'personal, grandiloquent, offensive'.[16]

A Cabinet dominated by Salisbury was well aware of the need for both firmness and courtesy in viceregal exchanges with the Amir in Kabul. In early August, Lytton had in fact been reluctantly authorised to send a British mission to Kabul, but not to insist on Sher Ali receiving it. Salisbury wanted Lytton to respond to Kaufmann's moves – indeed he instructed the Viceroy to dispatch the British mission via Kandahar as a hint that there lay the point of prospective danger. Salisbury did not, however, want Lytton to raise the stakes.

One may question the wisdom of so equivocal an instruction to a viceroy of Lytton's stamp. (Twenty-eight years later Balfour was also to equivocate in allowing Curzon's agent Younghusband to commit aggression against defenceless Tibetans.) That is not the point: the Cabinet had, belatedly, intervened in the arbitration, not only in the conduct of Indian frontier policy. Lytton could abide by the Cabinet's decision, or ignore it. He chose not only to ignore the decision but to make Sher Ali's rejection of the mission a *casus belli*.

Lytton's choice of Sir Neville Chamberlain, commander of the Madras Army, to lead the mission indicates that Sher Ali was no mere cab to be summoned off the rank. Lytton explained to Cranbrook: 'His selection will, I think, be agreeable to Lawrence and the whole Punjab school.' On the face of it, that was true enough. Chamberlain personified to a rare degree the frontier soldier of which Lawrence had been the prototype. Apart from a record of unsurpassed bravery in action – he had been wounded six times in the First Afghan War alone – he was also generally regarded as the model of common sense and straight dealing. He knew Sher Ali personally and, although this was certainly no recommendation in Lytton's eyes, had much sympathy for that sorely tried ruler. Further, Chamberlain was that rare thing in the Anglo-Indian military establishment, a Liberal in politics and a firm believer in Britain minding its own business so far as possible. He responded to Lytton's August overtures cordially enough and agreed to lead a mission to Kabul, but he stuck to a view expressed earlier in the year: 'Neighbours we must have on our North-West Frontier, but we shall not find the better ones by going through the Passes . . . we know the result of our interference in Afghan affairs in 1838–39.'[17]

Chamberlain was straight. Unfortunately, Lytton was not. Immediately on receiving Cabinet permission to send a mission to Kabul, Lytton told Chamberlain: 'I have obtained telegraphic permission to insist now on the Amir's immediate reception of a British Mission'. Content with this falsehood, Lytton then ordered Haines to give an appreciation of the forces he thought necessary to invade Afghanistan via the Kurram Valley and Bolan Pass. The objectives to be attained by these routes were Kabul and Kandahar. On 10 August, Haines replied, giving an estimate for the proposed operation of 20,000, but stressing that such a force, if given a double axis on which to advance, would need to be supported by twice the number in lines of communication troops. Indifferent to operational realities, Lytton ordered Haines to prepare a field force. Having settled such seeming trivia to his satisfaction, Lytton wrote on 14 August to Sher Ali. In the meantime, Owen Tudor Burne, Lytton's propagandist at the India Office, worked on the Secretary of State,

Cranbrook. The result was an official protest to Giers about Stolie-tiev's mission couched, according to Burne, in 'blood and thunder' language but, in fact, designed merely to maintain the diplomatic proprieties. It is, perhaps, characteristic of the lack of communi-cation between London and Calcutta that Lytton was not told of the protest. Had Lytton been told, *his* hand would have been weakened; he intended to try a fall with Sher Ali, and sought no role from higher authority.

The letter to Sher Ali was, for Lytton, conciliatory. No demands were made. An experienced native agent, Gholam Hussein Khan, known to and trusted by Sher Ali, delivered Lytton's letter on 17 August – all to no avail. Sher Ali wanted nothing of Lytton. His son and appointed heir, Abdulla Jan, died on the day the letter was delivered. The death was coincidental, but Sher Ali knew that Lytton had intrigued with another son, Yaqub Khan, in order to install him as Amir in Kabul and the Viceroy's tool. Sher Ali received Gholam Hussein civilly but, gave no indication that he would admit Chamberlain to Kabul, or even let him march through the Bolan Pass. Sher Ali had established a non-committal relation-ship with Kaufmann; he feared to initiate even that with Lytton.

Whilst Chamberlain prepared his mission, convinced that he was representing the British government, not just the Raj, in demanding that Sher Ali receive him, Lytton solicited approval in the one quarter where he was confident of a sympathetic response. On 31 August Lytton wrote a letter to the Queen, which so completely expresses his failure to distinguish between pomp and circumstance that only giving it in its entirety will explain why Disraeli and Salisbury were, in due season, so comprehensively to disown him.

The Russian army of the Caspian is, with the acquiescence and support of the Persian Government, rapidly advancing down the Attock Valley, absorbing the Akhal country, and thus approach-ing Herat . . . the Russian forces in Turkestan have been moved to strong positions along the right bank of the Oxus. These positions, if permanently held, will render the Russian frontier conterminous with the whole northern boundary of Afghanistan, and Russian influence predominant throughout the upper Afghan provinces . . . General Abramov with a military escort, variously reported as numbering from two to three hundred mounted men (Cossacks and Usbegs) and accompanied by one or two other

Russian officers of high rank, appears to have crossed the Oxus, reaching Kabul some weeks ago . . . The Amir, who little more than a year ago flatly refused to receive at Kabul a British mission of any kind, has now been publicly entertaining at his Court, with marked honour and distinction, a large Russian embassy of high rank charged with a direct communication for his Highness from the Czar himself . . . These facts are now known throughout all Central Asia and India; where they are, of course, popularly regarded and commented on, as a serious check to the policy and power of your Majesty.

In these circumstances, I have recommended to Your Majesty's Government the immediate despatch (at any risk), by the Government of India, of a British mission to Kabul. That recommendation having received the sanction of your Majesty's Government, I have appointed General Sir Neville Chamberlain . . . to take charge of this important mission . . . Sir Neville will be instructed, in the first instance, to demand explanations of the Amir as to his reception of a Russian mission after his refusal to receive a British one; and then to use every endeavour to effect, if possible in concert with his Highness, a pacific solution of the difficulty of the position in which we find ourselves now placed.

But it is quite possible that the Amir may still refuse to receive our mission, possible even that it may be fired upon by his orders. This risk we must now run . . . such are the difficulties and anxieties of the position in which we are landed at last by seven years of the policy pertinaciously imposed by Mr Gladstone on successive Governments of India, in the conduct of their relations with Afghanistan. A small stitch taken in time, even a few years ago, would have certainly saved the nine big ones which may have to be taken now . . .[18]

Falsehoods to Chamberlain were bad enough; deliberately deceiving the Queen was Lytton's most striking move towards self-destruction. The Queen read Cabinet papers carefully. She knew Lytton had not been authorised to impose a British mission on Kabul. She disliked Gladstone; reminding her of the fact was no business of Lytton. From this time onwards, two episodes developed. In London, Disraeli and Salisbury belatedly drew plans for limiting so far as possible the damage which Lytton's folly was likely to cause.

In Calcutta, and at Simla, a rather puny war machine cranked into action. The Queen noted in early October: 'The Cabinet has been much concerned with this alarming Afghan affair. Lord Lytton should not have sent the Mission, having been forbidden to do so by the Cabinet.'[19] The Queen was nearly right; had Salisbury known Lytton better, the mission's despatch would certainly have been forbidden.

Lytton had, however, already crossed his Rubicon. A month before the Queen alerted Disraeli and Salisbury, Lytton ordered Chamberlain to Peshawar. Salisbury's instruction for the mission to move via Kandahar was flatly ignored: Lytton could counter Sher Ali refusing to allow Chamberlain to enter Kabul by marching through the Khyber Pass. Lytton told Cranbrook of his intentions, assuming the latter's compliance. This move also boomeranged: on 13 September, Lytton was ordered to pause, and to stay his hand until Loftus had seen Giers. Lytton did pause, for five days. Chamberlain was then ordered to march, not to await further clarification, or orders, from London. This was the act which Disraeli was to comment on so bitterly five days after Chamberlain's rebuff at the Afghan border on the 21st: 'When V-roys and Comms-in-Chief disobey orders, they ought to be sure of success in their mutiny. Lytton, by disobeying orders, has only secured insult and failure . . . To force the Khyber, and take Kabul is a perilous business.'[20]

Prophetic words, especially from the Prime Minister whose desire for 'a man of ambition, imagination, some vanity and much will' was to discredit them both. If Disraeli had known the full story his words might have been more bitter still. On 19 September Chamberlain at Peshawar was handed a letter from Sher Ali in reply to Lytton's, sending condolences on the death of Abdulla Jan and pressing for the reception of a British mission at Kabul. This letter from Sher Ali was ignored at the time, and has been overlooked since; from the point of view which regards the Second Afghan War as an essential stage in the evolution of imperial strategy, one can see why.

Sher Ali had received Lytton's letter, replied and had it delivered within a week. He had treated the bearer of these letters – Gholam Hussein yet again – with marked courtesy. Above all, Sher Ali's tone was conciliatory, or would have been to any recipient still aware of realities. He wrote: 'I do not agree to the mission coming in this manner' – that is, by way of the Khyber. It might be supposed that Sher Ali's rejoinder was unhelpful and evasive since Lytton had not, in his letter of 14 August, directly browbeaten him about receiving a mission. Sher Ali must, however, have known what was in Lytton's mind, because he added: 'The Russian envoy has come, and has come with my permission'. Sher Ali then stressed that 'the mission . . . would be honourably sent away after the Id of Ramadan' (approximately the end of September in 1878).[21] He concluded by saying that 'His Highness claimed the right to have time to consider the matter as to its [the Chamberlain mission] reception, and that, if after reflection its reception should prove agreeable to him, that he would fix the time for its arrival and make suitable arrangements to receive it honourably.'

Chamberlain told Lytton of this letter but suggested it should be brushed aside, and that he should march to the Khyber and force the issue. Chamberlain wrote: 'It is now quite evident that the Amir is bent upon stretching procrastination to the utmost, and determined upon asserting his claim to total independence of action by making the acceptance of the Mission dependent upon his sole pleasure, and dictating when it shall be received . . . The Amir is bent upon upholding his will and dignity at any cost to the dignity of the British Government.'[22]

This was not the Chamberlain who had counselled delay who, but a week earlier had said: 'The question is whether, for the sake of a day or two's delay, we should risk the certainty of an open rupture with all its consequences, or give the short additional time in the hope that it may enable the Amir to act with reason whilst (according to Afghan ideas) preserving his dignity.' Between these two letters Lytton had made no new approach to Chamberlain, or pressed upon him more empty compliments. The chemistry of imperialism, made more potent by the atmosphere of 'face' which Lytton had deliberately contrived, had done its insidious work. Chamberlain, the paladin of the frontier, found himself in total agreement with the Viceroy's lofty assertion that the existence of the Russian mission in Kabul was 'a studiously insolent and significant advertisement to all India and all Central Asia of the impunity with which he [the Amir] could slight the friendly overtures and brave the long restrained resentment of the British Government'.

Chamberlain was to eat his words in the coming two years, but the real tragedy of his abrupt change of heart in September 1878 is that he knew then, with his great experience and essential sympathy for Sher Ali's position, that forcing the issue would do no good. If anyone had a right to judge frontier operations, it was Chamberlain. On learning that Cavagnari would form part of his mission he had hoped they would 'pull together'; however, he soon regretted the Deputy Commissioner's impetuosity – although it is doubtful whether the old soldier ever grasped how that unfortunate man's latent vanity was aroused by Lytton's flattery. Chamberlain spoke truly of Cavagnari when he discerned that 'He was by nature a man of high spirit and great determination, but perhaps too much inclined to trust to the power of his will and the power of our arms'.[23]

On 20 September, however, when Chamberlain and Cavagnari rode to Jamrud, at the mouth of the Khyber, their common mood was exactly suited to Lytton's purpose. Chamberlain and Cavagnari rode to their encounter with Faiz Mohamed Khan, Commander of the Afghan outpost at Ali Musjid and an old frontier friend and enemy, not only in a mood of imperial self-righteousness but at a time which Lytton could not have chosen better. The Cabinet had dispersed to grouse moors and country houses; the Queen-Empress's 'policy and power' was entrusted to a couple of agents determined on clearing all obstacles from their path.

There is no doubt that Cavagnari deliberately provoked an incident on 21 September. Even before he met Faiz Mohamed, Cavagnari, 'ardent, headstrong, void of fear',[24] took twenty men of the escort and, ignoring the protests of Afridis who were (or who had become) Sher Ali's men, pushed his way past them and rode to meet the Afghan Commander. When he met Faiz Mohamed, Cavagnari decided he would select the spot where they would talk. He then insisted on being allowed to pass the frontier. Faiz Mohamed pointed out that he had no authority to let him. 'He was only a sentry . . . unless he received orders from Kabul he could not let the mission pass his post.' The escort Commander, Colonel Jenkins, describes how the glove thus thrown down was picked up:

> Major Cavagnari said to the Sirdar [Faiz Mohamed]: 'We are both servants; you of the Amir of Kabul, I of the British Government. It is of no use for us to discuss those matters. I only came to get a straight answer from you. Will you oppose the passage of the Mission by force?'
>
> The Sirdar said: 'Yes, I will; and you may take it as a kindness

and because I remember friendship that I do not fire upon you for what you have done already.' After this we shook hands and mounted our horses; and the Sirdar said again: 'You have had a straight answer.'

On 22 September Chamberlain wrote to Lytton: 'My Lord – The first act has been played out; and I do not think that any impartial looker-on can consider that any other course has been left open to us consistent with dignity than to openly break with the Amir.'[25]

Salisbury's reaction to Lytton's folly was characteristic: 'The time for war has been chosen with singular infelicity'. Even for him, these words were, in two senses, a considerable understatement. The time for war was, indeed, infelicitous. Salisbury was seeking ways to regain some role for Britain in the arbitration of European affairs while simultaneously, and secretly, acquiring Cyprus as *une place d'armes* in the Mediterranean to watch the Straits and guard the Suez Canal. He could do without a Russian riposte to Lytton's war, one which would be made at a time and place of the Czar's choice. Yet Salisbury also sensed that a direct order to Lytton forbidding further provactive acts regarding Sher Ali would be ignored. The requirement in London was nominally to support Lytton whilst propitiating St Petersburg.

A complementary requirement was to deny Lytton material support, while accepting that the war could not be prevented. The overriding requirement, so far as India's Northern and North-Western Frontiers were concerned, was an amir in Kabul who would maintain his throne without threats from Calcutta or overtures from Kaufmann in Tashkent. The Cabinet accepted Lytton's description of Sher Ali's reply to his original letter – of 14 August – as 'insolent', although in fact it referred solely to his sense of grievance, his shock at the 21 September affair, and his fear of Cavagnari's actions in inciting Afridis by buying their services. As a result, and on 19 October, Disraeli authorised an ultimatum to Sher Ali. The ultimatum was deliberately designed 'to strengthen the *casus belli*', by insisting on Chamberlain's reception in Kabul. By 9 October, however, the three columns which were to invade Afghanistan had already been formed. Although Cavagnari's suggestion of a surprise attack on Ali Masjid was dropped, the columns had been concentrated by the 15th opposite the Bolan, the Kurram – and the Khyber.[26]

Between 25 and 30 October the Cabinet finally caved in and supported Lytton to the hilt. On the 25th Disraeli half-heartedly suggested further delay. Cranbrook, constitutionally indecisive, disliked the permission Lytton was given to go ahead with military preparations, and Salisbury remained unconvinced that the issue bore any relevance to politics as he knew it. But, on the 30th, after 'a stormy Cabinet session' as Disraeli reported to the Queen, Salisbury gave in. A final ultimatum was sent to the Amir: in form a demand, in truth a declaration of war.

By 15 November the three columns were ready to march, and the last curtain was about to be rung up. Perhaps some apprehension that it was all a ghastly mistake had by then begun to penetrate Disraeli's tired old brain. Loftus at St Petersburg and Thomson – the Minister at Tehran – made it clear in a series of reports in October and early November that Russian moves did not presage major military operations. Gorchakov's 'friendly assurances' to Loftus that Russia disclaimed all interest in Afghanistan were doubtless taken with more than a pinch of Disraelian salt, but the triumph of Berlin was already fading nonetheless. On the 20th the Prime Minister refused to discuss matters with Lawrence, the greatest public servant which British India had bred. It was said that Disraeli even insulted Lawrence with his inimitable sarcasm about the length of his letters to *The Times*. The following day much that Lawrence and his devoted band had worked for went up in flames.

The onset of the Second Afghan War, its course, and conclusion – an undivided Afghanistan with Abdur Rahman as Amir, a ruler acceptable to both Calcutta and Tashkent – is, in fact, mainly important in political terms: Salisbury's enforced acceptance of Lytton's aggression, followed by a steady search for compromise established a precedent. Lansdowne and Balfour followed much the same policy concerning Curzon's aggressive designs on Tibet, although with vacillation and ambiguity. In 1904, however, Balfour supported Lansdowne's search for something better than mere compromise with St Petersburg: while Curzon allowed Younghusband to dig his grave in Tibet, Lansdowne laid the foundations of an Anglo-Russian *entente*, ratified as a Convention on 31 August 1907. Younghusband's folly in Tibet did not prevent the Balfour government from seeking to put relations with imperial Russia on an entirely new footing at a time when Germany had emerged as the major threat to what remained of the Concert of Europe.

Salisbury, infinitely more gifted and perceptive than Balfour or Lansdowne, was unable to regulate Indian affairs in such a fashion. Salisbury wished to give European issues a priority in the formulation and execution of British overseas policy as a whole – precisely because he also saw imperial Germany as a threat to peace – but was unable to do so. In 1878 Britain's imperial role, if not the potency of imperial sentiment, forced Salisbury to concede more to Lytton than was good for India's Northern Frontier security or the office of viceroy. Salisbury made his concessions, moreover, well aware that a Russian riposte was inevitable sooner or later. He was also politically sensitive to the possibility that if Disraeli was replaced by Gladstone, a Liberal Party nominee as viceroy would concede more than was healthy for India – or Afghanistan.

Both Salisbury's assessment and forecast were accurate. Gladstonian compromise, moreover, was followed by a return to the forward policy, setting in train events which led to Younghusband's singular conduct concerning the Pamirs in 1890 and 1891. The main reason why compromise defines the conclusion of the Second Afghan War, however, is the series of blows to British prestige and policy which characterised its first eighteen months. Kabul was entered by May 1879; the Russian mission had decamped; Sher Ali had fled; Yaqub Khan was installed in his place. British agents were to be stationed throughout Afghanistan to ensure that Yaqub Khan's fealty – bought for a £60,000 annual subvention – would be supported by tribes hitherto notable for practical independence of Kabul.

Thus far the pattern of the First Afghan War had been repeated. Subsequently events were repeated in terms of blood and sacrifice. The bulk of the invading force was withdrawn – on grounds of cost. Cavagnari, nominated British Resident by Lytton, arrived in Kabul with an escort of 70 Sepoys from the Guides on 24 July 1879. Cavagnari, now Sir Louis, and a made man, took up his quarters in the Bala Hissar. He was not to enjoy his triumph for long. On 3 September, the Residency was attacked by Afghan troops either mutinous from lack of pay or incited by mullahs. After a day-long defence in the classic manner, the Residency was overrun, Cavagnari and the escort dying to a man. Yaqub Khan made no effort to intervene, although he unctuously informed Calcutta of the disaster.

69

The situation was partially redeemed by Roberts fighting his way through to Kabul from the Khyber. Six months later he held Kabul in his strong grasp, but Yaqub Khan had decamped, preferring the security of abdication – and the loss of £60,000 annually – to the risks of being Lytton's creature. This blow to his pride finished Lytton. In January 1880 he wrote to Cranbrook: 'The kingdom . . . has fallen to pieces at the first blow; and it would now be a difficult if not impracticable task, even if it were politically desirable, to reunite these fragments under any single ruler.'[27] Thus Lytton threw in the sponge, indifferent to what Roberts might achieve, ignorant of the fact that Abdur Rahman, uncle to Yaqub Khan, a refugee under Kaufmann's protection since cast out of Afghanistan by Sher Ali, was prepared to replace Yaqub Khan – and was a man who knew how to bide his time.

Gladstone's overwhelming victory in the April 1880 General Election finished Disraeli also. The new government only wanted to end the war. Roberts, no Liberal, but an educated soldier nonetheless, agreed. Lepel Griffin, Roberts' chief political officer in Kabul – an official from the Punjab, a determined exponent of Lawrence's convictions, a committed Liberal in politics – convinced Roberts that Abdur Rahman was the man to rule an undivided Afghanistan. 'An approach was made to him and after several months of rather difficult negotiations, on 22 July [1880], at a grand durbar at Sherpur camp, a proclamation was made naming him as new Amir.'[28]

Griffin's arrival in Kabul preceded the Gladstone government but, in practice neatly coincided with it. Griffin set about persuading Abdur Rahman and other Afghan chieftains that the new broom in London and Calcutta intended to sweep very clean, to clear away the mess made by Lytton, and to create, above all, a united Afghanistan. It is unlikely, however, that Griffin would have succeeded in persuading Abdur Rahman to accept the throne if he had not promised that British agents would not be stationed in Afghanistan – that clinched that matter. No agents meant no interference. With Lytton's insistent demand for a British presence gone, Abdur Rahman had some chance of keeping, not merely accepting a throne.

It was nevertheless a very odd end to all but the final stages of the Second Afghan War – Abdur Rahman, the protégé of the Russians, proclaimed Amir after Lytton's candidate had preferred asylum to a throne, and the 'moonlight steeplechase' had ended in crushing electoral defeat at the hands of the Party which had made much at the hustings of the iniquity and irrelevance of the forward policy and the conflict to which it led. Lytton had written to his old friend Fitzjames Stephen in 1879 of 'the fancy prospect I had painted on the blank wall of the future of bequeathing to India the supremacy of Central Asia and the resources of a first rate power'. Now all was dust and ashes or, as Disraeli, whose noise and splash led Lytton so sadly astray, would have quoted 'mere leather and prunella'.

7

Agents of War and Peace

The six years between Lytton's extinction in 1880 and Francis Younghusband's advent as the most notable player of the Great Game are marked by three developments, all reaching a decisive stage during 1885: the Russian riposte to Lytton's invasion of Afghanistan, forecast by Salisbury, ineptly handled by Gladstone; the first Anglo-Russian Boundary Commission – proposed in March 1884 by Granville; a deliberate attempt to complement the purpose of this mission – demarcation of Afghanistan's northern frontier – by welding the states south of the Hindu Kush into a defensive system whereby tribal rulers would owe allegiance and swear fealty to the Raj rather than a maharajah of Kashmir or an amir in Kabul.

These three events were preceded by a period of 'masterly inactivity', reflecting the outlook of Gladstone's viceroy Ripon. A more positive stage was initiated in 1885 by Ripon's successor Dufferin, an experienced pro-consul, whom Salisbury trusted. Dufferin was influenced by Salisbury in the evolution and execution of a policy which attempted to maintain an Anglo-Russian *rapprochement* on the roof of the world whilst redefining a feasible British sphere of influence in Afghanistan, Kashmir and the hill states. But Ripon and Dufferin, viceroys of political power and inclination, were swayed by the turbulent state of domestic affairs throughout 1885 and 1886. Gladstone resigned in June 1885. Salisbury succeeded him – but only to February 1886.

A short-lived Liberal Ministry was, however, replaced by a Conservative government in July 1886. Ripon left India in December 1884. Dufferin arrived during the last days of Gladstone's government, becoming, in effect, Salisbury's nominee. Dufferin settled into office as Salisbury and Gladstone played box and cox, then set himself to prosecute a moderate forward policy once the dust at home had settled. The consummation of this policy was the Boundary Settlement of August 1887. Afghanistan's north-eastern frontier was, however, left undemarcated – as both the Russian government and Calcutta wished – leaving a major problem for Salisbury and Dufferin's successor Lansdowne. This gave Francis Younghusband a chance to play the Great Game with a vengeance – at the cost of losing his credibility as a trans-frontier agent and intelligence officer.

Indian affairs were bound to be affected by political turmoil in Britain, a factor conveniently illustrated by the closure of the Gilgit Agency in July 1881 and its re-establishment in November 1889. The Agency then remained a distant outpost of the Raj until independence in 1947. Closing the Agency was due not only to Calcutta's difficulty in maintaining contact with Biddulph, or any successor, but also to Gladstone's rooted dislike of agents at a distant point. Re-establishing the Agency reflected the factor that Salisbury, disliking agents' tendency to overplay their hand, believed in the necessity for the Game to be played nonetheless. He derided Russophobes, but he did believe that Gilgit should mark a point at which British influence must prevail, stiffened by a garrison rather than dependent on an agent playing the lone hand.

The six years leading up to Younghusband's entry into the Great Game were thus a prelude to his early career on the Northern Frontier, Kashgaria and the Pamirs. Of greater importance in this context, however, is the hand of the Home government – or, rather, Salisbury's hand – shown by degrees, but indicating nonetheless that Calcutta's sway was progressively being replaced by decisions made, however belatedly, in London. Salisbury – Prime Minister and Foreign Secretary at all material times – was strengthened in his determination to keep viceroys and agents in check by hard-won experience, imperial and domestic. Dufferin prosecuted a forward policy, but only up to a point, never beyond it. Lansdowne, influenced by Younghusband, and others, pushed beyond that point – until Salisbury recalled him, and his subordinates, to order. By intervening directly, if tardily, in the early 1890s, Salisbury ensured that a second Boundary Settlement in 1895 prevented that co-terminity between Russia and India which so many viceroys, players of the Great Game, and Russophobes opposed and thwarted. The Settlement has stood the test of time: Russia and Pakistan remain separated by the Afghan Panhandle of the Little Pamirs.

Younghusband never appreciated political realities – indeed, was unaware of them – unlike the principal characters in the field during the 1880s: Ridgeway, Lumsden, Lockhart, Woodthorpe, Elias and McNair. Younghusband simply lifted his eyes to the hills, whence undoubtedly came his spiritual strength. His six predecessors kept their eyes on the job in hand. They were level-headed, not to say hard-headed, late Victorians. Elias and McNair were officials, explorer and surveyor rather than agents in the traditional soldierly mould. Their compatriots were soldiers, but although certainly men of action, also of a calm, reflective stamp. Ridgeway and Lumsden succeeded in their protracted and arduous duties on the Afghan Boundary Commission. Lockhart and Woodthorpe deluded themselves somewhat about the feasibility of welding the hill states into a defensive system but never let the issue go to their heads. Neither success or relative failure denies the fact that all six agents thought clearly and with some objectivity about the limits rather than the extent of British imperial power.

The Victorian high noon had passed. It was an age in which only Hayward's ghost haunted the passes of Gilgit and Chitral. Indirectly, change was revealed in these agents' accounts of adventure, hardship and achievement. In particular, narratives of the Boundary Commission, and much detail in the Lockhart-Woodthorpe Report, convey in unadorned language a sense of tasks faithfully executed amidst the wilds. Narrations evoke the desert and the *sowar*; Lockhart and Woodthorpe domesticate their mountain eyrie. The cumulative effect of reading such accounts is curiously reassuring: these men were at peace with themselves, and saw no need to strive for the unattainable. By contrast and despite the strength derived from playing a lone hand in his own fashion, Younghusband's every action is curiously unnerving.

The Russian riposte to the Second Afghan War was unambiguous: invasion of Afghan territory in March 1885 at Penjdeh, on what purported to be, but had not been demarcated as Abdur Rahman's northern-western frontier. The invasion was a brief, limited affair, inflicting casualties on Afghan troops and causing some loss of face to British members of the Boundary Commission. The purpose of the riposte was threefold: to serve notice that Russia's final conquest of the Turkomans posed a contingent threat to Afghanistan's western frontier – and British India's exposed flank west of Quetta; to test British support for Abdur Rahman; and to serve notice that a Boundary Commission would not cramp the Russian style on the Pamirs.

The riposte had its desired effect. Gladstone did not support Abdur Rahman, despite rhetoric in the House of Commons on 27 April that 'We must do our best to have right done in this matter' – in Bismarck's derisive phrase, 'pure Offenbach'[1] the Boundary Commission successfully completed its tasks, but Dufferin then proceeded to insure against possible Russian 'sapping and mining', as he called it, south of the Hindu Kush by despatching Colonels Lockhart and Woodthorpe in the summer of 1885 to what was designated, with a generous vagueness, the Northern Frontier. Abdur Rahman, despite, or because of, Dufferin's blandishments, was left to reflect on a British policy which brought him into virtual co-terminity with imperial Russia on his northern and western frontiers, denying him thereafter any vestige of compensation – or influence – amongst those hill states of which Chitral was chief.

The Russian riposte was not only unambiguous, but was based on two well-perceived factors: knowledge of Ripon's reluctance to authorise intelligence operations, comparable to those carried out by the second Forsyth mission a decade earlier, north of the Hindu Kush; and a conviction that no amir in Kabul could lay effective claim to territory on the right bank of the Oxus, and that any lands therein, formerly feudatory to Bokhara were, in fact, Russian. Territory on the left bank should be demarcated; Giers, more assertive in Central Asian affairs than Gorchakov, was willing to sustain amicable relations with Abdur Rahman provided the latter knew where the power lay.

Elias, a member of the Indian Political Department, was dispatched to Kashgar early in 1880, but Ripon refused to countenance him, or anybody else as British Agent there. Ripon ignored pleas that the Russian Consul in Kashgar, 'the argus eyed Petrovsky', should be watched by Elias, whose earlier travels in Chinese Turkestan abundantly qualified him for the appointment. By the same token, Ripon refused to allow any intelligence operations into what was still believed in Calcutta to be a buffer area north and south of the Oxus headwaters. He therefore ignored Russian activities in this area, and only had his eyes opened when William McNair, an official from the Survey of India, penetrated Badakshan from Chitral.

McNair's opposite numbers, Mataviev and Severstov, included in their Survey of Russian-claimed territory the provinces of Badakshan, Shignan, Rushan and Wakhan. All these were trans-Oxus: if 'masterly inactivity' was not to become synonymous with a Russian advance to the Hindu Kush, something on the lines of the Granville-Gorchakov Agreement needed to be revived. The fact that Abdur Rahman had not abandoned his claim to these territories only added urgency to the issue. What was the point of a Liberal government clearing up the mess left by Lytton if no attempt was made to reach agreement with St Petersburg on the extent and limits of the British and Russian Empires at these most distant points?

In March 1884, Ripon accepted the logic of this argument. He wrote a long dispatch for Kimberley, the Secretary of State for India, concentrating on 'certain proposals for demarcating the boundaries of Afghanistan in consequence of the new advance of Russia towards her frontier'. Given that the Russian advance at the time in question was towards Herat – in February, the Turcomans at Merv had finally submitted to General Abramov – Ripon actually meant that Afghanistan's north-west frontier should be demarcated. As a result, Ripon's words signalled the first stage in a long process whereby the Great Game was progressively replaced – if never wholly supplanted – by boundary commissions and the like. Younghusband, who commenced his intelligence career in February 1886, came to his inheritance rather late in the day.

Ripon claimed that Kimberley took insufficient notice of his dispatch, but even a Liberal government led by Gladstone could not ignore the implications of Merv's reduction, and the consequent threat not only to Herat but to the entire British defensive glacis west of Quetta. The Nestor of the Secretary of State's Council, Sir Henry Rawlinson, wrote: 'the people of England at last began to realise that there were no "pathless deserts" or "stupendous mountain ranges" between the Russian frontiers in Transcaspia and the British outposts in the Pishin Valley'. The people of England realised nothing of the kind, and would have been hard put to it if asked the whereabouts of Merv, Herat or the Pishin Valley. The Home government did, however, begin to understand dimly but collectively, that either indifference or agitation about the Northern

Frontier was irrelevant if 'Russia's advance' could menace India from the desert roads of Seistan and the Helmand.

'Mervousness' was thus in the air as Gladstone, locked into his Egyptian and Sudan imperialism, sought compromise over the Russian advance to India's frontiers. No British support was proferred to the Turcomans, even although 'the Merv people . . . have declared that they will act with England and have gone so far as to manufacture a broad VR and Crown with which they are marking their horses'.[2] No British troops were mobilised to defend Kandahar, nor was Gladstone disposed to help Abdur Rahman by other means. Inactivity nevertheless, however masterly, has its limitations. News of the reduction of Merv came to the Foreign Office via Reuters and the *Daily Telegraph*, hardly sources likely to be welcome in Whitehall. Such sources were no more agreeable than Lyall's suggestion to Abdur Rahman that knowledge of his frontiers might be improved if he studied 'Walker's latest maps, which can be bought in shops in Calcutta or Bombay'.[3] What Abdur Rahman wanted was reassurance, not footling suggestions from the Secretary of the Indian Foreign and Political Department. Abdur Rahman had not gone over to the Russians; he had kept his word to the Raj. Would he be rewarded?

Ripon was in no position to offer reassurance or rewards, but the genesis and explanation of the March 1884 dispatch to Kimberley is Abdur Rahman's warning of a year earlier that Herat would fall to the Russians unless the British Government took some action. If that government continued to hesitate, he, Abdur Rahman, would mount his own riposte by seeking to establish a claim to territory on both banks of the Oxus and, more to the point, garrisoning Penjdeh in order to defend Herat. The threat of an Afghan riposte to Russian pressure did the trick: in the same month that Ripon proposed demarcation, Granville suggested to Giers a joint Anglo-Russian Commission to survey and delimit 'the boundary between Russia and Afghanistan from the Khoza Seleh westward to the Tedjend'.[4] Giers promptly accepted: Khoza Seleh was an area across the upper reaches of the Oxus *east* of which St Petersburg wanted no demarcation – as yet. West of Khoza Seleh to the area north of Herat, however, suited the Russian book nicely for delimitation purposes. Merv had capitulated: an Afghan boundary could be demarcated; a prospective threat to Afghanistan – and British India – would remain.

Six months elapsed before the Boundary Commission took tangible form. On the British side the Commissioners – Lumsden and Ridgeway – had a long march ahead of them to the Oxus; a substantial escort was required; and Afzul Khan, of the second Forsyth mission, now native agent in Kabul, had to spend much time squaring Abdur Rahman in order that the mission could march through his territory unimpeded. For his part, the Amir garrisoned Penjdeh and awaited developments. The delay, if inevitable, was unfortunate in certain respects. Granville, with his unique tendency unwittingly to play the Russian game, insisted that 'the Commissioners alone should decide upon the region of their enquiry'.[5] Giers mounted a minor riposte to this ambiguous condition by declaring via the Russian Ambassador in London, de Staal, that 'our movements in Central Asia have been dictated in the first place by our own interests'. In other words, General Zeloni, the senior Russian Commissioner, would stake out a territorial claim, then virtually force Ridgeway and Lumsden to accept it.

While these exchanges continued, Russian parties pushed right up to the Afghan outposts at Penjdeh, thus establishing a *de facto* frontier. The War Office toyed with plans for a pre-emptive attack on Russian forces in Transcaspia. That this was merely an exercise in fantasy is suitably illustrated by the recommendation that 'one or two carefully selected Russian speaking officers should be sent to reside as sportsmen or artists in the neighbourhood until the necessary data has been obtained'.[6] Neither the neighbourhood to be investigated nor the data to be acquired was defined with any precision. Proponents of the pre-emptive strategy were always notable for ignoring awkward realities.

Fortunately, neither Lumsden nor Ridgeway lived in the clouds. Both appreciated that marching the 500-strong escort through western Afghanistan to meet Zeloni at Sarakhs – a point on the map claimed neither by contending powers nor minor potentates but tactically of advantage to the Russian party – would test the feasibility of a Czarist offensive or of British pre-emptive operations. But the British Commissioners were mainly determined to arrive in good order and on time – the rendezvous was to be on 13 October. What a joy to be in the wilds after four years tied to Ripon's apron strings! Holdich, senior surveyor to the British Commissioners, recaptured that experience. There was the delight of the night march – 'the pure fresh, invigorating air, air that may be eaten, as the

Lord Auckland muses on a fall with
Dost Mohammed

6 George Hayward, who wanted to
try 'the effect of cold steel across . . .
[his] throat'

7 Members of the Gilgit mission, 1885–1886: Colonel Woodthorpe,
Captain Barrow, Colonel Lockhart and Captain Giles

8 'A gaudy and theatrical ambition' –
Lord Lytton as Viceroy

9 Colonel Grombtchevsky, Assistant
Governor of Ferganah

10 The Baroghil Pass

Natives say'. The 'mere physical sensation in living was a delight in itself'. Holdich was no poet of the desert. He was pre-eminently a soldier of his time yet, in the prosaic enough context of a Boundary Commission marching to its objective, we can feel again something of the mood which made action so infinitely preferable to the cantonment and the office desk.

There is the purple starlit sky, alight with familiar constellations that come back like old friends at the appointed time; and the soft talk of the desert wind, which breaks rippling over the tops of the sand waves with a sound like the sound of a far-away sea. The glint of the guiding fire ahead, flashing into sight or dropping back to darkness, is an object of intense interest, especially when it has disappeared for any length of time. It seems so close, whatever the distance may really be; and only the weird look of figures around it, as they grow from little black sand sprites into full-grown human shadows, measures the intervening space. I possessed that inestimable treasure, a horse that could really walk. Over the flats, where sand was not, he walked at night, when alone, with a swing such as he never seemed to possess by daylight. Far away behind me I would sometimes hear the click, click of another horse's hoofs, and the clang of scabbard against spur as another rider came on to the course. It was a sort of challenge.[7]

When Holdich and his compatriots reached the Herat valley, another sort of challenge awaited them. 'The Russians were not only in possession of Sarakhs, but forty miles south of it.' Russian parties were also astride the Murghab river; Penjdeh was virtually invested. Worse, there was no Russian Commissioner at Sarakhs. Zeloni had pleaded illness, while his masters arranged a less obvious kind of delay to fool Granville. The men on the spot were in a cleft stick. Fortunately Lumsden, Ridgeway and their staff were professionals. They had not marched 600 miles from Quetta to play games. Their party was too large to be inconspicuous, too well equipped in various ways to be idle. Making a frontier was seen as an honourable objective to attain, in due season. Holdich's surveyors worked on the country west of Sarakhs as far as Meshed and north-east of the Herat valley up to the Oxus – and beyond.

Holdich pushed on to the north – 'a gallant effort was made to find out the whereabouts of Khwaja Salar [Khoje Saleh]. It was an important position on the Oxus which was to be the termination of the boundary (when we found it) . . . ere we reached the depths of that Arctic winter, Peacock and Merk were sent out on the quest. They came back with a stirring tale of exploring ventures, but without any solid assurance that the 'post' of Khwaja Salar yet existed. It had existed in the days of Alexander Burnes. What had become it it?'[8]

Holdich was driven to this question not only by the Russians' absence but the British Commissioners' belated realisation that a mission representing 'the prestige of India's wealth and luxury' was in a cleft stick. The British Commissioners did not know that Giers had concluded his riposte to Granville by asserting that Russian policy was also governed by 'the hostility towards us of which the English Government has given proof', but all concerned in London and Calcutta were well aware that Russia's reaction to Lytton's folly had assumed a menacing form. In Simla Roberts did not get up a Penjdeh scare but, for the first time, the pre-emptive strategy was given serious consideration.

Gladstone agreed to the dispatch of 11,000 troops from Britain to India in March 1885 – 'a horrible necessity'[3]. Only absolute Russophobes believed that a war between Britain and Russia over Indian frontier security would be other than a strategic disaster. On 13 March Gladstone attempted to extricate the government from Granville's blunders. Gladstone reported to the Queen: 'They [the Cabinet] think that the country between the Russian line and the English line should be treated for the purpose of the enquiry, as a separate zone, marking out northward and southward, the extreme limits to which the enquiry shall extend.' This was nonsense, making the confusion still worse. There was a Russian line – on the Oxus: there was no English line, only an encampment. The British hand, such as it was, had been forced. St Petersburg wanted a frontier to suit imperial purposes, and was determined to get it.

Lumsden and Ridgeway, moreover, could not simply sit still. If they supported Abdur Rahman at Penjdeh, and were defeated in a Russian attack, war between Britain and Russia would be inevitable. If Lumsden and Ridgeway ignored Abdur Rahman's pleas for support, the consequences in terms of humiliation could be equally serious. Accepting rather than fearing loss of face, Ridgeway sent Captain Charles Yate and Surgeon C. W. Owen to Penjdeh on 26 March, with orders to intercede with Russian forces facing the

Afghans, and failing that to return to the British camp. Gladstone could utter nonsense to the Queen. Bismarck – from whom Gladstone also sought intercession – could, with relish, 'publicly denounce the loquacious futility of Downing Street as making negotiation with it intolerable'.[10] The men on the spot were still left in the lurch, despite Dufferin's reception of Abdur Rahman at Rawalpindi and his telegraphed query to Kimberley on 25 March: 'Whether the Government will *defend Herat* and whether they consider advance of Russians over disputed ground [warrants] declaration of war'.[11]

Dufferin brought Gladstone up short. He was to indulge in rhetoric at the dispatch box a month later, but replying immediately to Dufferin, he made the British government's belated acceptance of reality quite plain:

> We are not in favour of such an expedition, at the present time, to Herat, as you describe. Such a demonstration as the dispatch of 25,800 men from this country as soon as they can be got ready would render continuation of negotiation [with Bismarck] extremely doubtful; and, apart from this, would not the Russians be sure to advance at once when they saw us preparing to move forward with so great an army? If so, how could we be in time? The Amir should, if attacked, make [the] best defence he can at Herat, and we shall be ready if war breaks out to give him military support in such manner as may appear best, but we do not think you should pledge yourself now to undertaking an operation at so great a distance at Herat, or that you should, at the present time, extend your preparations beyond what may be necessary to take up a military position nearer our own frontier, such as you mention under the head of your second question. An attack on Herat will mean war between us and Russia everywhere, and the Amir must leave us to fight the battle in the way we think most likely to secure success.[12]

Further telegrams to Dufferin throughout April rammed this unpalatable message home: there would be no war with Russia; Lumsden and Ridgeway must avoid traps; and Abdur Rahman should defend Penjdeh to the best of his ability but, if defeated there, he must cut his losses. The British mission escort reformed at Gulran, some hundred miles south of Penjdeh. Yate, observant enough to notice that the Arctic winter at Bala Murghab had been replaced by 'the whole prairie . . . bright with the scattered gifts of spring' sat out anxious days.[13] He had an unpleasant, perhaps an humiliating task in front of him. He could not advise the Afghans to retreat before being attacked. If they were defeated, Yate had to choose between recommending retreat to Herat, or a further defence between that city and Penjdeh.

In the light of history we must applaud Yate's discretion and courage. The Afghan troops were ready enough to fight, despite the misery of sodden trenches. On 29 March Komarov sent the Afghan Commander, Ghaus-u-Din, an ultimatum; the Afghan force, some four hundred-strong, must be withdrawn from the left bank of the Kushka. Ghaus-u-Din refused. The bridge over the river was 'the bridge of heaven', and he would defend it to the last. (The fate at the Amir's hands of Afghan generals who surrendered doubtless also weighed with him.) Yate directly intervened with Komarov at this point, and sought a stay of execution. 'Yate, still hoping for the best and realising the Russian appreciation of good cheer, invited Zakrchevski [Komarov's Chief of Staff] and his officers to an entertainment. It was given in the open between the two lines of mounted men who were only a few yards apart, and one can imagine the feelings of the two sides as they watched the British and Russian officers toasting one another in courteous fashion, and wondered what the upshot would be. For hosts and guests alike it was a memorable banquet possibly coupled with a sense of impending tragedy.' But, despite the courtesies and the flow of champagne, 'the Russians were not to be denied; and it was impossible [for Yate] to do otherwise than counsel resistance in case of attack. The pity of it was that our good offices ended with good advice.'

So it proved: three hours after the banquet ended, a dismounted Cossack regiment, flanked by Turkoman militia, fell on the isolated Afghans. 'Wet to the skin, with the damp permeating their rifles and ammunition', the Afghans, in Komarov's words, nonetheless 'fought like men, firing as they retired'.[14] Yate stuck to this battered force, and sent a message to Alikhanov, Komarov's Chief Political Officer, that Surgeon C. W. Owen should be allowed to tend the wounded. Alikhanov replied to this humane gesture by ordering Turkoman militia to capture or kill the two British officers. Perforce, discretion had to be a kind of valour. Yate and Owen rode to Gulran in three and a half days. Another round had been played, and without doubt it had gone to Russia. Komarov held the ground he had won, but attempted no further advance; the Afghan troops struggled back to Herat. Four brass guns, engraved with the cypher of George IV, had been captured by the Cossacks on 30 March. These were displayed in triumph in the Cathedral Square at Ashkabad. The ancient cannon, which Ripon had included in his subsidy to Abdur Rahman, aptly symbolised the limits of Britain's commitments to that troubled monarch.

Between the Russian stroke at Penjdeh and Gladstone's defeat in June, the situation became one of stalemate. Gladstone made his speeches; Dufferin continued to press for reinforcements; Holdich and his brother officers entered Herat – the first Englishmen to do so for forty years – and strove to improve the city's defences. Abdur Rahman wrote off Penjdeh and began to consider what compensation he might find or be provided with elsewhere. Bismarck, however, arbitrated the issue. In May he made it known that 'Germany, supported by the Continental Powers . . . would support Turkey in keeping the Straits closed to British warships'.[15] This touch of the iron hand shattered any idea of a British stroke at Russia's under belly of Transcaucasia. This had been seriously contemplated in March, but the realisation that Bismarck would openly thwart Britain over an issue quite outside Germany's sphere of interest forced British government and Opposition into an unusual mood of strategic realism. Bismarck, although refusing to mediate directly between Britain and Russia, kindly let it be known that he would not object to St Petersburg proposing that the Boundary Commission be convened at last.

This was a pill which a government less at odds with itself than Gladstone's might have found hard to swallow. The chance of a settlement was, however, eagerly grasped. Granville continued to hope for a revival of the mood of 1873, but the tide of events was against him. No longer was there dissension in the Cabinet as to the rights and wrongs of imperial objectives; all were agreed that the defence of India and Egypt were parts of a whole which formed the very substance of British foreign policy. The recognition of such an objective was enough. The task of translating it into policy would pass to other hands.

Salisbury, supreme realist, salvaged much from the wreck of Gladstone's masterly inactivity. Come late in July 1886 to his inheritance as Prime Minister with undisputed control of his Party and the Commons, Salisbury was, for all practical purposes, Foreign Secretary also. In December, he became so in fact, combining both offices with ease and dignity for the next seven years. Two years after Salisbury had become Prime Minister, 400 miles of common frontier between Russia and Afghanistan had been surveyed, demarcated, established. This may seem insignificant today; it did not seem so at the time to men in London and Calcutta who had come to accept the folly of trying conclusions with Russia at a distant point.

The achievement was, nevertheless, due to the men of the Boundary Commission, Russian no less than British, who were not immune from, but were indifferent to, political considerations compared with the good work of making a frontier. Before the curtain is rung up on Francis Younghusband and his solitary adventures, the work of the First Afghan Boundary Commission should be recorded. It forms something of a counterpoint to the efforts of Lockhart and Woodthorpe to build a defensive system below the Hindu Kush between 1885 and 1889.

The mission and its escort remained isolated. Physical strain had become commonplace. During the spring of 1885 the mission had experienced 'the "shamshir", the blizzard of the north that occasionally wraps up men and animals in the cold embrace of blinding, freezing hurricane, and leaves them helpless on the open steppes . . . Now and then a runner would be caught and frozen into a heap, along with his letter-bag and mails, whilst crossing the passes of the seemingly gentle Paropamisus.' In April, while spirits were still depressed by the Penjdeh affair, a blizzard of especial ferocity struck the mission camp. Only the hardiest survived unscathed: 'all next day and the next there came crawling into camp lame, frost-bitten and all but helpless units of that great company. Over twenty men perished and many mules. All the dogs with the caravan were dead, but so far as I can remember, no horses. Yet some of the 11th BL chargers got slowly to their legs the day after the disaster, literally sheeted with ice, as an ironclad is sheeted with steel.'[16]

Mental strain was still more taxing. 'At that time we did not know (it was impossible that we should know) what was the exact disposition of Russian military resources on the Oxus frontier. Penjdeh was occupied, but days and weeks passed, and there was no sign of any further advance southwards; no appearance of any attempt to rush Herat, to capture that place by a *coup de main*, which would not, in truth have been very difficult to accomplish then. Whether Russia was politically prepared or not to plunge into war with England was of course a matter of speculation . . . In the state of tension which then existed between the two countries it seemed at that time almost impossible but that war should ensue.'

As spring turned to summer, and as Salisbury tried to make Britain count again in European affairs, the Commission settled down, in dust and heat, to wait and hope. The resolution of Ridgeway and his companions was doubtless maintained during these anxious weeks by a desire not to be brow-beaten, by admiration for the bearing and discipline of their escort and, perhaps, by a belief that a Britain led by Salisbury would not land them in an utterly impossible or humiliating position. Ridgeway and the surveyors in his party were also sustained by their determination to make a frontier, to bring some order out of chaos, to define if not to tame the wild places. To do this was in itself good, in itself a factor for peace, in itself preferable to cloudy strategic theories or the Great Game.

This faith is expressed very clearly in what Ridgeway and others subsequently wrote about their work. In October 1887, when success had crowned his efforts, Ridgeway argued for his beliefs, in words which Younghusband could well have pondered.

As objection has been taken . . . to the compromise on military grounds, I may as well incidentally remark that there are no strategical considerations involved. No military man of light and leading will pretend that it matters one straw whether or not the Russian frontier under this settlement is advanced another ten miles towards Herat. It would indeed be straining at a gnat after swallowing a camel if we, after allowing Russia to advance some thousand miles towards Herat, were to break off negotiations for fixing a line across which she engages herself by an international undertaking not to encroach, because the only line possible would place her on a level desert road half a march nearer the city which is imagined to be the object of her ambition.[17]

Ridgeway concluded his argument by stressing the advantages of delimitation and co-terminity: 'If the frontier were left undefined, then indeed the peace of the world would be at the mercy of any ambitious frontier officer, and a series of Penjdeh humiliations would probably have been the result . . . our responsibilities have certainly been defined, but that seems to me one of the chief merits of the demarcation.'[18]

The signing of the Protocol authorising the Boundary Commission, ensured that 'demarcation went on merrily' in September 1885. Komarov and Alikhanov departed to fulfil their ambitions elsewhere. Their places on the frontier were taken by men like Colonel Kuhlberg, 'hard-headed men of business, who were keenly aware of the enormous advantage in demarcation proceedings of a close intimacy with the geographical details of a country before commencing political discussions'. A genuine accord and respect, refreshingly different from political phobias, developed between the British and Russian officers and their escorts, the latter now reduced to a mere squadron apiece of Cossacks and Bengal Lancers. As 'the poplars and pistachios turned red and yellow about the edges of the Hari Rud . . . and the bare acres of brown stubble land spread out where cornfields had been', the two parties settled into the routine of constructive work. Lessar, the most resourceful of Russian explorers in Persia, joined Kuhlberg; Mortimer Durand, the Foreign Secretary in Calcutta, had his brother Edward among the British party; thus foundations for diplomatic understanding were laid, which were to stand well in subsequent cold war blasts.

Another winter passed amid 'A wild, white wilderness of untrodden snow; a thin blue line of jagged hills in the far distance; a deep (intensely deep) canopy of blue sky above'.[19] The cold was both a killer and a seducer, mounted work a constant strain, not least because 'the monotonous click, click of spur and scabbard seemed to possess a soothing faculty, like the ticking of a grandfather's clock'. To be lost on the steppe, however, meant death in sleep. Fortunately, both parties had learned how to survive, even to live reasonably well. Holdich recalls: 'I found the Russian topographer ever ready to welcome any English colleague in the field of geography, and only too glad to place his little *tente d'abri* and his really excellent camp cuisine at his disposal'.

By the end of May 1886 'the boundary to the north of Maimana and Daulatabad had been marked out by pillars as far eastwards as the wells of Imam, some miles to the north of Andkhui'. The two parties, working together, were marching north-east to the Oxus, a mere 50 miles distant. Was that river, as Ridgeway and Kuhlberg urged, to form the boundary or would so utterly unequivocal a territorial division alarm Abdur Rahman because of its implications for further delimitation to the east? The question was too fundamental for the Boundary Commissioners to arbitrate. A compromise, whereby the Oxus was accepted as the boundary, but without prejudice to the Amir's notion of what was territorially his in the regions lying across its upper reaches and headwaters, was urgently necessary. The Amir, after nearly three years of patiently observing the two great enemies administer his affairs, was beginning to get restless. The negotiations were transferred to St Petersburg, away from the Oxus, where 'the heavy ferry boats ply all day long, bringing Bokhara merchandise to the great trade routes to Afghanistan, either Kabulwards, or in the direction of Herat and Persia'.

Ridgeway's men kept their camp by the Oxus for many months more and then, after three years of making peace in the wilds, marched back to India. In Kabul, on their way to Lahore, the Amir received them kindly, keeping certain thoughts to himself. In Russia's northern capital, in July 1887, after a year of negotiations, the boundary was finally settled at the Oxus. Ridgeway, who assisted in the St Petersburg negotiations, reckoned that Abdur Rahman should be satisfied; the Amir declared himself 'much obliged . . . inspired with hope . . . the knots in the thread of discussion with the Russian Government, which were tied with regard to the Afghan frontiers, have been untied and opened with the tips of the fingers of excellent measures'.[20]

Despite Abdur Rahman's urbane statement, neither Dufferin nor Roberts was prepared to renounce the forward policy because 400 miles of Afghanistan's north-western and northern frontier had been demarcated. Indeed, delimitation, to some in Calcutta and Simla, simply emphasised the fact that India's northern frontier lay open to Russian penetration elsewhere – from the Pamirs in particular. McNair's exploration of Kafiristan throughout 1883 was given renewed attention. Demarcation, following so shortly on Russia's final subjugation of the Turcomans, also convinced those British officials and soldiers in India who remained alarmist that the entire area west of Quetta was susceptible to assault.

In consequence of these alarms, India's north-west frontier became a defensive complex; communications were improved throughout the Punjab although, oddly enough, not in Baluchistan. Well before such schemes matured – leading to a substantial increase in the number of British troops committed to and stationed in India – Dufferin ordered Colonels Lockhart and Woodthorpe, accompanied by Surgeon G. M. Giles and Captain E. G. Barrow of the Indian Intelligence Department, 'to determine to what extent India is vulnerable through the Hindu Kush range between the Kilik Pass and Kafiristan'.

Lockhart and Woodthorpe's 'Mission to the Northern Frontier' took sixteen months, from June 1885 to October 1886. The mission's main achievement was the re-establishment of the Gilgit Agency. But, in the eyes of the hardy quartet who re-occupied the Agency bungalow during much of their sojourn in the wilds, the mission also succeeded in bringing Aman-ul-Mulk to heel and, by reducing strife amongst the hill states, making the British presence felt at yet another distant point. Younghusband later became convinced that such a presence was essential to deter Russian intrigues, and could be effected easily enough without garrisons if men of the right stamp joined him in trans-frontier intelligence operations or maintained British prestige from the Agency bungalow. Younghusband was wrong, but he erred in the company of distinguished seniors.

Despite Lockhart's deserved reputation – he rose to be Commander-in-Chief in India – his conviction about the British presence was not matched by any definite or lasting achievement. Indeed, a rather fugitive British presence in the area, and the consistent unreliability of Kashmir's 'Imperial Service' troops, led to campaigns during the 1890s which, in severity, all but matched those on the North-West Frontier. If not as sanguinary in their nature as expeditions against Pathan and Afridi, the Northern Frontier operations imposed comparable strain on the manpower and logistic resources of the British and Indian military establishments.

'The relief of Chitral' in April 1895 earned plaudits for the defenders – and admiration from Younghusband, who was on the sidelines – but this small Victorian war was, in reality, an apt illustration of the fact that such campaigns did little or nothing to secure India's frontiers. To the extent that they appeared to do so, a disproportionate strain was put on Simla's capacity to maintain and commit a field force in India, on its frontiers, or anywhere else. The upshot of the siege and relief of Chitral was that which Russophobe cold warriors and players of the Game so fervently opposed –

another Boundary Commission, derived from Younghusband's escapades on the Pamirs in 1891 and 1892, but gathering momentum from Salisbury's insistence on *rapprochement* with imperial Russia and an end to Indian scares.

None of these painful realities was grasped by Lockhart, his companions, or predecessors. McNair, for all his energy and resourcefulness, had only put his nose into Kafiristan – or what today is more usually called Nuristan. He had been tasked to provide 'information . . . that the Russians are moving as far as Shignan on the Badakshan border',[21] but failed. A presumption – valid enough, though requiring reliable raw intelligence to confirm – was turned into an assumption. McNair's exploration was mainly in territory south of the Hindu Kush – Dir, Swat, Chitral. No more than Hayward or Biddulph, could McNair say clearly how Russian penetration among these states and their neighbours could be effected. Lockhart assumed the possibility, and danger, of penetration. He therefore assumed that a combination of emollient words, bribes and assurances to Aman-ul-Mulk and his comparably rough-neck neighbours would ensure a deterrent against Russian parties – or deliverance of them into British hands. Rudyard Kipling's *Kim* was not published until 1901, but the notion of Russian agents portrayed therein had its unfortunate genesis in Lockhart's mission to the Northern Frontier.

McNair had endeavoured to propitiate Aman-ul-Mulk with presents: 'A Waziri horse, two revolvers, a pair of binoculars, several pieces of chintz and linen, twenty pounds of tea, sugar, salt and several pairs of shoes of Peshawar manufacture, as well as trinkets for his zenana'.[22] The Mehter would not, however, be caught by putting salt on his tail. A substantial bribe was required. Bazaar – and Secretariat – rumours in April 1886 of 'the suspicious behaviour of Russian officers in India' concerned with 'secret agencies in conjunction with two well-known travellers and a French banker in Bombay' gave Lockhart's Agreement with Aman-ul-Mulk of September 1885 the characteristic of a deal made in the kind of atmosphere which Lytton fostered and created. Lockhart would have preferred outright military occupation of Gilgit; Durand agreed with him. By the 1880s, however, the close frontier policy was a thing of the past.

The weakness of Lockhart's recommendations sprang, paradoxically enough, from the restrained nature of his appreciation. Having surveyed the passes, both direct and lateral, he doubted whether anything other than 'lightly equipped forces' could enter the new buffer zone south of the Pamirs. Despite his instinctive feeling that Gilgit should be adequately garrisoned, and his advice that the Dorah could 'rapidly be made fit for wheels', Lockhart argued that if Aman-ul-Mulk was cozened and coaxed sufficiently he would watch his passes for any signs of suspicious characters; if they appeared, the Mehter would round them up.[23] This was to put a high premium on the loyalty of a ruler who, at the best of times, sat uneasily between Kabul and Jammu, was hated by rulers still more obscure – a point which native agents had been making for years, even during Ripon's time – and had kept his throne only by murdering aspirants. Such a one might also be receptive to Russian gold; Russian bribes might buy his loyalty – and his silence. A Russian party could go to ground; a more heavily equipped force, supported by artillery, would show its hand whatever the Mehter did.

Perhaps Lockhart was too prosaic. Perhaps he needed a touch of Hayward's imagination, of Biddulph's cynical awareness of what loyalty meant in tribal politics. Lockhart memorialised Hayward: 'a solitary, weary man' who 'receives his death stroke from the sword of his treacherous friend whose honoured guest he had so lately been' – but when he came to business there is a total lack of sentiment. Hayward, on the Kuen Luen at 19,000 feet, felt the power of high mountains, 'stretching far away on every side in all their solemn grandeur'; Lockhart, surveying the Dorah from 17,000 feet, noted: 'The day was fine and the view splendid . . . Surgeon Giles took some excellent photographs, and the day was altogether a great success. The lake [beyond the Pass to the east] received the name of Lake Dufferin from its first European visitors, and was thus entered on the map.'[24]

The mission spirit domesticated all things. At Gilgit, during the winter of 1885/1886, the party settled into a routine inherited from Biddulph. Woodthorpe wrote: 'Usually the mornings were occupied by us variously; by Colonel Lockhart in political matters . . . by Captain Barrow in learning Persian . . . by Dr Giles in attending to his many patients . . . by me, in painting the portraits of my fellow-missioners . . . or occasionally assisting Dr Giles in some elaborate operation. In the afternoon, we walked, or played polo, or went out shooting till dark. Persian lessons were then taken up till dinner time, and a quiet rubber closed the peaceful day.' Hockey, that great

cold weather standby of the British in India, was taught to the
younger generation, who 'played with great spirit, skill and good
humour, notwithstanding the frequent whacks which they received
on their bare little shins'.[25] Such combats were followed by juvenile
tea parties, at which Woodthorpe benignly presided.

All this was very pleasant, but to treat some 12,000 square miles
as an Englishman's private estate was to assume a tranquillity which
did not fit the facts. This want of imagination comes out in several
ways, in dealings with Aman-ul-Mulk and lesser lights, and, most
clearly in attitudes towards Abdur Rahman. Lockhart's so-called
Agreement with the Mehter was simply verbiage: 'I, an eater of the
salt of the English, will serve them, soul and body. Should any
enemy of theirs attempt to pass through this quarter, I will hold the
roads and the passes with my loins girt until they send me help, and
I will put the Ishkoman route into a fit state for the passage of
English troops, by making the necessary bridges. I will provide
supplies for the troops moving in my dominions to the best of my
ability.'[26]

This was meaningless; the Mehter's territory, and that of his
neighbours, needed the sappers of a field force to bridge and make
roadworthy. (This was appreciated in Simla, but nothing was done.)
Lockhart dug further pits. He believed that the people he was
dealing with were 'to be won over and are worth winning'.[27] In
truth, however, the Mehter and his like had other ideas. The ruler
whose loins were to be girt on Britain's behalf was really fairly
candid. As reported by Lockhart, the Mehter demanded guarantees
from the Viceroy 'that my present possessions shall descend to my
line intact, from generation to generation'.[28]

This was just the kind of pledge which no agent – or viceroy –
could honour. If sought by an amir of Afghanistan, the stakes were
raised too high – to the level where the cold war might turn hot; if
claimed by an Aman-ul-Mulk, or any other ruler of the Northern
Frontier, the fragile and complex relationship between British India
and Kashmir was at once in peril. Since Lytton's day, Kashmir's role
had been to do that which no viceroy would do: play the rulers of
the Northern Frontier against each other, and strive to subdue them,
by fair means or foul. The centre of any British presence on or near
the Northern Frontier had to be Gilgit, since it was a natural focus
of direct and lateral routes. Gilgit was, however, through a process
of propitiating the Maharajah in Jammu, feudatory to Kashmir. In

order further to conciliate and, which was worse, allow Kashmiri troops to undertake the security tasks which Lockhart urged but Simla refused, Chitral was to be made over to Jammu also. This trick was not new, but none the better for it.

Even Hunza, from which Lockhart entered what he called 'Afghan Wakhan' over the Kilik Pass, had to be sold to Jammu. The ruler of Hunza wanted pickings too, however, if Lockhart was to use him to watch the most northerly outpost of all. Lockhart went on calmly performing his balancing act, noting Hunza's claims to Chaprot and Chalt, hinting that Kafiristan owed some sort of allegiance to Chitral, asking Durand to take 'the most special care' of the Mehter's sons when sent on a tour of British India, despite their sportive habits, exemplified by setting fire to Surgeon Giles' little hospital at Gilgit.

Propitiation, or bribery, of Aman-ul-Mulk could scarcely go further, but Lockhart's schemes and juggling for all that he strove to establish a *cordon sanitaire* in businesslike fashion, were not only ultimately but essentially futile. Abdur Rahman was affronted by the mission; he particularly resented Lockhart's return by way of what was claimed as Afghan territory in Badakshan. Abdur Rahman, forced to accept a frontier with Russian Turkestan and British incursions into territory west of Quetta, was unable to prevent Lockhart's Agreement with Aman-ul-Mulk. He did, none-theless, strive to prevent the cold war stakes being raised in an area where further Russian claims were more likely than not.

Ridgeway and Elias understood Abdur Rahman's fears: they kept out of the Upper Oxus. Both sensed that Abdur Rahman's claim to territory on the right bank was untenable; neither soldier nor explorer was prepared to put their suppositions to the test. Lockhart wanted to acquire some reliable intelligence on this issue; he failed. He spent more time attempting to bamboozle Abdur Rahman – by giving misleading indications of his routes – than in acquiring either geographical knowledge or political intelligence. As a result, Dufferin's forward policy was weakened by lack of information of Russian moves, and the validity or otherwise of Abdur Rahman's claims to territory in the Upper Oxus area. Russian *claims* were known well enough, and had been since General Soboleff asserted in 1882 that:

On the North-East the [Afghan] boundary line touches Kashmir, and on the north side of the Hindu Kush it runs side by side with

Chinese Turkestan and the Russian Pamirs. This frontier, is, however, but little known, and is more or less undefined. From the point on the Pamir plateau up to which Russian topographical surveys have been carried and where there was once a Russian detachment, to the last settled point belonging to Afghanistan on the extreme east, the distance is 53½ miles. *This intermediate space is uninhabited, but it may be reckoned as a portion of the Russian Governor-Generalship of Turkistan.*[*29]

In January 1884 Durand had minuted:

if we examine our actual position in the matter it appears that we have no distinct idea of proper frontiers of Afghanistan . . . from the Afghan outposts on the Persian border west of Herat, round to the Oxus at Khoza Saleh, there is hardly a pretence of a definite Afghan frontier except for a few miles above Kuson. From Khoza Saleh eastwards there is a supposed frontier as far as the Victoria Lake, that is practically the whole way up to Chinese territory. *But this frontier is now known to be faulty – the stream of the Oxus not being in point of fact recognised either by the Afghans or by Bokhara as their real line of demarcation.*[†30]

Three years after Durand's honest admission, one ambiguity was removed. The Boundary Commission had completed its work over toasts in St Petersburg. But, all the ambiguities and cold war dangers lurking within Soboleff's claims and Durand's admissions were to reach a climax with the advent of Francis Younghusband. The year 1886, when Elias made his great survey of the Pamirs and wrote a report which deplored any attempt to extend British influence in that grim region, was the year when Younghusband set out on his travels. There was another Englishman travelling in the wilds whose path crossed Younghusband's, untimely.

In 1886 a young Member of Parliament, George Curzon, after a few months spent observing the Russian Empire in Central Asia wrote: 'the Russians still entertain the idea of despatching a column, should necessity arise, by the Baroghil; the column would divide on reaching the Yarkhun [sic] valley, one half proceeding to Mastuj and Chitral, the other to Yasin via the Darkot Pass.' This prognosis, dismissed by Lockhart and his colleagues, was but part of that

* Author's emphasis
† Author's emphasis

93

notion of Anglo-Russian relations which the young MP was to describe as 'a chessboard upon which is being played out a game for the domination of the world'. In 1886 Younghusband set out on a quest for the great destiny for which he believed himself to be singled out. It was to end in Lhasa eighteen years later, culminating in rejection for the agent – and for his Viceroy, George, Lord Curzon.

PART TWO

FRANCIS YOUNGHUSBAND

'All men dream: but not equally. Those who dream by night in the dusty recesses of their minds wake in the day to find it was vanity: but the dreamers of the day are dangerous men, for they may act out their dreams with open eyes, to make it possible.'

T. E. Lawrence: *Seven Pillars of Wisdom*

8

Novitiate

Younghusband had arrived in India in August 1882. He was to spend many years as a servant of the British Empire but, although he occasionally saw the higher political and strategic command in action, he never gained any real understanding of the motives and methods of those placed in authority above him. As a recluse, he had no urge to become conversant with the ways of society and therefore appeared an innocent to the last. Underneath this exterior, he did, however, carry a guilty conscience which he himself was unable to analyse. He simply did not fit in and his letters home made cautious fun of the Kipling world he found on his arrival in Asia: 'Lady Bright is generally so awfully heavy that it takes all that the three Miss Brights can do to neutralise the effect'.[1] From the first, he was seeking release from this constraining society. It was found four years later. The brief period of intelligence duties in 1884 and a leave spent walking in the Himalayas had eased his heart and cleared his mind. He was ready for the Game, and the first big part he played in it remains in some ways his most astonishing achievement. Between April and October 1887 Younghusband walked and rode from Peking to Srinagar, a journey of 4,000 miles over a route hardly traversed by a European since Marco Polo's day.

Much of the time Younghusband was quite alone, save for guides. He was in constant danger from the perils of the road and, at the end, when even his reserves of emotional and physical strength were running low, in acute peril when crossing the Mustagh Pass. The pass had not been surveyed before, and although Lockhart had noted its importance – a note which Younghusband saw when engaged on intelligence duties in 1885 – no British agent had been in the area since Shaw and Hayward's day. Typically, Younghusband not only

97

explored the area but, despite his extreme fatigue, examined its lateral offshoots to check whether they increased or reduced its strategic importance. It is not surprising that when Younghusband returned to his regiment and sat down to dinner in the Mess, he 'felt in a sort of maze'.[2]

The journey had, or came to have, two objectives; to toughen Younghusband mentally and physically for bigger things, and to see what kind of assessment he could make of China's strategic position generally in relation to Russia, especially in Sinkiang. The first objective was attained. Of Younghusband's determination to be physically tuned up to concert pitch, there had been little doubt since his Sandhurst days. Like so many small men, Younghusband had reserves of stamina which carried him through the acute perils of the Mustagh Pass with equipment no better than that used by his uncle in the same area nearly twenty years before. He arrived in Srinagar 'Dressed in a Yarkand sheepskin coat and long Yarkand boots, and with a round Tam-o'-Shanter cap as the only European article of dress about me, and with a rough beard, and my face burnt by exposure in the desert and cut and reddened by the cold on the glaciers.'[3] Younghusband was in no sense worn by his experiences, and pushed on to Murree and Rawalpindi, where his regiment was then stationed, with scarcely a moment for rest. He had learned that he could travel for months alone, with virtually no company but his thoughts, and emerge from the experience more certain of himself. 'My utmost hopes had been fulfilled, and I had reached that destination which, as I rode out of the gates of Peking, had seemed so remote and inaccessible.'[4]

In intelligence terms, Younghusband's first operation under his own steam is much harder to assess. That he was carefully groomed for the expedition is clear from his letters home. Well before the party had set off for Peking, Younghusband had been preparing for the journey and his account of this stage is a candid description of how he was chosen for the Game. On 7 February 1886 he wrote to Emily:

Programme gradually getting clearer . . . the Chief [Roberts] said he wished he was young enough to go himself with us and sent a message to me that I was not to be a bit afraid about leave – I might have as much as I liked and the Q.M.G. was to give me every assistance. I am to get the appoint[ment] in the Intelligence when I return and I am to be nominally on leave in India while I am on the journey. This is in order to save Govt. should there be a row on. I have had various telegrams from the Q.M.G. about the expedition. One was to tell me to go to Simla and look up all records in the Intelligence and at Calcutta I am to see the Q.M.G. On March 17 I leave Calcutta by opium steamer which goes direct to China at a great rate . . . I only hope the India Office at home will not kick up a row if they know of it. The Conservatives would not but these Liberals might make themselves objectionable. Whatever you do don't say a word about my having gone to China as I am on leave *in India* and Govt. will recall me if it gets into the papers where I am going to.

With such a basis in deception and with Colonel Mark Bell, a Deputy Quartermaster-General and an experienced intelligence officer, as his mentor in China and India, Younghusband was primed for a journey which was to set him on the road to bigger things. Even in Peking, Sir John Walsham, the Minister, a somewhat dyspeptic opponent of the Great Game in all its political and strategic manifestations, 'placed all the archives at [Younghusband's] disposal in order that he might complete his military report'. This related only to the Amur Provinces of Manchuria, bordering Russia, which Younghusband had visited during the latter part of 1886. What he said about Sino-Russian relations and strategic dispositions there gives us a clue as to why his journey across China to India was so important to him, and why it gave his second major operation in 1889 a particular significance. Although Younghusband travelled quite openly in Manchuria – as he was always to do on every expedition in lonely places, once his superiors had provided the necessary bureaucratic cover – he was able to observe a great deal. What he saw convinced him that, wherever Russia and China touched or nearly touched, the former would be the dominant element.

Younghusband reported to Bell in January 1887: 'You will see from this [account of Chinese and Russian garrison, defences and communications] that China has the *will* to defend Manchuria – but when looked into it appears these preparations, with the exception of the telegraph, do not add greatly to her strength . . . the troops cannot use their rifles efficiently and the new troops lately raised look poor in physique, young and raw.' The Russian troops, however, impressed Younghusband – 'hard, strong-looking men, fair in complexion, with cheery good-natured faces . . . there was about them a workmanlike air, which gave one the idea that they could and would turn their hands to anything'. The Russian officers were 'strong, robust men, bursting with health', who treated Younghusband with soldierly courtesy – and sent him on his way very thoughtful about the capacity of his hosts to make a settlement and a frontier in the wildest places.[5]

It is likely, although it cannot be proved, that Bell and the Quartermaster-General, MacGregor, as the soldiers primarily concerned with training agents for intelligence duties, would prefer to have turned Younghusband into an expert on Sino-Russian relations for what was then, as it has remained, the potentially explosive Amur border area. Little was known in India about the territory; the British Legation in Peking was averse to remedying this situation. The Chinese factor in the cold war was becoming of increasing significance as Russia consolidated its grip on the Pacific coast. An agent there of Younghusband's potential calibre would have been very useful.

In 1887 there were other agents and travellers who were bringing back intelligence of Sinkiang, or preparing for their part in the Game. Elias was assessing the situation south and west of Kashgar with his habitual detachment; the merchant-adventurer Andrew Dalgleish, accompanied by a young Indian civilian, A. D. Carey, had already spent a year on a great journey through southern Sinkiang and northern Tibet; Lieutenant Hamilton Bower of the Bengal Cavalry, was planning a march across Tibet which was to form the basis of a revived strategic interest in that perplexing country. Lockhart's Gilgit mission was taking its course, one which was to send Mortimer Durand's youngest brother Algernon to 'the isolated little bungalow at Gilgit' three years later.

Other agents were being recruited and trained for service on the Northern Frontier. Younghusband was convinced, however, that there was a role for him in Sinkiang. When Bell arrived in Peking at the end of March 1887, Younghusband succeeded in persuading him that an exploration of the Karakoram and Mustagh Passes was long overdue. Younghusband went further; he argued that '. . . the general military inefficiency of the Chinese nation . . .' was a strategic factor which bore directly on Russia's pressure against India's Northern Frontier. He believed that the Chinese 'were quite unable to assume an offensive against the Russians, and in Turkestan [Singiang] would not even be held to their own; the Russians would have little trouble in conquering the whole of Turkestan.' Younghusband concluded: 'I had no opinion of China as an ally against Russia.'

Bell was a discerning sapper with a great deal of varied experience on frontier operations. He nonetheless submitted to Younghusband's argument, not only because single-minded young men can be very persuasive, but because the plan of exploring the Karakoram and the Mustagh would neatly complete Lockhart and Woodthorpe's Gilgit mission's survey. Younghusband's motives for a journey were not primarily strategic, however. They were personal. 'Here was the opportunity for which I had longed. Here was a chance of visiting that hazy mysterious land beyond the Himalayas, and actually seeing Kashgar and Yarkand, with whose names I had been acquainted since I was a boy through letters from my uncle, Robert Shaw.' In later life, Younghusband reflected on his first mission, 'It was a venturesome proceeding to start off alone on . . . a journey of nearly four thousand miles, half of which . . . through unknown country. But with the confidence of extreme youth I did not doubt that I should get through all right. If difficulties rose I would rise to meet them.' Above all 'There was great spaces before and around me. And every evening I had the sight of glorious sunsets, and afterwards communion with the stars . . . And always there was the thought of adventure ahead, and new countries to be seen, and fame and name to be won.'[6]

High mountains eventually became Younghusband's obsession. The Mustagh Pass, at 19,000 feet, was a personal challenge not a strategic objective. Indeed, although the result of Younghusband's travels in Sinkiang strengthened his conviction about the ineptitude of the Chinese officials there, the feebleness of their troops, and the vigour and drive of the Russian Agent Petrovsky in Kashgar, the importance or otherwise of the Mustagh was not a factor in his travels: later he was to regard the pass as 'impracticable as a military route'. A route there had to be, though, because only then could the lone agent's role be justified; only in playing this role could a man free himself from the world. That such a personal quest chimed with the strategic requirement to furnish evidence of the continuing Russian intention to cross the Northern Frontier was coincidental –

but it was coincidence which made Younghusband the most committed agent of them all.

Early in 1889 Younghusband had hoped to explore Tibet, but a recall for duty in Sinkiang served his purpose equally well. The Tibetan exploration was put aside for another day. After two years with his regiment, Younghusband was recalled to intelligence duties. It was, moreover, Mortimer Durand, Secretary of the Political and Foreign Department in Calcutta, and not Chapman, the new Quartermaster-General in Simla, who asked for Younghusband. The agent was no longer a pawn; he was to be involved in a political castling, whereby further exploration of the passes was to be combined with, and indeed given the cover of, a mission to bring Hunza and the entire Northern Frontier still further within the British orbit.

Younghusband's mission to the northern frontier of Kashmir as officialdom deceitfully called it, is the least known but, in some ways, the most important of his intelligence operations. It marked a basic stage in his psychological development; he played a lone hand, and a decisive one, to a far greater extent than in 1886 and 1887 or on the Pamirs in 1891. Younghusband also played his second big round in the Game at a moment when, with Lansdowne as Viceroy, Chapman as Quartermaster-General in Simla, Brackenbury in London, Director of Military Intelligence of increasingly Indian views, a new kind of forward policy was being implemented. Ostensibly a different, complex and indeed menacing situation was developing in relation to India's external security. By 1889, however, MacGregor – the most outspoken champion of the forward policy – was dead and the wildest strategic excesses had been curbed.

Paradoxically, however. MacGregor's death in 1887 marked a further stage in Roberts's strategy, which combined support for a close frontier with the conviction that intelligence operations beyond any defined boundary must be continued. Roberts argued his case with moderation and he avoided propaganda of the kind which earned MacGregor stiff official rebuke. The Roberts technique developed a process whereby the strategic debate was conducted in bureaucratic privacy. Salisbury unwittingly contributed to this process by excluding the Secretary of State's India Council from the 'Very Secret' distribution list in September 1888. Men like Alfred Lyall (who became a member of the Council in 1887) were therefore left to fire their salvoes without the benefit of strategic range finders.

Even soldiers who studied Russia's overall strategic strengths and weaknesses increasingly came to assume that it remained a military power second only to Germany in terms of forces available for immediate mobilisation and superior to it in terms of manpower and natural defensive assets.

The rapid development of the Russian railway system throughout the 1880s led to a further spate of detailed appreciations by Brackenbury's staff in 1888 and 1889. The substance of these was that, considered in the widest context of the cold war, from the Mediterranean to the Pacific, a Russian threat to India was increasing, however relatively small might be the field force available for operations south of the Hindu Kush and the Karakoram. In order to prevent the threat growing still further not only Kandahar and Kabul but the whole of British India's Northern Frontier must be sealed against Russian encroachments. All assessments assumed the defence of India was paramount in relation to foreign and imperial policy.

On the diplomatic front not much progress had been made in Persia, despite the ardent execution of Salisbury's policy for economic development by Drummond Wolff, the British Minister at Tehran. Russian agents were as active as ever south of the Caspian and a direct invasion of Persia was considered logistically more feasible than of Afghanistan. In spite of the recommendations of Defence Committees and Sandemann's promptings, no railway from Quetta to Kandahar or west to Kerman and Isfahan had got beyond the planning stage. Wolff's commercial diplomacy was respected by Salisbury, but by nobody else. Even the advent of a Russian Consul at Meshed was disliked.

The entire Chinese situation, not only over the Pacific coast but much nearer the Indian frontier, was increasingly seen as one where Russia could put pressure on Sinkiang. It is doubtful if Chinese weakness being considered as a cold war factor owed anything to Younghusband's views; a twenty-five-year-old cavalry captain might be a promising agent, but his task was intelligence, not policy. China was a factor in the Game partly because of a demonstrable decline in the Manchu power to rule, partly because strategic obsessions required nourishment. In the specific case of Kashmir's northern frontier, Peking's reaction to Hunza being brought within the British orbit could not be entirely overlooked, however marginal its authority.

Unfortunately, the British attitude to China throughout the latter half of the nineteenth century effectively ruled out any chance of an Anglo-Chinese alliance. The Manchu Empire was not only more sick than the Ottoman, less able even than the latter to deny Russian expansion, but it was also helpless before the advance of British commercial imperialism on the Pacific coast. Such a situation was hardly one where Britain could combat Russian pressure on India by seeking Peking's aid. Even if any sort of alliance or understanding had been possible – and in the spreading labyrinth of the British War Office such schemes could be found – it would have been neutralised by Manchu bureaucrats, by China's sheer size, and by the fact that Sinkiang, on which Calcutta's attention was concentrated, was virtually independent of Peking's control.

The extinction of Yaqub Beg, the self-appointed ruler of Sinkiang, had not been followed by any vigorous assertion of Chinese authority. On this fact those temperamentally opposed agents, Elias and Younghusband, were quite agreed. The Anglo-Indian bureaucrats of Calcutta and Simla, together with their compatriots in Whitehall, saw Sinkiang only as a cold war factor. In relation to this territory and to British India's Northern Frontier, 'the British frequently acted in a way which the Chinese, and their subject rulers, considered to be in defiance of established rights'. Only Salisbury, however, and possibly Morier in St Petersburg, saw that this attitude worked to Russia's advantage, and that in it 'lay the basis of many a boundary dispute'.[7]

Boundaries and co-terminity were not believed in or supported by those who made of the revived forward policy a binding strategic commitment and not a mere political or party plank. Those to whom Younghusband, fulfilling his own personal quest, became officially answerable, saw Russia strong and growing stronger; Persia weak and growing weaker; and Afghanistan the scene of vicious internal strife – the fragmentary intelligence of which, arriving in Peshawar by means as devious as they were outmoded, only added to general perturbation about Abdur Rahman's capacities and loyalties.[8] Kashmir, with Ranbir Singh dead and his successor, Pratap Singh, far from secure was considered a territory which needed British agents and their quasi-military presence.

Sinkiang was perhaps the most baffling problem. After a brief show of amity in the early 1880s Peking had refused to allow a British consul in Kashgar. George MacCartney, son of a British adviser to the Manchus who had married a Chinese lady, was allowed to reside in Kashgar, holding a watching brief for Calcutta, but unable to compete with Petrovsky in influence or status. By 1889 Elias had left the Pamirs and Dalgleish had been murdered after concluding in 1888 'one of the most adventurous journeys that has ever been made in Central Asia, a journey right round Chinese Turkestan and into the very heart of Tibet'.[9] Petrovsky reported that 'the Chinese authorities have not shown any inclination to institute an inquiry into the matter'. Everywhere British India was, apparently, menaced; were British agents redressing the situation? This was a question which Younghusband, aged twenty-five, decided to answer after his own fashion.

Younghusband's superiors did not need to justify faith by deeds. With Algernon Durand established in Gilgit, a pragmatic policy, with its own momentum, was developing and doing so without much reference to Lansdowne or Mortimer Durand, divided as he was in his loyalties between support for his brother and caution about commitments. Mortimer Durand, by no means a weak man or a negligible official, struggled hard to maintain a balance between defending India's frontiers and keeping buffer zone commitments down to a reasonable size. Instinctively he rejected the whole idea of India's frontiers being menaced by a Russia incapable of using agents to spread internal disaffection and revolt.

In January 1887 Durand, repeating his defence of Russian officers in India of the year before, went so far as to write to the Queen, arguing 'No doubt there may be Russian emissaries at work, but [I do] not believe they have any influence in the Native States at present which are much more in our hands than they were, and from whom we have nothing to fear, unless we are badly beaten in front.' Only two years later, however, Durand had become a partisan of the forward policy, particularly in relation to the Northern Frontier. He greatly admired Lansdowne: '. . . the straightest man I ever saw . . . He has a really remarkable knowledge of all that is going on . . . he is naturally bold and forward, but he is by no means as people seem to think in the hands of the military authorities.'[10] But, apart from his admiration for Lansdowne, Durand was increasingly in the hands of those who advocated a bold policy on the Northern Frontier. He had a deep respect for soldiers; he was emotionally stirred by the idea, if not always the effect, of risky enterprises. Above all, Durand, by the summer of 1889, was convinced that the susceptibilities of British India's northern neigh-bours were as nothing compared with the security of the Northern Frontier. Durand, although he refused to agitate himself on Lock-hart's behalf in 1886, had encouraged the latter to assume a British sphere of influence in Chitral, even if this annoyed the Amir in Kabul.

A mission to the Tibetan frontier in 1888 had reminded Durand of the stir and bustle in beleagured Kabul when he was Political Secretary to Roberts. Such reminders, and a revived forward policy gave Younghusband his chance. In June 1889 he was sent up to the Karakoram on a mission which reflected the convictions of the younger Durand in Gilgit and his fellow agents that British India's strategic frontier was on the Pamirs, and that of the three main routes which led to the Punjab from the north – over the Hindu Kush; through Hunza; by way of Yarkand and Leh – it was the second which must be secured. Aman-ul-Mulk in Chitral had promised to close the first; exploration had ruled out dangers from the third; it remained only to secure Hunza, by one means or another. If China protested, so be it.

Younghusband, however, interpreted his instructions in a typi-cally individual way. His three months among the passes from the Karakoram in the east to the Mintaka in the west were less a mission to see where the British strategic frontier should run, and up to what point Algernon Durand at Gilgit should extend his sway, than a personal quest to unravel some of the mysteries of solitude and the sense of awe and peace which came to him only in high altitudes. Between August and October Younghusband, accompanied by a *sowar* (trooper) from the 11th Bengal Lancers, who was trained in surveyance, and an escort of a havildar and 5 sepoys from the 5th Gurkhas, spent virtually all his time within an area of approximately 20,000 square miles. This area was bounded on the east by the entrance to the Karakoram Pass; on the north by Shahidulla, the course of the Yarkand river, and Tashkurgan; on the west by the Kilik and Mintaka Passes; and on the south by the Shingshal Pass and its maze of lateral offshoots. Exploring this barren waste Younghusband did comply with his official instructions which were:

I. To go to Shahidula via Leh, and enquire into the case of the Kirghiz, who had come to us for protection from the Kanjuti (i.e. Hunza) raids.

II. To enquire into the means of defending the Leh-Yarkand road from further depredations from Hunza.

III. To obtain guides from the Kirghiz and with their aid explore the main range of the Mustagh Mountains, from the Karakoram Pass to the Kilik Pass at the bend of the Hindu Kush, from which point westward the main range had been explored previously by Colonel Lockhart's Mission.

IV. To make a rough survey of the regions explored.

V. To return to India via Hunza and Gilgit, so as to meet with Captain A. G. A. Durand's Mission, who likewise were under orders to visit Hunza from Gilgit; and thus by entering his country from both directions to produce a good political effect upon the Raja of Hunza.

VI. Finally, to write a report upon the strategical value of this northern frontier with a view to any possible invasion of Kashmir from the direction of the Pamirs or Yarkand.[11]

To read Younghusband's private journal of this mission, however, is to get a very different picture of its objectives. A note attached to his manuscript copy of the expedition's map states: 'Exploration of the Karakoram Mountains made by Captain F. E. Younghusband, King's Dragoon Guards, in 1889. The latitudes may be taken as accurate. The longitudes were dependent on observation to a peak which was supposed to be K2 [Godwin-Austin] but which must have been some other peak.' Younghusband's map – or strictly speaking Sowar Shahzad Mir's – is remarkably accurate, also most revealing in the light of subsequent events. Nevertheless, the comment on latitudes and longitudes is pretty cavalier; Younghusband was less interested in clarifying his position on the map than in his quest. In order to follow that he trespassed and explored.

For the better part of three months, and at altitudes rarely less than 18,000 feet, often at 25,000 and more, Younghusband searched one glacier-baulked valley after another. His amazing physical endurance, and his gift for inspiring those immediately about him to strive as he did, meant that a thorough survey was made of an area which had never been explored before from all points of the compass. Younghusband's instructions called for no effort on this scale; no Russian party or reconnaissance force, however covert, would deliberately choose a route over summits and through ice-filled valleys running laterally across its path and, where traversable

– or even visible – at all, a dreadful drain on the strength and will of men and beasts.

Younghusband, although, occasionally he flagged – 'I started off this morning full of zeal, ready to go anywhere and do anything, but finished up utterly tired out and careless of what may happen'[12] – went on searching. The Karakoram, the Saltoro, the Mustagh – all were rejected. No less than 16 passes were explored. It was the Shingshal Pass, sought and discovered after Younghusband had concluded much of the political part of his mission – namely the production of evidence that Hunza raids justified British intervention on the Pamirs – that was the fulfilment of the agent's private mission.

It was not the pass itself which mattered – 'we could have ridden ponies over it had we wanted to do so'[13] – but the consummation of a search. 'When I first started travelling, it was the outward aspect of the world that interested me. Now it was the inner character and motive. I wanted to discover the deepest springs of life, to get behind the outward appearance and find the reality which underlies it, as we try to find the real man behind his surface looks.'[14] When in imminent danger of death from an avalanche on the Saltoro Younghusband had 'felt the hand of God sparing me for my task';[15] during the weeks of weary seeking for a way through the mountains, the sight of a new glacier 'marvellously beautiful' would lead him on to caverns of 'opaque white ice, of every fantastic form and shape'.[16] When nearly dead with fatigue, and when even his sturdy, merry escort and 'grave Pathan' Shazad Mir were downcast, Young-husband could be 'transported away from every hardship into the heavenly region of the spirit' by 'the loftiest mountain summits where all is shrouded in unsullied whiteness'.[17] This was a genuine journey of the spirit, but its effect on intelligence operations was unfortunate, to say the least.

Younghusband made two specific recommendations when report-ing on his mission: to establish the Shingshal Pass as a relatively good route south; to protect the nomads traversing south-west Sinkiang from Hunza's depredation. Action in consolidating British influence on the Pamirs would follow. Even here, however, his increasingly personal and subjective view of the agent's role led him into some rather strange paths. There is an intensity in Younghus-band's dealings with the nomads of the Pamirs and with Hunza robber chiefs which is understandable enough, given the loneliness and dangers of his role. To impress the nomads and the recalcitrant

Safdar Ali of Hunza with the might of the British Empire by holding an impromptu durbar wearing the full dress uniform of the King's Dragoon Guards, escorted by Shazad Mir with drawn sabre, was perhaps natural enough. The Khan of Hunza declared himself impressed with Younghusband's display, and promised submission. Whether that grisly man did more than engage in a charade is, however, doubtful. He asked the Gurkhas to demonstrate their musketry on live targets, produced among his subjects for the occasion. When Younghusband protested at this barbarity, Safdar Ali lost interest in the proceedings. Regimentals and the shibboleths of imperialism cut little ice on the roof of the world.

Younghusband nevertheless persisted in the conviction that this idiosyncratic imperialism, gallant but dated, would justify what was certainly his trespass of Chinese and, arguably, Russian territory: the agent needed a territory of his own, marked by no boundary settlement. It was significant that, at Shahidulla during the early stage of his mission, and before any dealings with the Hunza raiders, Younghusband pledged nomads, whose only home was the Pamirs, with Britain's protection. Neither Mortimer Durand in Calcutta nor his brother in Gilgit wanted a commitment in a buffer zone. Paragraph one of Younghusband's instructions was a cover for an extension of Algernon Durand's authority – but only over Hunza. Younghusband, in his innocence and bent on his own quests, interpreted the instruction all too liberally as a mandate to trespass on Chinese territory, and authority.

Younghusband was so imbued with 'the fact that I was an Englishman, that I stood for the British Empire . . . and to those people I was the embodiment, the incarnation of the spirit which animates England' that he reacted to the plight of the nomads as emotionally as he had to the presence of great mountains and a vast loneliness.[18] A durbar for Safdar Ali had been intended to impress, the clinking sabre and Gurkhas firing volleys was intended to reassure 'the timid, red-faced Kirghiz; the Tartar-featured Ladakis; the patient, long-suffering Baltis' that the British Empire, personified by a solitary agent, could range across the Pamirs at will.[19]

This was chivalry, not strategy. Younghusband's pledges that the Hunza raids should cease, made on behalf of 'the Great Lord Sahib' at various points on his march where he met nomad encampments, was part of an even wider, or wilder view of the Pamirs. His map, and its comments, were designed to argue that Chinese authority in the area of Shahidulla and the Yarkand river, and thus north of the passes, was weak or non-existent, and that it was all the more necessary for Britain to fill the vacuum. For this purpose, a solitary agent would answer very well, and it would be his task to secure the allegiance of the Kirghiz and repudiate the jurisdiction of any Chinese authority. Younghusband confided to his journal as early as 23 August that he was not sure where 'our boundary should be' but then comforted himself with the reflection that China could do little to protest at any extension of British authority, and that 'a Great Power which we are ought never to heed any complaint of theirs'. The following day Younghusband held a 'grand durbar' to further comfort the nomads and dispel doubts as to the length of Britain's arm.

This subjective interpretation of Mortimer Durand's instructions might nevertheless have remained at the level of gesture if, on 23 October, after sending word to the Gilgit Agency from the Shimshal, that he was marching south to make his report, Younghusband had not turned north and met Captain Gromchevsky, 'a tall, fine-looking bearded man in Russian uniform'. This meeting of two agents just north of the Yarkand Valley, contending for wardenship of the Pamirs, was a climacteric for Younghusband. Even when dismissing the Chinese and encouraging the nomads, it was an unknown Russian agent reconnoitring the Pamirs which had dogged his thoughts and filled his journal. The durbar had been held consciously or unconsciously as a challenge to Russia. 'This ended the proceedings. The guard fired three volleys which frightened the Kirghiz out of their wits and put a good wholesome awe into their heart, and they then departed thoroughly happy and the British Government though not having yet nominally taken them under their charge yet has them as firm as could ever be wished and the Russians have little chance of making a footing here.'[20]

For Younghusband, contact with his version of reality, whether a looming glacier or a fellow adventurer in the wilds, was initially so absorbing and stimulating that it delayed reflection and assessment. Meeting Gromchevksy north of the Yarkand river, and doing so moreover at the latter's suggestion, should have dispelled any notion that the Russians could not make a footing in the area; they had made one whatever the final outcome in conflict or co-terminity might be. The Pamirs and the mountains which rimmed it, from Qala Panja in the west to Shahidulla in the east, from Murghab in the north to the major passes in the south, was no longer a no-man's land.

Whatever view Younghusband's – and Gromchevsky's – superiors took of the 1873 Agreement, and whether or not Sobolev was justified in his territorial definitions, the fact of the matter was that British and Russian agents were operating in an area which had shrunk from a huge buffer region to a relatively small zone where no writ ran, Russian, Chinese, British, Afghan, robber chief or Kirghiz nomad. There could be endless argument about buffers and boundaries, natural, customary, diplomatic or ratified by treaty. There could be no argument that Gromchevsky and Younghusband's meeting was a kind of Anglo-Russian co-terminity.

The meeting, however, was first felt by Younghusband as an experience in its own right. He had met a fellow searcher, if not his *alter ego*, then at least one sharing the same objectives. 'We are both playing at a big game, and we should not be one jot better off for trying to conceal the fact.' Younghusband had to see the encounter as an adventure; Gromchevsky, a Pole who had served for many years on frontiers and who was well known as a Russian agent and explorer, saw it merely as a pleasant meeting between Europeans of common outlook. Younghusband liked and admired Gromchevsky from the first – indeed they became close friends – but he read into this chance encounter a significance which was too personal to have much relevance to the real strategic issues of the cold war. Gromchevsky, who was ten years older than Younghusband, returned his instinctive overtures with detached kindness and cordiality. The British agent was entertained to dinner, where Gromchevsky teased his travelling companion, a German naturalist called Conrad, and banteringly told his guest that Russian soldiers were only waiting for the word that would send them streaming through the passes of the Pamirs into India.

Gromchevsky was not playing games, but we may infer that he found something endearing in the intensity and seriousness of this British agent. Gromchevsky was a big man, a man without a home, travelling openly in uniform with his Cossack escort, not in order to make promises or publish blandishments and warnings, but to reconnoitre and report. He had done this in Hunza in 1888, and although great exception was taken to this move in Calcutta, and he was refused permission to enter Kashmir proper, the War Office in

London, concerned with the larger view, had seen nothing to object about.

When Younghusband did reflect on and react to his encounter with Gromchevsky it was in ways which were to lead in the following two years to a rapid intensification of the cold war; to the mobilisation by Roberts of the Quetta Division; and the reluctant issue by Salisbury of a cutting protest to St Petersburg. Younghusband's reactions were twofold and simple: to explore the Pamirs in depth, and to make doubly sure that Hunza was held fast in the British grip. His first act after leaving Gromchevsky was to repay courtesy with what, in a different context, might well be called treachery, explicable only by accepting the premise that honourable men governed by obsessions can do dishonourable things.

Younghusband admired Gromchevsky, but he was quite ready to play him a dirty trick. Convinced that a Russian agent who had got south of the passes into Hunza – and was allegedly setting up a listening post in Baltisan – was the spearhead of something far more formidable, Younghusband 'conspired with the friendly Khirghiz to lead the Russians well out of harm's way on a fruitless journey far to the east'. This move in the Game, as Younghusband reported to Parry Nisbet, the British Resident in Kashmir, was planned to 'cause extreme hardship and loss' to Gromchevsky's party. Younghusband succeeded so well that 'Gromchevsky lost all his horses and returned destitute to Shahidulla on foot'.[21]

Younghusband was silent about this act in all his private correspondence and diaries; like many single-minded men he had the knack of ignoring uncomfortable truths. Gromchevsky had treated him well, not only with hospitality but with the more practical gift of how to handle Safdar Ali, advice which proved to be sound. In return, Younghusband had sent a rival, but one met in the open, to what might well have been a lonely death. The two agents had talked freely; Gromchevsky was no spy but a senior member of the Turkestan administration. As Assistant Governor of Fergana, he was in a position to know and to state with authority that his tasks on the Pamirs were exploratory, not subversive or acquisitive. For subversion the Russians had little use; for conquest they used troops.

Gromchevsky knew, far better than Younghusband, the actual situation on the Pamirs; trouble brewing again between Tashkent and Kabul over Shignan and Rushan; the implications of the British Agency at Gilgit; the advantages of co-terminity; and the internal security problems of Turkestan. Gromchevsky was no paragon of an agent, but it is impossible not to feel that his understanding of what was at stake was better than that of his earnest young rival. All that Younghusband would ever say was that 'Gromchevskys were a nuisance and must be prevented from dropping in of their own sweet will upon the peoples inhabiting valleys on the Indian side of the great main watershed of Central Asia'.[22]

It was, however, perfectly in order for Younghusbands to drop in upon the peoples inhabiting valleys on the other side of that great watershed. Immediately after putting Gromchevsky into the hands of those Khirghiz whose aid had been so cheaply bought, Younghusband marched to Tashkurghan, well inside Chinese territory, and far outside any possible British sphere of influence. Even had the area of his travels been neatly bisected from west to east, with Russia paramount to the north and British India to the south, Younghusband had undoubtedly entered Chinese territory. At Tashkurghan, Younghusband met Bower and a Lieutenant Cumberland, who had travelled north from Leh and Shahidulla. Younghusband then turned south and west, crossing what is now the frontier between Russia, China and Afghanistan in order to explore the Little Pamir, or the Wakhan Panhandle. Whether he entered Russian territory in his march to an area where, two years later he was arrested by Colonel Ianov, and which was to be adroitly demarcated in 1895 as one of virtual co-terminity between British India and Russia, is academic. Younghusband genuinely believed he had the right to go where he pleased in order to make the Pamirs a British preserve.

For what it is worth, Younghusband apparently thought that the area he was traversing was still nominally under Chinese jurisdiction. Since, however, the Taghdumbash Pamir from which Younghusband was removed in 1891, had but three hundred odd inhabitants, the victims moreover in some cases, of Abdur Rahman's raids into Shignan, the notion of sovereignty was rather hard to establish. In this instance, Younghusband did not try to do so, nor did he attempt to replace Chinese jurisdiction by a British pledge. He pushed on for the Mintaka Pass, noting only that 'the Pamir is so easy that one can ride everywhere'.[23] By early November Hunza had been entered, and Younghusband was preparing for his encounter with its bloody-minded ruler. As has been seen, by dint of pantomime, Safdar Ali was sufficiently induced to give Younghusband and his escort a safe passage to Gilgit. By the first week of December Younghusband was sitting down to dinner with Algernon Durand. A hard march through Kashmir awaited him, but the mission had been completed.

9

Crisis on the Pamirs

Younghusband returned to India from the Pamirs more than ever
convinced of having been chosen by providence for the execution of
some great task. The tangible signs were rivals to be thwarted and
robber-chiefs to be subdued. These manifestations were always to
be important in Younghusband's world, with Gromchevksys and
Safdar Alis on the Pamir and, 'filthy lecherous lamas' in Tibet.
Younghusband's official report and dispatches on his 1889 mission
avoided the personal note, but his summary and recommendations
were nonetheless peremptory – and markedly subjective. They came
to this:

(a) A hostile force leaving Russian territory at Osh, proceeding
no doubt by the Baiyik and Mintake Passes, would reach the
northern frontier of Hunza with the intention of demonstrating
against Gilgit only to find themselves in a country beset with so
many natural difficulties that if the Hunza people offered any
opposition at all, further progress would be impossible. On the
other hand, if assisted by Hunza, such a hostile force gained a
footing to the south of the passes in the Hunza Valley, our
position at Gilgit would be most insecure and perilous, and our
operations in the direction of Chitral [would] be paralyzed by the
danger of a flank attack. It is therefore essential to secure the good
behaviour of Hunza.
(b) The proffered allegiance of the Kirghiz of Shahidulla should
be accepted, and also their application for the permanent location
there of a native official to represent British authority, and that a
few good arms be given to them. The Kirghiz themselves would
largely profit by such a friendly alliance, as it seems almost certain

they would then proceed to reclaim the fertile valleys of the Yarkand river between the Mustagh and Kuen Luen mountains, which would render them independent of any subsidy from us, and more than all prevent the Russians gaining a footing in a valuable tract which, if they once obtained, they would never abandon, but push forward their influence so as to dominate Hunza and mischievously intrigue all along this border.[1]

These recommendations were forwarded to Calcutta by Nisbet. Residents in Kashmir habitually tended to be at odds with agents carrying out intelligence duties in the most remote areas, since any proposals for extending the Maharajah's dominions in order to provide further buffers on the Northern Frontier were as liable to arouse jealousy as gratification in Jammu. On this occasion, how-ever, Nisbet had nothing but praise for Younghusband's 'tact, judgement and ability'.[2] Similar sentiments were entertained in Calcutta and Simla. Younghusband was introduced to the viceregal circle, was congratulated by Roberts, and was attached to the Foreign Department to prepare his full report. In Durand's depart-ment, Younghusband had the opportunity to get a wider picture of Anglo-Russian and Anglo-Chinese relations and realities than was possible at Simla. He looked carefully; what he saw dismayed him. Britain and Russia were becoming virtual neighbours on the Pamirs, flanked by Afghanistan and China, two states whose eastern and western frontiers were as vague as their jurisdiction was uncertain.

Younghusband saw in this situation a chance to play the Game with a vengeance. His idea had a revealing simplicity: close the gap between the Afghan and Chinese frontiers and thus keep the Russians off the Pamirs. This could complete the work of securing the allegiance of those fragmentary inhabitants of the Little Pamir. Younghusband never understood that his great plan would precipi-tate exactly the kind of situation which the Gromchevskys wanted: definition, demarcation and, co-terminity, or as near to it as was diplomatically feasible. Convinced that Russia meditated some great but furtive stroke against India, Younghusband, like his superiors, never grasped that Gromchevsky and the administration of Turkes-tan were as little interested in the empty steppe of the Wakhan Panhandle as were their colleagues in Transcaspia over Zulficar and Penjdeh. In fact there was an interest, and a very keen one; it was with defining and then securing a frontier, behind which the Russian notion of empire could be maintained with full vigour and severity.

Subjective views and lack of diplomatic experience apart, Younghusband's misconceptions only reflected the distortions which decades of cold war and confrontation had given to the picture of Anglo-Russian relations as seen by British agents of varying degree. Their notions, moreover, were accepted as true in essentials by governments and their bureaucracies in Calcutta and London. The misconceptions were not all on the British side. That Gromchevsky, an experienced and intelligent agent, could declare to Younghusband that 'the Natives of India were thoroughly disloyal, and on the first appearance of the Russians would rise against [the British]',[3] only shows where fancies lead. It did not necessarily follow, however, as Mortimer Durand was the first to point out, that Russian agents were engaged in subversion. He might have added that these agents had their work cut out keeping Turkestan quiet. Durand did not make this point either because he did not know it himself, or if he did, could not grasp that imperial problems in Tashkent were not much different from those in Calcutta.

This failure to see the situation objectively, this habit of living in a looking-glass world, where the other side, so to speak, did everything left-handed, not only gave agents their chance to play the Game – Younghusband was surprised, to see in Durand's department no 'dark, deep-laid plots and cunning devices for combatting the Russians' – but gave a totally disproportionate emphasis to the entire issue of defending India.[4] Keeping Russia on the other side of the Pamirs became a fixation, wasting Britain's strategic strength in the process. Younghusband's idea of closing the gap between Afghanistan and China fell on receptive ears. It was not in fact original, and to see why it is necessary for a moment to look at the wider picture as it was before Younghusband set off on a journey to the Pamirs – 'to see what the position there was' – which was to force Salisbury once more to intervene in Indian affairs.[5]

'As ever, the Government of India was dangerously short of both political and topographical information about the real situation on the Upper Oxus.'[6] Thus the authoritative Dr Alder of the situation in the summer of 1890, when Younghusband again set off for the Karakoram Pass. This was not strictly true, since Younghusband had been shown a map by Gromchevsky in which the area south of the 1884 Sino-Russian boundary by the Uzbel Pass was marked in

red, as indicating a zone in which Tashkent had a particular interest.
There were, however, two senses in which the Indian government
was short on information and intelligence: how far to the south
Tashkent had established a presence, even if itinerant; what local
forces on or adjoining the Pamirs could be utilised by Russian agents
in Fergana to make that presence permanent. Despite Ridgeway's
interest in the area east of Khoja Saleh, and the intermittent hopes
which were entertained by officials in the India Office that boundary
settlement could be made of the Upper Oxus region, no policy
existed for combatting or coming to terms with Russia in that large
and remote area. Failure to settle the vexed issue of whether
delimited frontiers were preferable to buffer zones or vice versa,
inhibited the development of consistant British policies.

Lack of a definite plan reflected decades of ignorance. Not only
was there an unawareness of Russian moves or failure to grasp their
purpose, there was also an inconsistency in the policy of successive
viceroys, their advisers and agents towards amirs in Kabul, and the
infinitely distant and difficult government in Peking. The problem
was rendered hopelessly complex by the lack of co-ordination in either
information or intelligence between the various departments of state
in London, the Indian government in Calcutta, and General Headquarters in Simla. In such a situation, agents with Younghusband's
views were bound eventually to precipitate a crisis, if not between
Britain and Russia, then within their own imperial establishment.

In the late 1870s the muted British hopes of Kashgaria being
reconquered as Chinese Turkestan or Sinkiang meant that relatively
little attention was given to the eastern Pamirs. Despite Gordon's
reports, it was not until the early 1880s that the picture became
detailed, being one where 'hundreds of miles dwindle it seems to as
many versts . . . Dr Regel [a Russian explorer] can run down to the
Panja (Oxus) from Tashkent and be back in a month'.[7] By then,
while the British maps had seen some confused adjustments –
Wakhan was placed on both sides of the Oxus, although only as far
east as Sarhad – attention was being mistily focused on the Little
Pamir and the growing Russian interest in Darwaz. This might not
have mattered much – Darwaz was so inaccessible that 'travellers
were swung along in baskets . . . suspended from the face of the
cliff', a mode of progression which the most ardent Russophobe
might well have pondered in logistic terms.[8]

Although it was still widely believed – or hoped – that Turkestan's southern boundary was Fergana, evidence was accumulating that the Russians thought otherwise, and were pushing on to see whether men and animals could move to the Hindu Kush and the Karakoram by conventional means. Not only were Russian explorers quite exceptionally active on the Great Pamir throughout the 1880s, but their maps, or those of their political and military superiors, began to mark in the interesting territories of Shignan, Rushan and Badakshan with the red wash of an area no longer credible as a buffer zone.

An inevitable consequence of this was a worsening of relations between Tashkent and Kabul. From 1883 onwards Abdur Rahman was beset on all sides. The Russians warned him off – and out of – Shignan and Rushan, although they accepted he had some sort of *locus standi* in Wakhan. When the Amir protested and, in growing exasperation, claimed that Bokhara had no rights in Darwaz, Russian troops not only flag-marched through Shignan and Rushan, but officials made menacing noises about Badakshan; with the nerve born doubtless of that unrivalled urbanity of deceit which so annoyed the Foreign Office in London. All that Sobolev had said about 'the Russian Governor-Generalship of Turkistan' extending *de facto* only to Sarikol was quietly ignored, while Russian officials declared to Calcutta that Afghanistan's provocations in the trans-Oxus territories were a breach of the 1873 Agreement. The Russians held the initiative in these years of Ripon's viceroyalty, and exploited it skilfully, invoking and dismissing the Agreement as it suited them. Mortimer Durand was reduced to admitting he had no idea where the Afghan frontier ran, the War office in London to producing maps which showed no frontiers at all.

By one of those ironies inseparable from this story, it was Ripon who concocted a scheme which appeared to checkmate what was so widely believed to be an inexorable Russian advance. On 11 March 1884, in the same dispatch which led to Granville suggesting a Boundary Commission for Afghanistan's north west frontier, Ripon calmly proposed that the Afghan territory to the east should be extended by some eighty miles further east to Nezatash, due south of Sarikol. By a further irony, the same dispatch that recommended this attempt to shut the Russians out of the central Pamirs declared that Abdur Rahman had been asked to keep clear of the right bank of the Oxus. This was a bold move considering that Rawlinson and others who were again coming to the fore at the time, argued that the Amir had jurisdiction on the right bank. There is little doubt that Abdur Rahman, for various reasons, thought so too.

Yet the biggest irony in the whole situation is what did not happen. By proposing an Afghan boundary well to the east of Lake Victoria, Ripon was in effect offering the Russian authorities in Turkestan the chance to regularise their position. Ripon was implying that Russia could reach the Oxus, provided a strip of Afghan territory, the Wakhan Panhandle, prevented that absolute and dread co-terminity of the two great rivals. If Granville and Kimberley had genuinely wished to reach an accord with St Petersburg, this would have been the moment. The chance – if it was ever seen as one – was missed and not until Younghusband's arrest in August 1891 provoked an artificial crisis between London and St Petersburg, did it return. Fortunately Salisbury was there to revive it. By early 1895 the boundaries of Russia and British India across the Panhandle had been defined and demarcated at last. Younghusband's escapade on the Pamirs led to precisely the kind of situation – defined frontiers – which he had striven to avert.

In 1884 a gradual growth in understanding between Tashkent and Calcutta might have come about if Abdur Rahman's relations with the latter had been either consistent or cordial, or if his own authority had not been constantly under attack from enemies within. It was the Amir's vulnerability which gave another handle to those who urged on Dufferin a new forward policy. It was the Amir's inability to contest the extension of Russian authority to the Oxus which made the situation look so menacing to Simla. Above all, it was the Anglo-Indian establishment's refusal to accept that Bokhara was simply Russian Turkestan's Kashmir – albeit one more tightly controlled and lacking any independent policy – which gave to the whole picture of Russia on the Pamirs so dark and menacing an aspect.

By 1885 Abdur Rahman was driven to say, 'If there had been no [Lumsden-Zeloni] Commission he would have kept Penjdeh, and if there be a commission [for his eastern frontiers] he would lose Shignan.'[9] To this Dufferin could make no reply; enough was known from Russian sources to demonstrate that what Abdur Rahman might want from an eastern frontier settlement and what those protecting British India's Northern Frontier wanted would be two different things; Abdur Rahman wanted to cross the Oxus at the nearest point to any undisputed centre of his authority. To do this would, however, play into Russian hands. Conversely, if the Amir was given an eastern frontier stretching away into the Taghdumbash Pamir, he would be hard-pressed to exercise any jurisdiction at all.

In Dufferin's time this dilemma became acute; when Lansdowne arrived, a new forward policy was set in train, but it was not one which could resolve the problem. The War Office in London reported that Russian parties were all over the area and that Captain Pokofilo 'of the staff of the Turkestan district' had shown not only that Bokhara exercised suzerainty over Darwaz, but also sought it south of the Oxus.[10] A Russian staff map of 1886 gave Wakhan to Bokhara. Lockhart saw this map, and was prepared to concede that although the Panhandle – or Little Pamir as it was generally known – belonged to Afghanistan, the area between Sarikol and Aktash was 'debatable'. The *Novoe Vremya* of 29 September 1886, commenting on the Boundary Commission, revealed the truth that Russian activity was to conserve rather than to expand when it said 'after the conclusion of the work of demarcation . . . Russia will proceed to formulate her rights and claims in this part of the Pamir [the Taghdumbash], rights whose maintenance is indispensable to the security of our frontier'.[11]

To dismayed strategists in Simla these words had a hollow ring. Not only were Russian parties exploring the central Pamir – the brothers Grum-Grijmailo prominent among them – but troops also had been concentrated at Charjui on the Oxus. The enterprising brothers were essentially explorers, as were the equally adventurous Frenchmen Bonvalot, Capus and Pepin; the latter, moreover, travelling from Osh, across the Alai and thence to Mastuj found the Pamirs in winter an experience they would gladly have missed. Although Lansdowne said their hardships were 'very excellent news' – as showing that movement was so difficult – his subordinates preferred to see the fact the Frenchmen had survived at all as further evidence of what Russians could achieve.[12]

The Russian concentration at Charjui aroused even stronger fears, even though it was known to be due to Abdur Rahman's growing troubles in Badakshan, where his punitive methods of rule had led to a serious revolt throughout much of Afghan Turkestan. It may be surmised that the authorities in Tashkent and Samarqand had a fair idea of their former guest's lack of real pretensions across the Oxus, but his internal problems provided an excellent excuse for a show of force. As Abdur Rahman's difficulties increased, so did Dufferin's. In August 1887 the Viceroy even refused the Amir's request for delimitation of his eastern frontier, because his insecurity – and apparent ambitions – seemed to be playing so obviously into Russian hands. The following year there were reports that the Amir had advanced into Turkestan, although it was not clear whether he had crossed the Oxus or not, or if so, where. By this time Lansdowne was Viceroy. The little Irishman was endowed with decisive habits; he quickly came to detest Abdur Rahman. Lansdowne was also active and bold. Russia was formidable in his eyes, not least by possession in Turkestan of a railway and telegraph system to rival anything in India.

The Viceroy encouraged Roberts, another leader small in stature, bold in thought. Younghusband was their man. When he recommended a British presence on the Pamirs – an agent, and Kirghiz armed with breech loaders – and reported that *Chinese* jurisdiction could be found to extend west to Tashkurghan and thence north, he said things most pleasing to the active viceregal temper. Younghusband had his doubts about the Taghdumbash; he too was constrained to call it a 'debatable area'; nor could he push the 'probable' eastern Afghan frontier further towards closing the gap with China than just beyond Buzai Gambad, some twenty miles east of the 'Last Afghan Post' at Langar. Younghusband, truth vying with desire, found it hard to decide who, if anyone, had jurisdiction at Buzai Gambad.[13]

These doubts and hesitations were seen as irrelevant. Peking's lack of interest in frontier adjustments to suit British purposes was dismissed; China's feebleness in relation to Russia forgotten; the view of the Foreign Office in London that nothing could be achieved on the Pamirs without Chinese co-operation, indeed that to eschew it would be 'useless and dangerous' was, quite simply, treated as the opinion of those who wanted boundaries and ignored the necessity for strategic frontiers. Abdur Rahman's refusal to let Younghusband operate in Shignan and Rushan – as defined in Kabul and Calcutta – only strengthened the case for a bold stroke further east.

On 23 June 1890 Younghusband was given his marching orders, officially discreet but capable of much latitude of interpretation by the man on the spot. Accompanied by George Macartney, he 'was sent to make an accurate survey of the theoretical limits of Chinese claims on the Pamirs, and to encourage the assertion of Chinese authority up to those limits'.[14] What happened between June 1890 and August 1891 was rather different. The official instructions contained one paragraph which allowed a very wide margin indeed: 'you should endeavour to impress upon the Chinese officials the necessity of strengthening and asserting their occupation, so that, if possible, there may be no grounds for alleging that *any unclaimed strip* intervenes between Afghan and Chinese territories.'

Having been given his cue, Younghusband took his time. Letters to his father and sister suggest he saw his third mission as a trial of strength with rivals on the Pamirs, one from which Russia's agents in Central Asia would in future recoil. Two emotions drove him on: love for a woman, the daughter of a certain Colonel Ewart, whom he feared was about to marry another man; love for his country, too ready to accept the niceties of diplomatic exchange or the wrath of a mere amir in Kabul. These sentiments were fused by an inarticulate belief in his destiny: his 'up and down state of mind', which made him unfit to 'act as the representative of the British Government ought to act', was strengthened by a conviction that a great issue was to be decided.[15] This mood led to a grandiose conception of the Game, in which the laggard Chinese, far from home and comfort, were to be warned off Shahidulla and the eastern Pamirs, but pushed forward, north and west of Tashkurghan.

Younghusband headed north from the Karakoram, spent a short time in Yarkand, sounding the views of Chinese officials – and meeting again the forebearing Gromchevsky – marched to a point south east of the Trans Alai, then north and east to Kashgar. On his 1889 mission map Younghusband had shown the Russian boundary as running just south of the Great Kara Kul Lake; in 1890, he 'went inside Russian territory for a march or two', as he freely admitted.[16] Yet Younghusband's route map of his 1890–1891 mission shows that he regarded Russian authority as extending still further south of the lake. Younghusband therefore conceded some Russian claim to the empty steppe, but was determined nonetheless to shove the reluctant Chinese as far west as possible, risking a Sino-Russian clash, with all its immediate and hidden consequences.

By the end of October Younghusband had arrived in Kashgar. He spent the next nine months alternately talking and waiting. This protracted stay among 'the hospitable Chinese officials, who [showed] us much friendly attention . . . [and] entertained us at a round of dinners' suggests that Younghusband was careful to persuade logically, rather than cajole, his hosts. Persuasion was certainly necessary if the Chinese in Kashgar were to extend their Empire for Britain's purposes.[17] There is no doubt that Younghusband had a strong gift for patient, protracted and courteous negotiation. Nevertheless, the nine months were not confined to enduring Chinese diplomacy, or in fencing with Petrovsky. Kashgar was a base for operations, not a winter refuge, nor a centre for meeting fellow explorers like the young Swede, Sven Hedin. Younghusband, using blandishment, and pointing out that some nomads met with on his circuit of the Pamirs declared an allegiance to China, succeeded in getting a Chinese post established at Somatash, directly in the line of any further Russian advance to the Little Pamir. Reporting this achievement to Mortimer Durand, Younghusband could claim some evidence for the validity of this policy. There were no Russian posts at Murghab, as had been rumoured; there was, at Somatash, 'the remains of a fort . . . and part of an old Chinese inscription'.[18]

Although the inscription 'apparently [described] the events of 1759' (over a century previous) setting forth 'that a Chinese force had pursued their enemies up to the borders of Badakshan', it sufficed for Younghusband's purpose. With the Chinese at Somatash, the race against time had been won.[19] Seven years to the day from Ripon's ingenious proposal for extending the Afghan frontier eastwards, Lansdowne informed Cross, the Secretary of State for India, that 'from Captain Younghusband's reports . . . we believe that we have now obtained sufficient trustworthy information to enable us to pronounce, with some approach to certainty, that the whole of this region is claimed and occupied, and that the boundary between China and the Afghan provinces admits of being defined with sufficient exactitude, for all practical purposes, from the frontiers of India to the Russian dominions.'[20]

The race had not been won, however, and with hindsight, it is not so very difficult to see why. There were two reasons, other than the very marked reluctance of the Chinese to play games. Younghusband was strung up to a mood of tense expectancy, brought about not only by news in February of Miss Ewart's engagement but, a few weeks later, of his mother's death. Most people would have suffered under such blows; men like Younghusband perhaps suffer more than those who share their joys and sorrows with the world. He responded to pain, admitted it to few and, renewed the struggle with himself. In the spring of 1891, in a city essentially alien, Younghusband had to fight hard not to give way to despair. At the end of May he wrote to Emily that he was still downcast, depressed by the endless formalities of Chinese officials, and irritated by the Russians and their demonstrative ways.

Even Macartney failed to satisfy – 'a good enough fellow in his way but he is not English and I find him of much more use in giving me the Chinese side of a question than in supporting me as an Englishman'. The respect shown him by the Governor of Kashgar, and the Indian government's recognition of his services in making him a Companion of the Indian Empire cheered Younghusband slightly. He was, however, intensely lonely; even the arrival of a certain Lieutenant Davison, who proved in his attitude to adventure and exploration more congenial than Macartney, did little to raise Younghusband's spirits. In consequence, keeping the Russians off the Pamirs became a fixation while ceasing to be a feasible objective.

The second reason for Younghusband's failure was, quite simply, that the Russians were not fools. Petrovsky was a vastly experienced agent, and he was in close touch with his colleagues in Tashkent, Samarqand and Margelan. Younghusband's activities, even if meshed in a cocoon and spun out over a nine months' stay, could hardly be treated as the eccentricities of a British traveller. How much Gromchevsky's colleagues wanted to equal the score with Younghusband is a matter for speculation. What is clear is that the Russian government had no objection to a boundary settlement, but the administration in Tashkent had the strongest possible objection to the Indian government attempting to establish a strategic frontier by the use of an agent whose single-minded notions had led him into some strange paths. Petrovsky knew that the Chinese in Kashgar had only half-heartedly supported Younghusband in his proposal to extend their frontier westward. The reaction of Calcutta and London to expelling Younghusband from the Pamirs could not be gauged but could, Petrovsky argued, be risked. He decided to act; the consequences are well described by Dr Alder: 'In the spring of 1891 a series of conferences was held between General Vrevsky, the Governor-General of Turkestan, and the Minister of War. Then things moved fast. Gromchevsky suddenly arrived back at Margelan early in June and the intention of the Governor-General to visit the Alai frontier was announced.'[21]

On 22 July 1891, Younghusband and Davison marched out of

Kashgar. Macartney was left behind to keep an eye on events, a task he performed so diligently that, rare leave excepted, he remained at his post for the next twenty-seven years. The two soldiers rode south for Tashkurghan, their object being further to establish Chinese and Afghan co-terminity on the Little Pamir. Some hundred miles south of Kashgar Davison and Younghusband parted company; the former, who was not quite the amateur explorer whom Younghusband supposed, but had been sent by Mortimer Durand to 'pick up' what intelligence he could, headed west for the Trans Alai.[22] Younghusband continued south. What then happened is best told in his words.

I passed on to Tashkurghan. After halting here for a day to collect supplies, I left on 5 August, and marched up the Tagh-Dum-Bash Pamir, intending to proceed to Gilgit by the Baroghil or some other pass leading into Chitral territory. All this time reports kept coming in that a small Russian force had entered the Pamirs, and proclaimed them Russian territory. I then descended into the basin of the River Oxus, and passed along the Pamir-i-Wakhan to Buzai-Gambad, which I reached on 10 August. Here I found a party of ten Cossacks encamped. They formed a guard over the stores which had been left here by the main party of Russians, which had gone on to reconnoitre in the direction of the Baroghil Pass.

On 13 August the reconnoitring party returned. As I looked out of the door of my tent, I saw some twenty Cossacks with six officers riding by, and the Russian flag carried in front. I sent out a servant with my card and invitation to the officers to come in and have some refreshments. Some of them came in, and the chief officer was introduced to me as Colonel Ianov. He was a modest, quiet-mannered man, and talked little. He showed me a map with the boundary claimed by the Russians coloured on it. This boundary included the whole of the Pamirs except the Tagh-Dum-Bash, and extended as far down as the watershed of the Hindu Kush by the Khora Bhort Pass. The Russian officers stayed with me almost an hour, and then went off to make their own camp arrangements, asking me, however, to come and dine with them that evening.

At the conclusion of dinner Colonel Ianov proposed the health of Queen Victoria, while I proposed that of the Emperor of

Russia. There were, besides Colonel Ianov, a staff-officer from St Petersburg, two Cossack officers, a doctor and a surveyor named Benderski, who had been to Kabul with the Russian mission of 1878, and had also surveyed the Pamirs with Ivanoff's expedition of 1883. Colonel Ianov showed me the survey which his party had just made, and the route they had followed across the Hindu Kush. They had crossed the Khora Bhort Pass, and then turned westwards up to the Darkot Pass, the summit of which they reached, and looked down into the valley of Yasin. Since crossing the Khora Bhort they were on the Indian side of the watershed, and in territory generally considered to belong to Chitral. We spent a long evening together, squatting on the floor of the little tent, and talking very freely upon subjects of mutual interest. It was not till after midnight that the dinner broke up, and Colonel Ianov and all the officers escorted me back to my tent, parting with many protestations of mutual friendship. On the next morning they left for the Alichur Pamir. I waited on for a few days, expecting Davison to rejoin me.

But three nights later, I heard the clatter of horses' hoofs on the stones outside my tent, and, on looking out, saw, in the bright moonlight, about thirty mounted Cossacks drawn up in line, with the Russian flag in the centre. Two or three officers dismounted, and I found they were Colonel Ianov and the same officers whom I had parted with three nights before. Colonel Ianov said he had something very disagreeable to say to me. He then courteously and civilly, and with many apologies, informed me that he had that morning, while at Lake Victoria, received a dispatch from his government, in which he was instructed to escort me from Russian territory back to Chinese territory. He said he very much disliked having to perform such a duty, for I was a military officer and he was a military officer, and this was a duty usually performed by police officials; we had, moreover, met before on very friendly terms, and he had been in hopes that I would have already left Buzai Gambad, and saved him from the necessity of carrying it out.

I told him that I did not consider that I was on Russian territory at all, and that, in any case, I was returning to India; but Colonel Ianov replied that by his maps Buzai Gambad was included in the Russian territory, and his orders were to escort me back to Chinese, and not British territory. I then asked him what he would do if I refused to go, and he said he would, in that case, have to use force. There was, of course, no answering this argument, for he had thirty Cossacks, while I had not a single soldier with me. I therefore informed him that I should have, in these circumstances, to submit to any terms he might wish to impose, but I should do so under protest, and should report the whole matter to my Government. Beyond that I had, therefore, nothing further to say. Next morning I packed up my things and started for the Little Pamir.[23]

Younghusband was depressed and tired – 'I am horribly sick of myself' – but the whole business had only strengthened his conviction that a showdown between Britain and Russia was inevitable. He saw himself as the catalyst: 'This will be a big business & I don't [know] when Govt. will be able to spare me & I only hope I may at least have the satisfaction of being of some use.' Younghusband fervently hoped there would be no Boundary Commission – an acknowledged device of Salisbury's to settle disputed frontiers: 'Let all the talkee talkee be done in London & on the spot let us have nothing but fighting. The mistake we made on the frontier of Afghanistan was that we sent gentlemen to talk with the Russians – expecting that they would also send gentlemen on their side. But they in fact do not possess any gentlemen in their political service, & if we are wise we will not let ourselves in for being insulted again but answer to their system of using force by using force ourselves & my belief is that they will cave in if they see we are in earnest.'

Brooding led to stronger feelings: 'These are things which not even a Gladstonian Ministry can overlook, and I shall await anxiously to see how Government take up this matter. But if full satisfaction is not obtained from Russia I shall never again serve under Govt. in a political capacity.' Nor were Younghusband's feelings confined to execrating the Russians and fearing the worst of his own government. The security of the Northern Frontier nagged at him like an old tooth. Even fellow agents were found wanting: 'Durand the agent at Gilgit quietly loafed off to Simla at the beginning of this month [August] – although I had warned Govt. to be prepared for emergencies this summer.'

Younghusband was determined that this slackness should be pulled up sharp before he got back to India. Unaware that Durand had been active in Simla, Younghusband drafted a scheme 'for the settlement of the frontier' which he hoped the former's assistant would be able to put in train 'without awaiting orders from Govt. as they may come too late'. By the time Younghusband, once more in company with a Davison similarly trapped and as kindly treated by the Russians, reached the Kilik Pass, there to be met by an old Cliftonian in the person of Lieutenant J. M. Stewart and an escort of Gurkhas, he was in a mood where he could write: 'The Russians have not heard the last of this business & they will one day bitterly regret that they dared insult English officers like this.'[24]

If warnings, threats, apologies and general noise and splash in the next few months meant anything, Younghusband's 'insult' was amply avenged. If a considerable shake-up of the entire Northern Frontier strategy in the following four years meant anything, Younghusband, at the centre of events there as Political Officer, successively in Hunza and Chitral, was a man with his case proved. If what Roberts, Brackenbury and Chapman said and did through-out the 1890s explains why the Anglo-Russian Convention of 1907 failed to change the course of British strategy, Younghusband did indeed carry governments with him. But the picture is not so simple, however, nor did the events following Younghusband's arrest and expulsion from Buzai Gambad do much good for the Afghans and Chinese. Beyond all the excitement was the incontest-able fact that Younghusband had precipitated exactly the situation which he, Lansdowne and Roberts most fervently wished to avoid – a boundary commission, with all that it implied for Anglo-Russian co-terminity on the roof of the world.

Lansdowne's dispatch of 11 March 1891 in which Younghus-band's closing of the gap between China and Afghanistan was so ingeniously, and ingenuously, explained, unequivocally expanded the irrational and deep-seated prejudice against Anglo-Russian co-terminity. 'We desire to add that, though we wish to encourage Chinese occupation of territory on the Pamirs up to Afghan and Russian limits, we should deprecate any steps being taken by H.M.'s Imperial or Indian Government to demarcate the line proposed. All that our policy requires is a one-sided assertion by China of dominion up to a specified line. A frontier mutually agreed to between China and Afghanistan would be quite superfluous; and indeed the less Great Britain places herself in evidence in any measure of delimitation that China may adopt, the less chance there will be of arousing the jealousy of the Afghans on the opposition of the Russians.'

Alas for prejudice; on 22 June 1895 another Boundary Commission, the enduring Holdich a prominent member, left Kashmir for the Pamirs; by mid-September the British and Russian teams had demarcated that no-man's-land at last. However, the British proponents of the cold war and their agents had already done much to weaken the effect of this settlement by their policy for the Northern and North-West Frontier. At the cost of two sanguinary little campaigns in Hunza and Chitral, the Kashmir frontier at last was pushed to the Pamirs, but it was not until Curzon's Tibet expedition that the tender plant of Anglo-Russian accord was nipped by the frost of unrelenting viceregal hostility.

As with the events preceding the Second Afghan War, there are many versions of those immediately following Younghusband's arrest and expulsion. To compare the versions is to be reminded of the agitating effect on officials of the activities of agents at a distant point, and of the degree to which a strategic chord in minor key can be introduced and sustained while the major political theme continues with few variations; while the wires hummed between Calcutta, London and St Petersburg, Algernon Durand and Colonel W. F. Prideaux, the Resident in Kashmir, were completing plans for the subjugation of Hunza and Nagar. What is most revealing about the vast amount of material on reactions to the events of 16 August is the evidence of Salisbury's imperturbability, and his determination that the deeds – or misdeeds – of a solitary agent should not be allowed to affect the even tenor of his policy towards Russia: neutral, cautious, detached, with emphasis only on the paramount importance, in a period of British isolation, of India and its strategic requirements. Because of this attitude in London, the idea of a Pamirs Boundary Commission quickly germinated; its growth in the next four years was slow, but even Calcutta's hostility did not suffice to stunt it.

There are two crucial dates in the period between Younghusband's arrival in Kashgar and 22 March 1892, when Lansdowne wrote to Cross: 'I was much pleased at receiving your telegram of 24 February about the Pamirs. The Russian *amende* is, I think, as much as one could have ventured to expect.' Those dates are 15 December 1891, when Currie, at the Foreign Office, drafted a telegram for Morier on how he should approach Giers for an explanation of Ianov's act, and 23 December when Morier reported to Salisbury. The telegram of 15 December was substantially altered by Salisbury before transmission, giving to the final version a content and tone wholly at variance with Lansdowne's suspicion of Russian policy and the alarmist note struck by the Intelligence Branch at Simla; the latter's situation report for September asserted, on the basis of bazaar gossip, that 'Russia is undoubtedly preparing for war in Central Asia'. Salisbury used his favourite technique of raising points to start or revive a diplomatic dialogue, and of pitching complaints in a key which could, if necessary, be sharpened.[25] The telegram that was sent merely stated that Buzai Gambad was not Russian territory, and went so far as to call Younghusband's arrest an act of 'lawless violence', one, moreover, which must not be repeated. This last point was included at the express wish of the India Office.

Those points apart, all was caution and conciliation. Morier was merely instructed to seek an explanation from Giers; Salisbury made it clear that he did not regard Ianov's act in itself as evidence that the Russians were claiming any new extension of territory; above all, Salisbury refused to be swayed by Younghusband's assertion that Ianov's party had penetrated Indian territory, and that it was, therefore, necessary for the British government not only to protest but to retaliate. On this point Salisbury was at his most disenchanted: 'that the violation was intentional can honestly be affirmed, [but] as the countries are not delimited [and] we cannot give the names of the officers on the date of the offence I think we had [better] ignore it'.

On 23 December Morier reported his talk with Giers. The Ambassador had made what was virtually a diplomatic overture, placing a trivial incident in its proper context, while leaving to the Russian government the onus of making the first positive move to a more stable Anglo-Russian relationship. Morier declared that the British government was 'animated by a warm desire to settle in a pacific spirit any difficulties which might exist and would not refuse to consider any proposals for delimitation that might be made to them in the same spirit'. Giers, reported Morier, had quickly responded to this hint: 'he believed himself that some form of delimitation would be found the most satisfactory method of settling the matter'. At a further meeting with Giers on 30 December, Morier sought an apology from Giers, and a 'disavowal' of 'the extravagance of a young officer on a shooting expedition'. This card was dealt in order to ensure that any question of delimitation should not be initiated on the basis of a Russian presence on the Little Pamir; the year closed with every prospect of Younghusband and Ianov being removed from the diplomatic stage.

The cautious British approach was not dictated solely by Salisbury's diplomatic style, but also by his desire to put Anglo-Russian relations in a context hitherto restricted by fears and suspicions and to do so by introducing a Boundary Commission. In the first place, Salisbury and his official colleagues were prepared to accept and even support an imperialist foreign policy, but they were not prepared to risk international crises in its defence. As far back as August 1886, when firmly in power for the first time, Salisbury had made it clear just how far he was willing to go in any showdown with Russia.

Writing to the Queen, who had complained with 'anxiety as to the inferiority to Russia which, in a diplomatic battle, we are apt to show', Salisbury had stated: 'As land forces go in these days, we have no army capable of meeting even a second-class Continental power: that is, we could never spare force enough at any one point to do so. The result is that, in all places at a distance from the sea, our diplomatists can only exhort, they cannot threaten; and this circumstance often deprives their words of any weight.'[26]

This harsh factor, induced by the demands of British imperialism and by the period in question, seemingly immutable, was blithely or blindly ignored by men of such intelligence and experience as Brackenbury and Roberts. But Salisbury although he failed to develop any relationship with this new strategic establishment, and indeed gave it its head, would not be budged from his cautious stance when Britain and Russia were brought face to face. It was all very well for Younghusband, on returning to India late in 1891 to meet Roberts, to have his arm squeezed by that forward warrior and to hear the fighting words: 'Now's the time to go for the Russians. We are ready and they are not. Keep the Government up to the mark.'[27] It was doubtless gratifying to Younghusband's hurt pride and patriotism to hear not only that the Quetta Division had been mobilised, but that, despite the Amir's opposition to there being any railways, ever, in Afghanistan, plans to complete a line to Kandahar were going ahead. The Great Game on the Pamirs had revived a greater concept – the counter-attack on Russia. Yet the excitement and the concentration of strategic resources was all on one side.

Throughout 1891 the Foreign Office had a pretty good idea of what Russia was up to on the Pamirs; some allowance must be made for the ingrained condescension which senior Foreign Office officials habitually displayed over Indian affairs, and their unawareness of how issues appeared to lonely men in tight corners. Morier's good relationship with Giers, and the overall view of the Ambassadorial Staff, military attachés excepted, that the Russian Empire in Central Asia was a great achievement, possessed neither of internal contradictions nor the power to threaten India, were also factors which made Currie and his like treat Younghusband's arrest as of no particular importance. The fact remains, however, that only in the Foreign Office was anything approaching an objective view to be found, achieved because Salisbury insisted on the Indian government's dispatches being compared with those from the Embassy at St Petersburg.[28]

For instance, Lansdowne's dispatch of 11 March 1891, in which Younghusband's success in closing the frontier gap on the Pamirs was described, had an enclosure from the latter which rather gave the game away.[29] Younghusband said: 'It is very important therefore that the question as to whom the Pamirs really belong should be definitely settled as soon as possible.' That one sentence was to stick in the collective Foreign Office mind through all the months and years which followed, cutting through the interminable India Office memoranda on places unknown, unpronounceable and, all too often uninhabited, supposedly belonging to Afghanistan or China, and apparently accepted as such since time immemorial – or that perplexing Agreement of 1873. Well before Younghusband's humiliation by Ianov the Foreign Office in London had decided that 'definitely settled' meant delimitation, not buffer zones. Despite problems on the Pamirs thereafter, neither Salisbury nor his subordinates budged from this conviction.

By early July, Morier was well aware that Russian pressure against Afghanistan was on the increase, not only over Shignan and Rushan, but also over territory not far west of Herat. Morier well knew that Giers was opposed to the Anglophobia of his Ministerial colleagues; it was a trait which had developed as Russia moved towards *entente* with France. Morier saw his task as encouraging the Foreign Minister to resist this threat; his method was to report the acts of agents like Kuropatkin – Governor of Transcaspia, a region directly responsible to the Minister of War – as irritants, not crises. Morier, like Salisbury, knew where Britain was strong, and where weak. Morier was occasionally forced to bluster – on 4 July 1891 he informed Giers that 'we had everything prepared to lay down a railway to [Kabul] and so get within striking distance of Herat far quicker than could be done by an equivalent Russian Army'. This was, however, shadow boxing or, at best, a means of sustaining an elusive dialogue between the two Empires.

Thus, when Younghusband's arrest became a problem for the Foreign Office to tackle, a technique was available to wring some slight advantage from it. The news did not come entirely as a surprise – as early as 15 July Hatzfeldt, the German Ambassador in London, told Salisbury that he had intelligence of a Russian expedition to the Pamirs, whose object was 'to seize a certain number of forts which protected the passes penetrating through the mountains into India'. Salisbury reacted sceptically – although he told the Queen – a sure sign that he thought something might be in the wind. More to the point, he told Lansdowne. On 27 July Brackenbury confirmed Hatzfeldt's information 'from a sure German source'. After some hesitation, Salisbury asked Morier to check the situation. On 30 July Chichkine, Giers' deputy and no friend of Britain's, said no expedition had been mounted.

On 5 August, however, Giers issued a statement which, despite a markedly disingenuous tone, could have saved a lot of subsequent irritation from Morier if its content had been checked with the India Office and whoever in Durand's office was keeping track of Younghusband's movements. Giers' message said: 'Russian frontier in that district has not yet been delimited, and a detachment of eighty infantry has been sent there to shoot game for rifle practice, and to note and report what the Chinese and Afghans are doing in those regions. Detachment left camp 22 July, and is to return 22 August. Russian Embassy in London were informed of expedition 18 June, so that they might furnish full details in case your Lordship [Salisbury] should question them on the subject.'

When news of Younghusband's arrest was received in London on 3 September, it clearly became essential for the British Embassy at St Petersburg to get at the truth if possible, not because of the affront but because the Indian government's reaction was so strong; Lansdowne believed Younghusband's message, sent from Buzai Gambad as early as 10 August, that a Russian party was making for the Hindu Kush, and approved Prideaux's instructions to Manners-Smith (Algernon Durand's assistant) that 'if Russians cross Hindu

Kush into Chitral or Hunza territory, they should be called upon to withdraw. No Russian parties to be permitted to descend the Ishkoman, Yasin or Chalt Valleys; the Russian officer commanding such party on meeting our detachment to be called upon to retire, and warned if he attempts force he does it at his peril.'

These instructions were in one sense superfluous, since, by the date in question and in advance of any alleged Russian penetration, Algernon Durand's policy for the Northern Frontier was already well developed; it was one which was designed to extend British authority up to the Pamirs and to back it by local garrisons. This was approved by Lansdowne in September – 'the bringing of Hunza and Nagar under complete control'. It is true that no frontier policy for so wild and desolate a region could ever prevent penetration by a determined agent or even a small party; this fact explains so much that is otherwise odd. On 26 August Lansdowne signalled to Cross that Manners-Smith had been instructed, reacting to a situation where the essential strength of imperial India's position behind the Northern Frontier states was forgotten in fears about its weakness among them.

Two conflicting policies – although not seen as such at the time – thereafter evolved; Salisbury's, for utilising Younghusband's arrest marginally to improve relations with Russia; the Viceroy's and that of his agents, backed and approved by Brackenbury and Roberts, of strengthening the Northern Frontier as part of a wider Indian strategy. The first Foreign Office reaction to the news of 3 September was to ask: 'Where is Buzai Gambaz?' This determination to decide the issue by fact rather than precedent governed Salisbury's approach throughout. The Viceroy's reaction, strengthening his approval of the instructions to Manners-Smith, was to provide Algernon Durand with a reinforcement of 200 Gurkhas. The two policies were taken up and propagated, with no appreciation by Salisbury, Cross, Brackenbury, Lansdowne or Roberts that a common objective might be sought and attained.

Throughout September and October Howard, the Chargé d'Affaires at St Petersburg, made enquiries of a situation 'so singularly at variance' with the picture given by Giers in August. Howard, fortified by reports which his colleague Charles Eliot had brought of the current position in Central Asia, indicated that the real issue was 'that the [Russian] Imperial authorities desire to bring matters to a crisis and force the delimitation of the Pamir district on Her

Majesty's Government'. In a spate of diplomatic double negatives Howard suggested that demarcation was worth consideration, and backed his argument by reference to the dangers of a state of affairs where the security of the Northern Frontier was dependent on the good will, complaisance – or ignorance – of China, a state whose 'army as a military body, is despicable'.

There is no mistaking the note of approval which Howard gives to the idea of rationalising a situation, expressed in General Vrevsky's words: 'I may be wrong in my views of Russian territory, but at any rate I wish to embody them in practical claims. The one thing I will not stand is that political adventurers should go careering over territory which we call, for the sake of argument, doubtful. I consider the said territory Russian, therefore I arrest these gentlemen. If you consider it British, you should support the view officially, and not by the intrigues of young officers. The matter is one which can only be treated between two Governments, and neither by me nor Captain Younghusband.'

Salisbury, and Rosebery after him, unwittingly adhered to this view throughout the remainder of 1891, and the disappointing four years which followed, while Anglo-Russian relations in all other respects became sterile rather than neutral – and as the British opponents of any end to the cold war moved further and further away from the realities of the situation which had been so clearly described by Salisbury to Queen Victoria in August 1886. The permanent officials of the India Office came increasingly to support the Foreign Office approach, not least because the Younghusband incident had revealed the absurdity, the impossibility of regarding the Pamirs as a Tom Tiddler's ground on the one hand and an area of the most jealously regarded rights on the other.

In November 1891, while the Embassy at St Petersburg was still probing, and the whole situation dark and confused – a Russian general reported to be intriguing at Bushire and Kerman, Abdur Rahman said to be contemplating a commercial treaty with Russia – Sir Stewart Bayley, the Political Secretary at the India Office, produced a memorandum of the most numbing erudition, but which, stripped to its essentials, laid bare the real weakness of Calcutta's case, not only in relation to Afghanistan and China, but in establishing to whom Buzai Gambad really belonged. Nobody knew, not even Younghusband. Moreover, all the arguments about Badakshan, Shignan, Rushan and Wakhan – to the elaboration of which Rawlinson, amending Bayley's memorandum, concentrated a lifetime of scholarship and prejudice – only strengthened the case for saying that the Oxus was a natural basis for delimitation, since one could talk until Doomsday and never reach agreement on any other.

Gradually a common policy was evolved by senior officials of the Foreign and India Offices, one based partly on a sense of realities and priorities, but strengthened as the War Office and the Indian government grew closer together in outlook and objectives. Delimitation of the Pamirs was now commonly believed to be something worth achieving. It was not, however, a policy that was easy to implement in a period when Anglo-Russian relations were reaching their nadir, and when, after Bismarck's fall, Europe's map of alliances and understandings was drawn anew. 'The system whereby Germany directed the affairs of Europe came to an end in 1892'[30] – when Russia preferred France to Germany as an ally, and thus in turn destroyed that Triple Alliance on which Salisbury relied as a European gendarme to free his hands for a policy of consolidation and expansion elsewhere. This huge shift in the balance of power still left Germany as the fulcrum; it did, however, make a wholly isolationist British policy impossible and adventures on the Pamirs impracticable.

Men like Currie at the Foreign Office and Lyall on the India Council had to struggle hard to achieve anything. In the first place, the course of negotiations between the British and Russian governments was beset by pitfalls of every kind. Throughout 1982 Giers and Chichkine allowed the forward school clustered about Alexander to consolidate its position on the Pamirs. The members of this school were far less influential than appeared at the time; although the Tsar rather spoiled the effect of Giers' apology to Salisbury for Ianov's activities by ostentatiously presenting the latter with 'a diamond ring engraved with the Imperial cypher', a forward policy for Russia in Central Asia was, by 1892, really a matter of consolidation, not conquest.[31] Russian troops bundled the Chinese out of Somatash in July 1892 and summarily defeated the Afghans there only a month later. That was, however, the end of the affair. To an extent, Younghusband's escapades had prevented co-terminity between the Russian Empire and India, but only because Salisbury had intervened to suggest a compromise Boundary Commission.

Not even the most ardent proponent of the forward policy suggested a major military riposte to Russian actions on the Pamirs.

Russian newspapers were inclined to be smug about the way matters had developed, and never ceased to infuriate some Russophobes by verbal nonsense; considerable forces on the Pamirs were referred to as 'sporting squads'. In January 1892 Morier, an able man but ailing, was driven to say that the excuses given him for Ianov's arrest of Younghusband possessed 'a character of arrogance, superficiality, contempt for facts, and offensive self-assertion which we might expect to meet in a missive of the Tsar to the Amir of Bokhara'.[32] The fact remains, however, that Indian plans to use China and Afghanistan as two doors closing on a Russian advance brought a diplomatic riposte from London – directed at Calcutta. Once Salisbury had accepted, in February 1892, the premise that delimitation ought to proceed, it would have taken an international crisis for the idea to have been wholly abandoned.

When Rosebery became Foreign Secretary in August 1892, he declared to the Queen that he knew nothing about the Pamirs but was worried about Constantinople – an inimitably Roseberyian combination of indifference and pessimism. A month later, however, having read a somewhat remote Foreign Office memorandum on the Pamirs issue, Rosebery came out clearly in favour of a Boundary Commission. Negotiations faltered however, and were in no sense hastened when Chichkine, in January 1893, said that any agreement on a 'Mixed Commission' for the Pamirs would have to accept as a pre-condition that the Oxus would be the basis for delimitation. In effect, he was repeating the one-sided argument which had been used before: Britain and Russia should draw up boundaries in order that Afghan territory should be restricted in the process. Chichkine insisted that if there was to be another Boundary Commission, Afghan claims to Shignan and Rushan would have to be abandoned. This was a nasty pill to swallow despite the Russian proposals in effect accepting that Wakhan was at least partly Afghan; Ianov's exclusion of that area from the Russian frontier – a point so frequently forgotten by Calcutta in the aftermath of Younghusband's arrest – had borne useful diplomatic fruit in providing Abdur Rahman with some compensation. What took hard swallowing was conceding *any* Russian claims to the Pamirs.

Salisbury was tepid on the Pamirs issue, and concerned only about its broader implications, but his judgement and experience reassured those who might otherwise doubt – and oppose – him. Rosebery, however, easily alarmed his advisers. He was moody, neurasthenic, ignorant and secretive. He had several times refused to be Foreign Secretary, and had only consented when Sir William Harcourt, the Chancellor of the Exchequer, had flattered him with the thought: 'A Liberal Government without you is inconceivable; with you it is merely impossible'.[33] Rosebery, a man with a psychological aversion to responsibility only exceeded by his need to be courted, failed to spot the taunt concealed within the bribe. As Foreign Secretary he frequently threatened resignation, and gave to what in any event would have been a testing period for British foreign policy, a nervous twitch remarkably like that which afflicted the Liberal government between 1882 and 1885.

Britain and Russia did, however, delimit the Pamirs, agreeing to do so in February 1895, and they did so for two reasons which were, at the time, complementary. The first factor was Britain's increasingly exposed, and not merely isolated position in relation to European combinations; the second was that even proponents of the forward policy had come to understand by the mid-1890s that delimitation was the only means of keeping the Northern Frontier secure. Realisation of Britain's isolation led to no positive move to establish a new relationship with its neighbours; the difference between Liberal Party assumptions of the early 1880s and those of ten years later is one of degree; formerly the Powers were to help Britain out of its imperial difficulties; now they were to overlook them, or relate them, in some arcane way, to a scheme for preserving British prestige on the cheap. Even Salisbury could still say after Bismarck's fall: 'our interests lie on the side of the Triple Alliance'. Rosebery was capable, in January 1895, of believing that he could play 'la haute politique', as he put it to the British Ambassador in Berlin, by reminding the German Government that 'Great Britain, if her policy be properly guided, holds the key of the [European] situation'.

This fatuous remark reflects what happened, although in a way precisely opposite to that supposed by Rosebery. Britain's isolation reflected the capacity, if not the inclination of its neighbours, to combine. Salisbury, after commenting on the Triple Alliance, added, '[but] it is most important to persuade the French, if we can, that England has no antipathy to France, or any partisanship against her'. This was a grudging admission of reality, not a positive move, and because thirteen years were spent in reaching an Anglo–French *entente* which was never to be very cordial, its opponents, in Simla as much as Whitehall, were able to rob it of real value. Salisbury, however, still meant what he said in August 1891; the time was out of joint for Roberts to have his war with Russia.

Between 1892 and 1895 it was Lansdowne and his successor Elgin who helped to make the delimitation of the Pamirs a possibility. This paradox is explicable only in relation to the disproportionate effort which went into executing Algernon Durand's frontier policy; to a compromise which his brother in 1893 succeeded in effecting with Abdur Rahman; and to a decision that any resentment which Peking might feel at the arbitrary and inconsistent nature of Calcutta's policy could be safely ignored. Although Rosebery, at one moment of strategic aberration, called Buzai Gambad 'the Gibraltar of the Hindu Kush',[34] a more material remark was Lansdowne's, in June 1894: 'We have no reason to fear a Russian advance through the Passes to the East of Buzai Gambad'.[35] This was doubtless true, although not for the reasons which Lansdowne advanced. Making the Northern Frontier secure, in Algernon Durand's terms, proved to be difficult, costly, unsatisfactory; it was neither politic nor possible to go beyond Hunza in executing the forward policy; thus, in September 1892, with affairs among the unwilling feudatories of Kashmir still very much in the balance, Lansdowne was driven to accept that delimitation of the Pamirs might be no bad thing.

Afghan territorial demarcation was a bigger issue altogether, and the Durand Line which the Foreign Secretary negotiated with Abdur Rahman in 1893 as a sop for the latter's disappointments elsewhere, proved to be a major cause of British punitive expeditions in the years which followed. Durand was genuine in wanting to accommodate the Amir; because the Indian government's Foreign Secretary always retained his doubts over the forward policy, he also retained, unlike Lansdowne, a complementary capacity to consider the Amir's invidious position. At the time, the Durand line – whereby Chitral passed to Kashmir but Abdur Rahman was rewarded, if that is the word, by minor adjustments elsewhere, on the North-West Frontier – was regarded as a masterly exercise of the Foreign Secretary's skill; in fact, all it did was to buy time. In place of the clarities inherent in a Boundary Commission and in delimitation, the Durand line gave further approval to the notion of buffer zones. It is true that defining, let alone demarcating, the

North-West Frontier of British India would have required a new John Lawrence – and maybe another Dost Mahomed – but the praise which was showered on Durand in 1893 was misplaced. Abdur Rahman was only temporarily appeased.

Peking, however, presented no problems; it proved possible, at the time, to pay less attention to the government of China than to an amir in Kabul. Salisbury provided Calcutta with an excuse. Despite what his officials felt about the China factor as a whole, Salisbury said categorically – and several times between August 1891 and his defeat at the hands of the Liberal Party a year later – that if the Indian government insisted on Hunza being regarded as vital to the security of the Northern Frontier, Chinese feelings should be brushed aside. By the same token, any resentment from Peking over the farce of attempting a presence at Somatash should not be heeded either. This advance and support was found most useful. Peking was ignored; in far off Kashgar Macartney was reduced to pleading for 'blue books, so that I may be better advised of the situation regarding the Indian Government's policy towards the Pamirs'. Macartney was ignored also. On the Pamirs, after so much noise and splash, another silence fell; in Chitral Younghusband awaited his next chance. His insult had not been avenged; four years among the Northern Frontier states had only strengthened his conviction that Russia and Britain were irreconcilable enemies; meantime the humiliated agent possessed his soul in patience.

PART THREE

THE AGENT AS VICTIM

'A man who had such a face had a tired heart.'

The Amir Habibullah of Afghanistan, on seeing
a portrait of Curzon, Kabul, May 1904.

10

The End of the Affair?

The The twelve years between Younghusband's capture on the Pamirs and his acceptance of a role as Curzon's standard bearer in Tibet mark the transition from the nineteenth to the twentieth century in more than merely chronolgical terms. Younghusband like other agents of his type and level of responsibility, failed to notice significant shifts – in personal and political values as much as strategic factors. Thus his bewilderment and anger late in 1904, when attacked by Balfour and Brodrick, the Secretary of State for India, for his handling of the Tibet expedition, was extreme.

The truth of the matter is that the difference between the Pamirs in 1891 and Tibet in 1903 and 1904 was the difference, short in time but profound in terms of Britain's international standing, between what the man on the spot could and could not do. After the Tibet expedition there were still to be many agents who played the lone hand; T. E. Lawrence and Orde Wingate were allowed a degree of independent action stemming from the traditional method which forms the substance of this story. They had many imitators, and it was their compulsion to treat parts of Arabia as Younghusband regarded the Northern Frontier, the Pamirs and Tibet that goes far to explain Britain's final loss of political and strategic credibility between the Mediterranean and the Persian Gulf.

Younghusband, far more than his successors, remains the agent struck down by those he served. Wingate, like Gordon and Lawrence, knew the ways of men pretty well. Younghusband played the Game rashly, but it was others who made him the scapegoat. Not much blame can usefully be laid at Balfour's and Brodrick's door; to ask for consistency from a failing government, yet one whose leader possessed to a rare degree the gift of appreciating his country's

strategic and diplomatic liabilities, would be foolish. The story of
the Tibet expedition, is one without a hero – nor has it a villain.
There was, however, one interested party whose conduct was
designed to ensure that he survived: Curzon. The 'most superior
person', whose conviction that he was destined to stop the Russian
steamroller had begun at Eton, and whose great contribution to
India's internal security should never be forgotten, treated Younghusband's fate as of no account at all. Curzon did much to urge
Younghusband forward; little to restrain him; nothing to save him.
In Curzon's view, whether consciously expressed or not, noblesse
oblige only applied one way. In the voluminous writings by and on
Curzon, Younghusband is treated as a mere appendage, mentioned
briefly and dismissively.

During his viceroyalty, the events which Curzon saw as significant, apart from his predominant care for India, were British
ascendancy in the Gulf, the establishment of a new relationship with
Abdur Rahman's successor, Habibullah, of a British presence in
Tibet. Compared with Lytton, whom he resembles in several
important ways, Curzon, once installed at Calcutta, was not merely
arrogant; he was supremely convinced that the fulcrum of Britain's
imperial policy was none other than his own viceregal hand. All his
energies – and they were great – and his talents – which were
impressive – were concentrated on thrusting the importance of India
on his erstwhile colleagues at home. When looking beyond India's
shores Curzon's eye travelled no further than the Persian Gulf, for
which he did have plans, and which he did bring to fruition.

In this area, Curzon's convictions and those of Balfour and his
colleagues were in harmony, and aroused moreover no opposition
from the Committee of Imperial Defence, an extension of that
'permanent government' in Whitehall whose members had done so
much to isolate Britain from the mainstream of international responsibilities. Indeed, Curzon's dismissal by Balfour in 1905 was due to
personal resentment rather than disagreement over policy. Curzon
was sacked because he was Curzon, not because he disagreed with
the government about Afghan policy, nor because of his row with
Kitchener over army reforms, least of all because of the Tibet
expedition.[1] Yet there is one sense in which Curzon's dismissal was
inevitable on other than personal grounds. It is not a point which
can be proved – as can the rancour and worse between Brodrick and

Curzon – but it is reasonable to suggest that the Viceroy's remoteness from international reality told at last on other men unwilling to end a policy of voluntary isolation from coalition or alliances which had become progressively less splendid as the years had passed. Younghusband's folly in 1891 led to a conclusion he opposed: delimitation on the Pamirs. His foolishness in Tibet led to an Anglo-Russian *rapprochement*, ratified in 1907 by a written convention. This was still more contrary to Younghusband's political ideals.

The basically minor issues of the Northern and North-West Frontiers enable us to understand the factor which is still overlooked – and was insufficiently appreciated by one as experienced and otherwise knowledgeable in Indian affairs as Curzon. The frontier campaigns immobilised in India not only the Indian Army but the British Army. The Chitral campaign of 1895, and those throughout the North-West Frontier which dominated the following three years, purported to strengthen those areas in case of an assault on Russia; in reality the campaigns had precisely the opposite effect; they inflamed the frontiers and led to a situation where British and Indian forces were on the defensive, not poised for attack.

All John Lawrence had done was forgotten; what his pupil Lyall said was ignored. It is to Curzon's credit that he appreciated the essential instability of this situation, and took bold steps to remedy it, by creating a new North-West Frontier province and the rudiments of administration in that area. It is one of the quirks of history – partly explicable perhaps by the strength of the 'permanent government' – that Curzon nevertheless not only clung to his notion of a hostile Russia but, in strategic terms, made much the same kind of mistake over Tibet in 1903 as Elgin, his predecessor, had made between 1895 and 1897 over Chitral and the country to the south.

The more particular interest of this period in its essentially Indian context is, however, its effects on Younghusband. Two things happened to him: he met a leader and saw, to his own satisfaction, fresh evidence of dangers from Russia. Younghusband also witnessed, albeit in South Africa in 1896 and 1897 and not on the Pamirs or the Northern Frontier, an advanced example of that playing of a lone, bold hand which he supposed was the right way to cut through the knots sedulously tied by an imperial bureaucracy. He had met Dr Starr Jameson, whose attempts to bring down the Boer Republics of Transvaal and the Orange Free State by a *coup de main* aroused Younghusband's greatest admiration, which was not in the slightest degree diminished by Jameson's subsequent humiliation from Salisbury's last government.

A major uprising in Chitral in the early months of 1895 found Younghusband hungry for participation in the affairs of men. Part of this anxiety to be in the thick of things may have been due to his absence from Chitral when, on New Year's Day, Aman-ul-Mulk's successor, Nizam-ul-Mulk, was murdered by his brother, Amir-ul-Mulk, and the whole elaborate scheme for turning the Northern Frontier states into an economical version of the North-West Frontier, devised so optimistically by Lockhart and Algernon Durand, was destroyed at a blow. Chapman, Brackenbury and Roberts – all opposed to the delimitation of the Pamirs – had supported Durand in building a defensive box, based on Chitral, Hunza, Nagar and Gilgit. The scheme had, however, many basic weaknesses, quite apart from the doubtful validity of the argument that it was necessary to balance the Peshawar-Rawalpindi-Quetta area – which owed fealty to the Indian Empire – by a comparable one, which should have the double objective of defending the northern passes and warning Abdur Rahman off Chitral. The scheme devised by Lockhart and completed by Durand was weakened by dependence on Aman-ul-Mulk in person; the difficulty of gaining accurate intelligence of movement towards the northern passes; the lack of communication between Gilgit and Chitral; and, more fundamentally between those places and Peshawar.

Even assuming Kashmir's support over frontier matters – although few agents did – the defensive scheme was also weakened by ambiguity over local objectives, attainment of which was rendered more difficult by lack of resources. The states in question were in such an ambiguous relationship with Kashmir, and thus in turn with the Imperial government, that security could only have been kept by the deployment of many agents or the concentration of reliable troops. The first course was ruled out because Calcutta preferred an equivocal relationship; the second on grounds of economy. Younghusband was not regularly on duty in Chitral – although, sensibly, he asked to be – nor was the Political Agency at Gilgit adequately garrisoned in circumstances where, for seven months in the year, it was connected with Peshawar only by telegraph.

There was, finally an overriding weakness in Durand's scheme, one which Lytton indeed had discerned nearly twenty years before, and which was to result in a situation where the Chitral uprising involved the northern half of the North-Western Frontier in the most serious conflict of its history. The states and tribal confederations lying south of the defensive box, but north and west of Peshawar, had been left entirely in a state of nature. They acted as a lightning conductor nonetheless. When, in April 1895, a division-sized force marched from Peshawar to put down the Chitral uprising a sputter of revolt ran along that conductor, lighting a fuse in Pathan and Afridi, whose allegiance to the British Crown had never been more than nominal.

Younghusband was in London when Chitral erupted. He had been replaced as agent by an officer much junior to him in service, and was in fact in that curious limbo of non-active employment which the Indian Political Service kept for such of its members who had, at one time or another, allowed their love of independent action to become an end in itself. Even now it is difficult to see why the system which Younghusband so much despised should have operated against him in 1895 rather than 1891. Bureaucratic nemesis had, however, struck. Younghusband's conviction that his personality guaranteed peace in Chitral had fallen on deaf ears in Calcutta; his enemies there – as he supposed them to be – retaliated by making their agent obey every line of their instructions, even to the extent of forcing examinations on him – 'examinations in International Law, the Indian Penal and Criminal Codes, Political Economy, Indian History. Until I passed them I was given no permanent position in the Political Department; and even when I did pass them I was put at the very bottom of the list.'[2]

In London, however, Younghusband found on the whole a more sympathetic atmosphere. He made little headway at the India Office, where indeed his memorandum on the Northern Frontier produced a significantly unfavourable reaction.[3] All that Younghusband did, however, was to point out that the premise of a Northern Frontier security policy, such as it was, rested on a continuing Russian threat; it followed therefore that good communications from Peshawar to that frontier were essential, that lateral routes should be developed, and that local levies should be increased in number. These were sensible arguments – *if* one accepted Younghusband's assumptions about Russian interests. He did no more than repeat the arguments of his military superiors regarding the North-West Frontier which had been urged on successive governments for the past nine years.

A Liberal Government – upholding a close frontier policy – was in office when Younghusband wrote his papers in February 1895. The government had just concluded a Pamirs Boundary Agreement with Russia, and was anxious to demonstrate the purity of its intentions. Campbell-Bannerman, the Secretary of State for War, accepted virtually all Chapman's pre-emptive arguments – a fact which the latter noted as if it were a matter of course – but there remained even in the War Office a notion that the Northern Frontier was a relatively minor affair. Indeed, if Salisbury had not succeeded Rosebery in June 1895, it is just possible that Chitral would have been entirely abandoned. In the India Office, feeling about the Northern Frontier was very strong. The idea of virtually occupyintg the area – for that was how the Younghusband case was interpreted – was rejected so comprehensively that even today those distant states remain cut off from the outside world.

Elsewhere in London Younghusband was welcomed with marked favour, and nowhere more so than at the Royal Geographical Society. Some of the welcome may have been due to the fact that the Society's president, that enduring Liberal Mountstuart Grant Duff, had been bitterly criticised by Kimberley in 1892 for his refusal to keep controversial – and, in officialdom's eyes, confidential – matters from the realm of public debate. An agent who had lived dangerously and operated secretly, who hated officialdom and had much to say, was guaranteed approval. Indeed, by the Society in general, Younghusband was regarded as 'a very old friend' and a prime source of information on remote places. His address, 'Chitral, Hunza and the Hindu Kush', to members on 25 March 1895 although disliked so strongly in the India Office, was something of a *tour de force*. The whole occasion was really a justification for his views on how the Northern Frontier should be made secure. He was warmly commended by Lord Roberts – and given an Augustan eulogy by the Hon. G. N. Curzon, MP.

The latter declared that 'he would not intrude upon that sphere, with which I have no right to deal', and then proceeded to dwell upon it at length. Curzon also described the pleasure which he had found in Younghusband's company when travelling in Chitral six months previously. The agent so markedly out of favour with his masters was given a kindly word by one also temporarily in opposition: 'From my own experience I can say that Captain

Younghusband is eminently gifted to win and to retain the confidence of the native peoples and their Chiefs with whom he is brought into contact.'[4]

In 1895 Younghusband had not yet chosen Curzon for his leader. Indeed, his condescension over the handling of wayward Chitralis may well have grated on Younghusband at a time when he felt sore at the refusal of Calcutta or the India Office to listen to him, especially when Dr Robertson, the Gilgit Agent, was himself besieged in the very fort of Chitral from which an attempt to express the British presence had been made. Younghusband did indeed recall meeting Curzon six months previously, and had found him 'both a pleasure and a trial. He was perpetually discussing frontier policy, which was agreeable; but he was continually disagreeing with me, which was irritating . . . we resented Curzon's cocksureness. His manner grated on us on the frontier.' A seed had been sown – all in all, on strategic issues 'I found that [Curzon] was entirely in accordance with my views' – but it was slow to germinate.[5]

Roddy Owen was a different thing altogether. Younghusband was refused permission to return to India in an official capacity and assist in raising the siege of Chitral; that task was entrusted to Major General Robert Low and a considerable field force. Younghusband went nonetheless – as *The Times* special correspondent. Reporters in those days were glorified camp followers; Younghusband was in a particularly odd position. He knew everybody – his brother George was in the relieving force – but had no official standing, indeed rather the reverse. There was nothing for Younghusband to do, yet he longed for action. Unlike the besieged force in Chitral, whose enemies had shown not only military aptitudes, but had been able to execute them through the provision of modern weapons obligingly sold by a Scots firm in Bombay, the force from Peshawar had primarily to contend with terrain and climate.

By the time General Low's troops had crossed the 10,000 foot Lowarai Pass between Swat and Chitral, Younghusband – deeply impressed by this feat of mountain warfare – was consumed with impatience. He did, however, find a confidante. Owen 'jumped at the idea . . . that we should ride on ahead straight through to Chitral in one day. We did not ask the General's permission, and he afterwards told us it was as well we did not, for he would not have given it.' The ride was a gallant affair, Younghusband's justification of his faith in the Chitralis, and of their respect for him. He made it with 'the man I came most to admire of all I have met in my life . . . just about perfect in body and spirit'.[6]

We can see why Younghusband was drawn to Owen. All who live in the wilds and are not oafs or dullards become hyper-sensitive to physical factors. It was not, however, because Owen was 'Beautifully built, tall and slim, slick and supple', that Younghusband found in him an ideal. It was Owen's power to charm – 'a forceful *compelling* charm – one which came after you and seized you. He was quite irresistible. You simply could not help doing what he wanted, and would do anything for him.' Owen was nothing so exceptional, however – for those days. He was almost the stereotype for an adventurous Englishman. He had won the Grand National on *Father O'Flynn* in 1892; he was a resourceful soldier, who, the very same year 'conducted a campaign against the Banyro [in Uganda] and made a spectacular dash down the Nile to Emin's old headquarters at Wadelai where he hoisted the Union Jack'.[7] What Owen also clearly had was extrovert self-assurance in full measure. Allied to what must also have been a very genuine charm, a compound of physical self-confidence, social self-assurance, and a happy disposition, his personality made the most powerful impact possible on the agent who lived by the will.

In 1895 that agent was sick and sore – not without some cause. Spiritual comforts were still fleeting; higher authority thwarted him; even, late in 1895 successfully arguing the case for the Northern Frontier and the retention of Chitral – 'It is well [that we have done so] for I afterwards heard that the Russians on the Pamirs had orders to march in if we marched out'[8] – could not compensate for a feeling that he had failed to find that 'great thing' which would mark his destiny. It was to come, but from the hand of another, who also lived by the will.

Tibet: Opening Moves

George Curzon was an enigma, but what is most pertinent in this closing stage of the Game is that he had a unique gift for antagonising his friends and a habit, scarcely less unfortunate, of unwittingly misleading his subordinates. By the time Curzon became Viceroy in 1898 he had, a mere forty years old, caused heads as illustrious as Queen Victoria's and Salisbury's to shake with concern. By the time Curzon summoned Younghusband to Simla five years later, his former colleagues at home were tired of him; his subordinates in India, despite his courage, industry and achievements felt more strongly. 'He is absolutely hated here'[1] Younghusband wrote from Calcutta in October 1903.

It is Curzon's personal characteristics that are more relevant here than his obsessions about Russia or his determined preparation to become the greatest viceroy India had known. In the final stages of the Game – before its revival in the First World War – British agents of high and low degree lost sight of the issues; they spent their time absorbed in personal compulsions. Paradoxically, it was Cabinets in London which kept the issues in sight – and kept the cold war going, though with a caution quite unperceived by their subordinates on and beyond imperial frontiers.

Curzon's will to fame is partly attributable to the obscurity of his political origins. In the landed sense the Curzon family was almost as old as Younghusband's, and in social terms enjoyed infinitely greater advantages. While the Younghusbands had made a name for themselves as servants of the Empire, the Curzons had remained minor aristocracy, beyond the pale of that political power enjoyed as an hereditary right until the end of the nineteenth century by Cecils, Cavendishs, Churchills and Stanleys, their friends, relations, and the nouveaux riches who married among them. Curzon, in pursuit of an admirable objective – finding out as much as possible about Russia, Persia and India, and doing so at first hand, albeit as a privileged visitor, travelling in style and meeting mostly senior officials – was, in his twenties and thirties, trying to do two incompatible things. He wanted to become an expert on the cold war, in its purely Asian setting, and he wanted political success. Trollope had, however, pointed out thirty years before that expertise bored the House of Commons; expertise on India emptied it.

This fact was unfortunate, and it is singular that the imperialism of Curzon's day had so little time for his ideal if self-opinionated version of it. Curzon felt alienated from his kind by definable factors – the isolation of ceaseless pain from curvature of the spine, which he heroically bore, not less than a sense that the political fruit was plucked by others. His dislike of the Balfour Cabinet – certainly a family affair – could only be expressed by satire, crude but true. We may suppose that he did sometimes feel nobody understood that the intensity of his concern for India – a land which, he declared, 'haunted him like a passion' – was something more than a pose. The compressed lips hid much; the prolixity of his books, speeches and minutes reveal little about the man who produced them. Curzon was a bad hand at communication. Curzon opened his heart to few. One was St John Broderick, an Eton contemporary and, in their youth and early manhood the 'Dear Boy' of a sustained correspondence.

Curzon was not made Viceroy by Salisbury as a consolation prize for lack of political advance. Nevertheless, Curzon was not an immediate or automatic choice when Elgin retired – Sir Michael Hicks-Beach, the Chancellor of the Exchequer, was Salisbury's first candidate – nor did his appointment enjoy universal approbation. Curzon's expertise could be suffered by ignoring it; but the views which it bred suggested a grandiose idea of Indian needs which, with a man of his temperament, might lead to an independent Indian policy – and so it proved. By the end of his viceroyalty the only point on which Curzon and the Cabinet agreed was on denying political advance to the Indian people. The point on which Cabinet and Viceroy most strongly differed was in their conceptions of the viceregal office.

To Cabinets in London, policy-making by a viceroy was allowed – provided that policy furthered party and governmental ends.

Curzon, however, believed that the viceroy 'is the responsible head of what is by far the most perfected and considerable of highly organised governments in the world'. Curzon lived with that belief to the end; indeed he expressed it in the words just given but two days before he finally left India in November 1905. The interpretation of that belief was one which led Curzon to acts and, what was perhaps more galling, their description in inimitably condescending prose, which suggested that he told Cabinets what to do and expected them to do it.

Nor was this all. Curzon left for India in 1898 with a good many question marks against his name. His views on Russia's advance in Asia – specifically, that it was an inexorable process, obeying, as it were, the laws of nature rather than politics or strategy – were acceptable enough in print but, when expressed in political debate and ministerial speeches, a sharp reaction set in. The corollary to Curzon's view of Russian expansion was that it would cease when it reached the sea. If that day ever came, Britain's supremacy in the East would end. About Russia's ambitions towards the Pacific, Curzon could do little. But, in his years at the India and Foreign Offices he extensively developed the argument that a Russian outlet into the Persian Gulf should be resisted at all costs. The 'permanent government' agreed with this – but its members did not live in Curzon's world. Those who did were repelled by his tone and alarmed by his outlook. Salisbury grumbled frequently. 'Curzon always wants me to talk to Russia as if I had 500,000 men at my back, and I have not.'[2]

Above all, Salisbury was concerned about Curzon's views on the Gulf. When the former returned to power in 1895, Curzon became Parliamentary Under-Secretary of State for Foreign Affairs. This was a junior ministerial appointment but, with Salisbury doubling the offices of Prime Minister and Foreign Secretary, and sitting moreover in the House of Lords, Curzon's post was unusually important. He at once used it to argue the case for British ascendancy in the Gulf; a naval demonstration there was urged, not only as a warning to Russia but to ensure that the Sultan in Constantinople, Abdul Hamid, was 'thoroughly frightened'; early in 1897, after more of the same, the Queen wrote to Salisbury about Curzon's lack of discretion. 'You should caution him', was all that she said, but the warning, from such a source, is indicative of widespread concern. Salisbury's eventual reply is revealing. Referring to Curzon's notions about Muscat, the Prime Minister said: 'The Residents are the most jingo and the most contemptuous of treaties of all Indian officials; and Curzon has fallen into their hands.'

Whether Curzon appreciated Salisbury's declining authority is uncertain; he rarely bothered to appraise men or, a more generous characteristic, calculate on the failings of others. (Calculations about governments and regions were another matter.) At all events, he was not deflected from his belief that British control of the Gulf and, still more important, its vigorous and explicit assertion, was one vital key to India's security. In February 1898, three months before his appointment as Viceroy was announced, Curzon wrote a long letter to Salisbury, in which he developed his ideas about the Gulf and its littoral to the point where he saw it necessary for the whole area west to the Mediterranean and north into Persia to be under British control. 'The predominance of Great Britain over the whole country from Alexandretta to Mosul is indeed unquestionable', declared the Viceroy designate. Russia could be allowed a sphere of interest to the north of Mosul, but none in regions where open country led to the sea. These ideas of Curzon's were to germinate in responsive soil a few years later, and in them we may trace the belief in Britain seizing and keeping a grip on the Gulf and the littoral in the face of rival claims (Russian above all), explaining much of what occurred in two World Wars, and until lately.[3]

In February 1898, however, Salisbury was determined to avoid extending more than one commitment at a time. But Curzon, on becoming Viceroy, immediately put his Gulf ideas into practice, refusing France coaling facilities at Muscat. Salisbury and Lord George Hamilton, the Secretary of State for India (and another of Curzon's few close friends), protested in far from soothing language at the Viceroy putting local issues before Britain's international policy. Curzon was unrepentant, and successful. The incident was important for several reasons. Curzon had demonstrated his independence of London, and had done so over an issue which, although it happened to involve France, expressed with notable simplicity the idea that India must be guarded at all points. We can, moreover, trace in the evolution of Curzon's Gulf strategy during the following four years clues to his decision that Tibet also required to be looked at anew – boldly, actively, independently – and as a striking expression of the forward policy.

Curzon did succeed in making Britain count in the Gulf, by bringing Bahrain and Kuwait totally within the orbit of the Indian Foreign Department, and by establishing a network of agents tasked to suborn the Sheikhs of the western littoral from their allegiance to the Porte. In Persia and Afghanistan there was no special triumph to record. The assassination of Shah Nasir-u-Din in May 1896, after a reign of fifty years, and Abdur Rahman's death in October 1901 – after twenty-one years of unbridled ferocity – revived all the old uncertainties regarding Calcutta's relations with Tehran and Kabul. Curzon's achievement in bringing relative peace to the North-West Frontier made a settlement of Afghan issues less urgent than the re-establishment of British influence in the Gulf. He was not indifferent to Calcutta's relations with Persia as a whole, but he was adamant in his belief that control of the Gulf came first.

A viceroy less well versed in the history of the cold war would not have laid such stress on the Gulf; a viceroy more sensitive to opinion at home and more concerned with wider international issues might well have chosen to ignore the area altogether or, at the least, to see it as a Cabinet rather than a viceregal responsibility. Durand, however, strongly supported by Curzon, now promoted to be Minister in Tehran, took precisely the opposite view. Durand was unpopular with his predominately diplomatic staff, who also had a low opinion of the intelligence activities of such young agents as Percy Sykes – destined to revive the old notion of a British quasi-military presence in southern Persia, and to do so up to and throughout the first World War. Durand and Sykes might have been unpopular, but they had Curzon's support, and that was what counted in those years.

By the end of 1902 Curzon, on his own admission, was looking for fresh fields to conquer. At one time it had seemed as if Afghanistan might serve the purpose. After Abdur Rahman's death, and despite the security brought by the new North-West Frontier province and the Malakand Agency, Curzon feared a Russian *coup* in Kabul. Writing to Roberts in November 1901 Curzon implied that a third Afghan war might be unavoidable. He knew of course that contingency plans existed for intervention in Afghanistan on Abdur Rahman's death, whether Russia reacted or not. Indeed, such plans legitimised the pre-emptive strategy. In fact, Habibullah succeeded his father in an atmosphere of unwonted, unprecedented calm; the new Amir made overtures to Calcutta; intervention ceased to be feasible even to the most ardent cold warrior, especially as the Indian government's Foreign Department was anxious to reply to the new Amir's conciliatory approach by suggesting an official visit to Kabul and the disucssion of a treaty.

Curzon thought little of this trend, and was scathing about his Foreign Secretary, Louis Dane. But even Curzon could hardly destroy the opportunity of improved relations with Afghanistan. Thus Tibet, where, as Curzon revealed at the end of his viceroyalty, 'I did not begin until I had been in India for four years' was chosen as the field for a culminating triumph.[4] The deepest inner motives for intervention in a land with which governor-generals and viceroys just as active as Curzon had rarely interfered remain elusive. It is possible that Curzon was overwhelmed by India, and sought release on its marches. Writing to Roberts in June 1901, Curzon admitted uncharacteristically: 'I never feel very sanguine or confident about anything in India'.[5] Tibet, however, was in most ways an unknown quantity; action there might dispel dark thoughts.

So much is speculation. But it is a fact that Calcutta's relations with Tibet in 1902 were no different from those obtaining at any time in the preceding hundred years. Only two things were certain; the country was politically unknown, despite the efforts of native agents and the results of sporadic exploration; emissaries of the Raj were unwelcome. There were two other factors, vague and hard to assess, requiring verbal manipulation to create additional reasons for intervention. The thirteenth Dalai Lama, spiritual and temporal ruler of Tibet, was said to be advised by one Dorjieff, believed by some, although presumably Tibetan, to be a Russian agent, a kind of Rasputin of the cold war. China was thought by Calcutta to be too weak to prevent any active Russian intervention.

On the fact of Tibetan indifference to closer relations with India Curzon manufactured an argument closely akin to Lytton's in relation to Sher Ali's 'insolence' in 1878; on the rumour of Russian intrigue, Curzon told a tale of that Power's ascendancy; to justify both argument and exposition, Curzon chose Younghusband to penetrate the unknown land and bring it within the imperial sphere. As to China, Curzon was confident that any protest from Peking would be swiftly dismissed by a government in London which had but two years previously exacted punitive revenge from the Manchus for their acquiescence in the Boxer Rebellion and the attempt to destroy the legations.

There is, of course, an idiosyncratic version of the Tibet expedition, its genesis and aftermath, which can be given; of a bold viceroy and a resolute agent pressing forward in defence of vital interests, and doing so despite a vacillating Cabinet, of which Brodrick, the one time 'Dear Boy', was the member most active for a policy of advance and retire. Such a version of what, on the essential facts and the few crucial dates, is a straightforward story, was subsequently put about keenly enough, not least by Younghusband himself. Since obstinacy did wrestle with vacillation, this second version is respectable enough – as a version. To understand the matter with some detachment, however, let us see how the cold war looked at the beginning of 1903 to the Cabinet presided over so urbanely yet uncertainly by Balfour. To Curzon all was simple: Russia was still the enemy at the bridge, and the simplicity of this belief was the greater in that he saw himself as Horatius.

To Balfour all was complex; Russia was indeed the enemy, and the Cabinet's collective hostility to it at this time must be borne in mind when considering Curzon's actions. Balfour, although – or because – he saw the European situation with great clarity, 'had no real faith in a lasting Anglo-Russian entente'. The Prime Minister was prepared to accept 'temporary arrangements; they smooth things for the time being',[6] but Balfour, like his colleagues, remained convinced that Russia could never be a friend of Britain; there was a gulf, which his philosophical mind, otherwise so keen on speculation, chose to accept as a fact of life. In what political, strategic and diplomatic context was this hostility set? Above all, were there any aspects of Indian foreign policy – for that, in effect, is what Curzon's notions of viceregal power had produced – which clashed with British foreign policy, executed, if not exactly conceived, by that former Viceroy, Lord Lansdowne?

There were in fact two such aspects in 1903. Curzon's policy over the Gulf had complicated negotiations for the Berlin to Baghdad railway, and had done nothing to improve Anglo-German relations; Curzon's contempt for China emphasised, even if it did not actually clash with, Britain's involvement in Far Eastern affairs, of which a hostile attitude to Russia's policy in Manchuria was the main ingredient. Both these complex issues were really subordinate to wider ones – initially seen as such by Lansdowne and Hamilton – but they impinged sufficiently on the central problem of where Britain stood in relation to its Continental neighbours for Curzon's method of executing his office to be viewed with increasing suspicion and mistrust in London.

Exacting tribute from the Manchus after the Boxer Rebellion still left many issues unresolved. Over Persia and Afghanistan Lansdowne and Hamilton had, at this time, no settled view, or determination to interfere. It is, however, one of the paradoxes of these two years (1903–1904) that the Cabinet came increasingly to support Curzon's policy over the Gulf and to differ little from him on his view of China yet, by the end of the period, to insist that policy towards Persia and Afghanistan should be taken virtually out of his hands. Policy regarding Tibet was taken entirely out of Curzon's hands.

Curzon's entire identification with the trivial issue of Tibet denied him, by 1905, the chance to execute Afghan and Persian policies which, in almost every sense of prejudice and assumption, could have been framed either in the Cabinet Room or the Viceroy's Council. By the end of 1904, moreover, with Curzon rebuked and Younghusband rejected over their Tibetan adventure, Balfour and his colleagues were still as unrelentingly suspicious of, and hostile towards Russia as had been any of their predecessors throughout the cold war. The Cabinet in London was, however, no longer prepared to let this hostility be shared by Curzon; indeed, on the face of it, Anglo-Russian relations had improved.

The fundamental contradiction in the Balfour Cabinet lay in seeking some accommodation between Britain and the other powers – including Russia – which should yet impose no check on the independence of British foreign policy; the latter was, for all practical purposes, a further extension of the imperial system. The contradiction was not new, indeed it was tediously old, but it deepened – and was accepted with far less equanimity by the powers – in 1903 and 1904 because of the fact that Britain's real strategic weaknesses had become exposed at last. In 1898, Britain had seemed immune from the challenges and requirements of collective security. By 1903, after a war in South Africa which had revealed British military inadequacies far more starkly than the Crimea and to a world quite unwilling to ignore the discovery, a situation existed which Alan Taylor has described thus: 'A European Power which made an alliance with Great Britain would be nearer war than before, not further away, for it would be involved in the burden of the British Empire'; moreover: 'the next few years were to show that it was awkward for the British Empire when the Powers of Europe were on even reasonably friendly terms with each other'.[7] In 1903, as it happens, those Powers were moving apart, and moving towards war; yet their hostility to Britain kept them in some kind of uneasy equilibrium.

Balfour was more acutely aware of the contradictions in Britain's policies than his colleagues – in 1904 he analysed the case for and against Britain supporting Japan over the latter's impending conflict with Russia in a display of such dazzling analytical prowess that his bemused Cabinet decided to do nothing at all. Balfour was, however, an imperialist; indeed he gloried in the name. It was imperialism solely of the 'White Dominion' variety, the creation largely of Dilke and Joe Chamberlain, given a rhetorical justification by men like Milner and John Buchan, whose South African experiences in putting down one European race to benefit another were quite beyond the ken of Curzons or Younghusbands.[8] To Bertrand Russell, one of the early critics of 'Randlord' imperialism, Younghusband was a man 'of immense candour of thought'.[9] This was not a trait which had anything in common with an imperialism whereby concentration camps for Boers and indentured Chinese labour working in the Rand gold mines were, by some alchemy, transmuted into a new version of the white man's burden. The new imperialism reflected the new age, in which, while radicals and socialists attacked the older imperial view, and a young generation began to break with their inherited beliefs, British weaknesses seemed disguised by the bounty brought from the world's four corners. As a result, an isolationist foreign policy persisted until sheer necessity replaced it by one of accommodation with Continental powers.

Balfour – and, for that matter, his critics – were less aware of these contradictions than they should have been. Thus, although Lansdowne, by early 1903 was seeking new accords with both France and Russia, Curzon was right to believe that his Indian policy and that of the British government were as one on all essential points. If, however, proper communication had existed between London and Calcutta, and if, above all, the role and power of the 'permanent government' had been appreciated by Lansdowne – who certainly sought improved Continental relations for Britain with steady persistence – the degree of difference in the execution of that policy might have been appreciated by Balfour. Since his imperial objectives took no concrete Indian form, and as, by this time, he had no friendship left for Curzon anyway, it is possible that good communication might not only have prevented the Tibet expedition but, in the process, have forced the Cabinet to consider what Britain could and could not do without increasing its strategic weaknesses – or alienating its neighbours. To see why none of this happened, and why, as Younghusband said, 'the mutual indignation of these two great men [Broderick and Curzon] spilt over on to my poor head',[10] the chronicle of events in 1903 and 1904 must be seen from various points.

In the first place, Lansdowne, in December 1902, had received 'a hint of an overture . . . from the Russians'.[11] Neither at this time, nor later, did the Russian approach make any impression on the Committee of Imperial Defence which, under Balfour's active chairmanship, argued that meeting Russia's threat to India was the first charge on Britain's strategic resources. The pre-emptive strategy no longer required formulation in Simla; it became the main preoccupation of a body whose supposed function was to define British strategy and see it whole. Brodrick, as Secretary of State for War (between October 1900 and 1903) shared Hamilton's developing conviction that Indian commitments should be kept in check. The CID pursued the even tenor of its way, nor did its deliberations take much note of the 1903 Esher Committee for the reform of the Army's organisation. The Committee accomplished 'some very speedy spring-cleaning of the War Office'; the strategic furniture was not replaced.[12]

Appreciations written by Chapman and Roberts and an 1886 invasion plan from the Governor-General of Turkestan, Kuropatkin, were produced as evidence that the essential aims of Russia's policy were unchanged. 'In England she sees the chief obstacle to the fulfilment of the destiny she believes marked out for her', stated a War Office memorandum of January 1902.[13] 'As Russia can nowhere put effective pressure on England except in Asia, it is there that the contest must be decided.' The danger of this situation was stressed in paper after paper. Russia was presented as an economically straitened empire by comparison with Britain's, but possessed nonetheless all but inexhaustible manpower resources, and was virtually immune from blockade. But, 'In fighting for India, England will be fighting for her imperial existence.' This was a situation to be deterred, or met by a pre-emptive strategy. 'We cannot doubt . . . that . . . whatever else may be left done or undone, the greatest and most determined effort will be made by Russia against India. Here alone can a fatal blow be dealt us. The loss of India by conquest would be a death blow to our prosperity, prestige and power. The damaging effects of even a near approach by hostile forces would be incalculable.'[14] The strategic neuroses of Calcutta and Simla had been translated *en bloc* to the War Office. The process had taken twenty years; its damaging effects continued to mature.

Appreciations proliferated to show that Russian troops could invest Herat at will and that diversionary operations could be mounted across the Upper Oxus by forces from the Transcaspian and Turkestan garrisons. The combined strength of these forces rarely totalled more than 50,000, out of a war establishment strength in these regions of some 90,000, and it was further assumed that these numbers could be matched by troops in India. Inherited Russophobia and a real sense of India's fundamental insecurity could nevertheless not be dissipated by consideration of Russia's true internal state, particularly in Turkestan and Transcaspia, or its actual international position. That troops could be concentrated in Turkestan; that the movement of the one reinforcing army corps considered necessary from European Russia (out of 20 odd deployed there), assisted moreover by the efforts of such men as 'Mr Wilson, a Railway contractor and a capitalist'; that all this could take place in a matter of weeks; these were issues to which much weighty consideration was given. Thus, a CID report of 31 May 1903 which encapsulated earlier reports concerned with 'The Military Needs of the Empire in a War with France and Russia', decided that the defence of India was the only issue of prime importance. Despite the invasion scares of those years – specifically that Germany might invade Britain – Balfour and Brodrick accepted the argument that:

(a) Britain had no effective obligation to maintain European security.
(b) Home defence could be left to the Royal Navy and appeals to British youth to join the colours.
(c) 'Three offensive Army Corps' should be made available for overseas operations. Two of these would be sent to India, to support the investment of Kandahar – as a preliminary to sustained offensive operations – and to raise 'the field army on the North West Frontier of India to a strength of about 192,500 men'. The

third corps would take part in attacks on the French Colonies, a process which, assisted by the Royal Navy's control of the sea, would, it was supposed, lead to speedy success – in any case an essential factor in British strategy. 'A series of disasters in the French Colonies would, it is thought, induce the excitable French democracy to upset their government . . . and to declare for peace.'
(d) The White Dominions and Colonies were not only to be increasingly responsible for their own defence, but were to assist in garrisoning Egypt (against which a Russian descent was feared) and India.[15]

It might be thought that appreciations so oddly compounded of fear and hope, and expressing so crudely their belief in the advantages of isolation, would have fallen on deaf political ears, especially as Russia's internal troubles were, by 1903, common knowledge. In March and May of that year, however, Indian forces had been increased. The number of British troops permanently stationed in India was to be raised by 30,000; the first convoy of reinforcements from Britian to India would, if necessary, sail via the Cape without a Royal Navy escort. Although Selborne (the First Lord of the Admiralty) and Brodrick argued about details, these arguments had their desired effect. Lansdowne no longer shared the defence establishment's view of the threat to India – his tone on that subject changed markedly after 1891 – but he believed Russia to be powerful, nonetheless, and he feared it. Russia, in 1903, was, as it is today, a great unknown. Despite the European world of Giers and De Staal (and their successors Lamsdorff and Benckendorff), plus the widespread British notion of a thrusting, westernised, industrial state, there was still an uneasy feeling among British policy-makers and their subordinates that all this was but the veneer for something older, more primitive, more dangerous.

Tsardom was seen as 'a many coloured amalgam of the bureaucracy, the police-army, the Orthodox Church, and the personal caprice of the sovereign autocrat. Side by side with such modern arms of imperialism as the Chinese Eastern Railway or the Loan and Discount Bank in Persia . . . you [had] the essentially old-fashioned viceroyalites of Trans-Caucasia and Turkestan . . . strange mixed types, such as the Court intriguer Badmayev, a Mongol medicine man turned railway promoter.'[16] Dorjieff was not just a figment of

Curzon's imagination; he struck a response in the breasts of men in London unable to decide whether Russia was powerful because of the iron roads spanning the country, or sinister due to methods of conducting business which seemed permanently subtle and devious. Just as the soldiers feared not only Russia's threat to India, a thing in itself, and were over-impressed by their opposite numbers' knowledge of Indian defence problems (a subject on which that widely respected public servant M. Lessar had become an acknowledged authority after twenty years at the Game), so Lansdowne was torn between an accord with St Petersburg and a *rapprochement* with Berlin, between the old and the new. A combination of the two was inconceivable – [17] which would prevail? In 1903, neither did.

In the spring of that year, despite Russian overtures the previous December, Lansdowne found it particularly difficult to set a consistent diplomatic course. He had decided to interpret the growing Russian interest in the Gulf as an expression of commercial rather than strategic objectives. 'Bandar Abbas [on the Persian shore of the Gulf] is the Vladivostock of the Middle East' an excitable Russian newspaper leader had said in 1901;[18] similar arguments appeared, which saw in the new Vladivostock a check to British 'pretensions' in Kuwait. In September 1902, however, another leader put Russian interests as 'the Dardanelles first and foremost, the Persian Gulf second, and Manchuria a bad third'. This declaration appeared in the *Novoe Vremya*, hardly a source of pacific sentiments. Russian interest in the Straits was a matter of course, and had to be lived with. If that in the Gulf could be confined to purely commercial objectives, Lansdowne saw no reason why a process should not be established whereby this area and, indeed Persia itself, would be divided into British and Russian spheres of interest which, nevertheless, would not prejudice legitimate commercial activities.

Manchuria, however, was a much more complex issue than the Gulf, raising in an acute form the question of how far Britain could protect its Eastern interests in isolation. In 1898 Salisbury had managed to achieve a settlement of differences with rival claimants to slices of Chinese territory by preferring to co-operate with Germany rather than Russia. In 1903 things were not so simple. Attempts to improve Anglo-German relations were constantly foundering on the rocks of mutual suspicions (and competing phobias), let alone on the more fundamental point that Germany's interests remained resolutely Continental, while Britain's could not, in Lansdown's eyes, be separated from imperial objectives, however much the latter were seen as an element in wider international relationships. The one point of similarity between 1898 and 1903 was that Lansdowne did not for long trouble himself with Peking's susceptibilities over Manchuria's future. Not only had the Boxer Rebellion weakened the Manchu government to the point where it could resist no demands from European states; the rise of Japan to unquestioned industrial and commercial importance had turned China into a kind of territorial carcass, on which national vultures might feed at will – provided they did not injure each other in the process.

Russia and Japan were, however, at loggerheads over Manchuria; the Cabinet, despite the Anglo-Japanese Alliance of 1902 – seen by so many as the end of isolation – was torn between support for Japan and co-operation with Russia. Balfour, Lansdowne and Brodrick, together with their advisers, believed Russia would win a war with Japan; on the other hand, a victorious Russia, one, moreover, still allied to France, would complicate Britain's relations with the latter; France, backed by a triumphant Russia, might become intransigent over negotiations for an improved relationship with Britain; these negotiations were in train and their main element was a *quid pro quo* over Morocco and Egypt: Britain would ignore France's claims over the former, France would accept British control of the latter.

This cat's cradle of competing choices and risks for Britain could only be straightened out by decisive action. A major diplomatic row with Russia was not regarded by Balfour as desirable or safe yet, at the dawn of this bloody century, crises moved more slowly to the brink; Lansdowne, as Curzon prepared to embark on his Tibetan adventure, struggled, and with temporary success, to keep his diplomatic options open. Benckendorff was consistently available; Cambon, the French Ambassador, was as consistently level-headed; to Japan's protests that Britain was dragging its feet regarding a positively anti-Russian policy, Lansdowne managed to return a series of singularly dusty answers. Isolation had its perils; it had not yet brought Britain to the edge.

Thus, on more than personal grounds, Curzon could feel justified in the decision to 'despatch . . . a "pacific" mission to Lhasa that was to be spearheaded by an armed escort'.[19] It is true that Hamilton had told Curzon in December 1902 – as Lansdowne sought to digest Russian overtures – that the Cabinet was opposed to 'any action which is likely to produce war or disturbances in any part of the British Empire'.[20] Hamilton, however, distanced himself from that view – or did so to Curzon's satisfaction. Even if Hamilton had urged any specific restraints on Curzon, there was the evidence of the Cabinet's uncertainties as to which diplomatic and strategic objectives to pursue. Indeed Hamilton was the source of this information; the Secretary of State was not only an old friend of the Viceroy's, but had held his high office for the unprecedented period of eight years. We can now see that Hamilton hoped Curzon would take a hint to proceed with caution over Tibet, about which the former was as well informed as a Minister could be.

The Viceroy construed Hamilton's December communications in quite another light. He did not hesitate. May 1903 was the month when Younghusband was roused to action but, 8 January 1903 was the moment when, 'in the breathless rush of the Coronation Durbar of King Edward VII',[21] Curzon composed the dispatch 'outlining a more active and definite policy towards Tibet'. Between 8 January and 6 November 1903, when Brodrick, newly come to office as Hamilton's successor, sanctioned a further advance in Tibet, Curzon had virtually a free hand. The Cabinet found more pressing international issues to tackle than Tibet; moreover, the calm and experienced Hamilton resigned (on the Tariff Reform controversy) in September. Thus, as in 1878, communication between London and Calcutta was noticeable by its absence throughout much of 1903.

Nonetheless, 1903 proved an intensely frustrating year for Curzon, and one whose summer months were to tell on Younghusband also. Curzon had got up a case against the Tibetans, but it was so weak, and also so involved, that the latter had no difficulty in settling down to protracted negotiations which got Younghusband nowhere. From the many accounts which are available, it is clear that the Tibetan plenipotentiaries, whom Younghusband encountered at Khamba Jong between July and October, were men who enjoyed a long talk for its own sake, and enjoyed still more the sight of a British agent having to make verbal bricks without straw. Younghusband did not find it enjoyable at all, which explains a good deal of what occurred in 1904. For our understanding of what happened in 1903, there are five factors to consider: Curzon's case against the Tibetans; the basis of the case for action; the wider strategic considerations; the intelligence problem; personal issues.

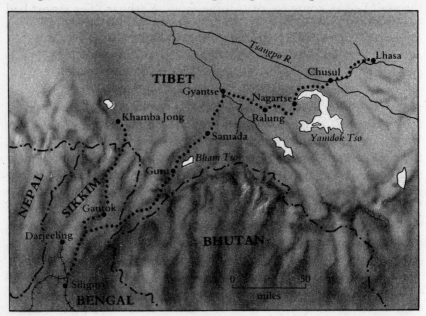

The route for the British expedition to Lhasa, 1904

Curzon's case against the Tibetans was very simple; the Dalai Lama refused to answer his letters requesting 'friendly relations';[22] his people refused to trade with Indian merchants. It is essential to make clear from the outset that both these assertions were false, and it is equally necessary to stress that there is a strong presumption that Curzon knew them to be. He may or may not have 'read everything', as Peter Fleming avers, but his appetite for memoranda was nearly insatiable.[23] Proof that the Dalai Lama had answered at least one letter from the Indian government, albeit indirectly, and that trade did exist, lay in reports which would almost certainly have found their way on to Curzon's desk. In March 1900, the Dalai Lama replied to a letter sent on Curzon's behalf by a native agent, one moreover, who had been used by the intelligence authorities on many occasions and was known, as far as anything in this field was ever known, to be trustworthy and well informed. Throughout 1902 the staff of the Intelligence Branch at Simla were completing a revised edition of the 'Military Report on Sikkim and the Chumbi

Valley; with some Notes on Tibet'.[24] The Tibet/India trade figures given in this are modest, but they bear comparison with that passing through Leh en route to, or coming from, Kashgar. The report had information other than trade which, according to view, put even that supposedly central issue in a wider, more challenging context, one where Curzon's self-admitted desire to move the strategic chessman about could be given free expression.

What is more, the Dalai Lama had refused to answer *his* letters; moreover, such reply as he had sent made it clear that he wanted no truck with the Indian government. The Dalai Lama also said of the Russians, 'They have repeatedly with the orders of China, wished to come within our boundary . . . We will not allow them on any occasion to come, and on this we are united, both lamas and laymen.'[25] To Curzon, that was neither here nor there. In fact, the Dalai Lama's dislike of Russia's interference was exactly the kind of remark which Curzon had to suppress if a more telling reason for intervention, and one which would keep London quiet, was to be produced.

A more substantial – or, at any rate, more elaborate – case for action had therefore to be formulated. The initial argument came to this: the Tibetans, especially those who inhabited the Chumbi Valley, a fork of territory thrust into Sikkim south of the Himalayas, were contumacious; they had ill-treated their Sikkimese neighbours, whom Britain was bound by treaty to protect. Since the 1890 treaty between Britain and China, which redefined China's nominal sovereignty over Tibet after clashes with Sikkim – and British troops – in 1888, the Tibetans had persistently shown a hostile and agressive attitude to their neighbours – or so Curzon was told. In 1902, however, Tibetans of the Chumbi had agreed to discuss boundary questions with John White, the Political Agent in Sikkim. Curzon argued that this event justified a mission to Tibet, which might result in the settlement of more fundamental differences. White had in fact refused to discuss anything with the Tibetans after certain boundary adjustments had been made, but this indulgence in 'face' was too trivial a point for the Viceroy to consider.

In any case, the Tibetans as such were essentially minor players; the case for action might rest on Tibet's dislike of China's suzereignty, China's inability to effectively impose it – and the possibility of St Petersburg stepping in where Peking feared to tread. Although Curzon was on weak legal ground in making these points – the 1890 treaty had specifically recognised China's suzereignty – he was absolutely right in his appreciation of the real situation as far as China and Tibet were concerned. The Tibetans did dislike their Chinese overlords, and the latter were as ineffectual in imposing their authority in Lhasa as they were in Kashgar. If Curzon did read the Intelligence Branch's 1902 report, he would have known that Chinese officials were not supposed to interfere in Tibet's internal affairs but, as the same report emphasised, this meant little. 'The Ambans [Chinese Officials, roughly corresponding to Political Agents] are detested by the Tibetans, which is largely owing to the reason that when they leave the capital on excursions or inspection tour they and their retainers exact food and money from the inhabitants to an exorbitant extent.'

All this was useful, but Curzon was still in the early stages of his argument. He came to the heart of the matter – the wider strategic considerations – when he argued that China's inability to exercise authority over Tibet must lead to a situation where Russia would do so – with results which would produce a situation on India's North-Eastern Frontier just as dangerous as that which, for generations had obtained for the Northern and, in lesser degree, the Northern-Western Frontiers. Curzon buttressed his case by references to Sinkiang, where Chinese authority was minimal – and Russian interest strong. He did not refer to Younghusband's exploration of the Pamirs, or to his airy assumptions as to China's capacity for extending, not merely exerting its authority in Sinkiang. Had Curzon done so, his case might have been wrecked from the outset. Younghusband's name would inevitable have cropped up; that agent was not well thought of in the Foreign and India Offices. When Curzon composed his dispatch, Younghusband was still in the wings, but what happened to him in 1891, and what Salisbury and Morier were forced to do thereafter, might have alerted Whitehall to the possibility that Curzon had a version of the forward policy in mind which would force the Home government to intervene.

At no point in marshalling his arguments – which, in one sense opened up a whole new cold war zone – did Curzon suggest that India could be invaded by Russia through Tibet and the North-East Frontier territories. Ardagh, – Director of Military Intelligence in London – had said in 1898 that, 'unless we secure the reversion of Lhasa we may find the Russians there before us',[26] but this assessment and those written thereafter by other members of the 'permanent government', kept close to the argument that it would be the effect in India of such Russian propinquity which was the danger – to be met by pre-emptive or punitive action in Tibet. If Curzon and the soldiers had stressed the dangers of outright invasion in arguing their case for a pre-emptive strategy in Tibet, the Cabinet in London might have listened, but certainly would not have acquiesced in a new forward policy. By concentrating on a contingent Russian presence in Tibet and by implying a new threat thereby to India's security, Curzon initially received the tepid support of the Cabinet in London. The support was given for an operation which was designed to warn the Chinese authorities in Lhasa. The Cabinet was indifferent to Curzon's wider ambitions, provided they did nothing to worsen fundamentally Anglo-Russian relations. By sanctioning a limited operation, the Cabinet unwittingly trapped Curzon and Younghusband in an impossible situation. Curzon escaped; Younghusband did not.

Curzon had, by this stage in his exhaustive advocacy for intervention (of which the 8 January dispatch was but a distillation) reached the point where evidence of danger from Russian intervention had to be produced. Fudging the evidence over Tibetan obstinacy and trade was one thing, but with the Cabinet not especially responsive to arguments about specific Russian threats, it was clearly necessary to produce something pretty telling to demonstrate that they did exist. Here Curzon faced a major difficulty, one moreover which was to dog Younghusband's steps throughout his Tibetan sojourn. Information about the country was scant; intelligence of Russian activities sparse. In 1903 Tibet was not wholly the uncharted land of popular imagination, but those who knew were not the kind who talked. A great deal was known in Simla about Tibet's geography: native agents had continued to operate there even after Montgomerie's death, and although the information which they brought back was intelligible only to a trained geographer's mind, it added up to a picture which revealed that the movement of men and animals was clearly possible.

By 1884, when the agent Kintup's report was produced (he was illiterate and dictated the results of his four and a half years' travels among and between lamaseries and on the banks of great rivers), Tibet had been pretty well surveyed. As with earlier operations by native agents, odd perils and strange encounters enlivened their narratives. One pundit – soldiers, for some reason, were never employed in Tibet – was delayed for four months 'owing to him falling in love with his host's wife'. Another agent, at one point on the road, noted that people are 'said to eat dogs, snakes, tigers, leopards, bears and monkeys'. Two others, in straits from robbers 'managed to raise a little money by pawning their instruments; the aneroid, which was a large one, proving very serviceable, as it was mistaken for a gigantic watch, and valued accordingly'.[27]

The adventures of native agents in Tibet do sometimes sound improbable – and sometimes were – but their geographical information proved to be remarkably accurate when, after 1904, the country was explored with tolerable frequency by British agents. Certainly the information brought back to Simla by Kintup and his comrades was far more reliable than that which their successors purveyed.[28] The agents traversed the country, whereas most nineteenth century European explorers were forced to stay on or near its northern boundaries. Bower, in 1891 and 1892 got within 150 miles of Lhasa – which enabled him to hear that 'Tibet was in no way under China' – but only native agents penetrated the Forbidden City itself.[29] For example, Deasy in 1896, was confined to the Aksai Chin. Finally, the enterprising and objective British Agent at Leh in 1899, Captain R. L. Kennion discovered – and reported – a fact adduced by all native agents, and one which Curzon might well have pondered. Trade with Tibet was perfectly possible; a political initiative by India was not; the Tibetans did not want it, and would resist its imposition.

This kind of intelligence would not serve Curzon's purpose. Something alarming was required. A little of this desire for a motive may have been due to the ease with which Tibet seemed to elude the processes of political intelligence. Except in the chastening terms just noted, neither native nor British agents were able to provide anything. The Tibetans, to British eyes a priest-ridden people, not only concealed the important facts with almost supernatural cunning, but operated their own intelligence service with considerable skills. A British officer who was engaged in the 1888 Sikkim operations noted: 'The Tibetans maintained a regular system of communication by means of their monasteries; we were at a loss to know how such good intelligence of the fighting reached Leh, until we made out that it was passed along from monastery to monastery.'[30]

Monasteries – or lamaseries rather – were to figure largely as centres of baneful power and influence in the intelligence diaries of the Tibet expedition. From the Dalai Lama downwards, the theocracy of Tibet was regarded by British officials with a curious mixture of fear and loathing. When one more than usual inspired report was produced to the effect that the Dalai Lama was 'cohabiting with a high-bred nun', it was conned with unnecessary zeal.[31] Rarely were Tibetan intelligence methods circumvented by British Staff Officers, although on one occasion during Younghusband's mission the Tibetans, having relied on a raven to spy out the land, discovered to their chagrin that the invader had, rather unsportingly, shot it down.

Any intelligence that was gleaned was always unsatisfactory. Bower, when he met Tibetan officials from Lhasa, tried to press upon them thoughts of friendly relations with British India. He was rebuffed. 'Tibet was forbidden ground to all strangers . . . as for friendship existing between the two governments it was no reason why the people of both nations should not stick to their own countries.'[32] Intelligence was sought from Nepal. The ruler managed to keep on reasonable terms with Tibet, China and British India, although there was no love lost with the first; an ambiguous degree of subjection governed relations with the second; and a mercenary relationship based on recruitment of Gurkhas for imperial service subsisted with the third. Answers of a sort came back to Curzon's expectant mind but, not surprisingly, they lacked consistency. Much of the information which the Nepal government's representative in Lhasa passed on to the British Resident in Kathmandu was too obscure even for that expert to unravel. When, in February 1902, something positive emerged via Kathmandu, it was distinctly unhelpful. The report was to the effect that 'British activity on the Tibetan frontier had been so bitterly resented by the rulers of China, Tibet, Bhutan and Ladakh, that they had formed an alliance for war against the British in India.'[33]

This was another piece of high-priced fiction, and even a man searching for a motive would have been hard pressed to utilise it. The report did, however, add something else, and it was enough for Curzon's purpose. 'The promise of Russian support had been secured, and hostilities were due to commence in 1904.'[34] Now this might or might not be nonsense, but it was an axiom of the British in India that any mention of Russia required investigation. Curzon certainly manufactured a case against a people who had done no harm to anybody, and he did it largely for personal motives but, no viceroy, not even Ripon, would have read such a report and ignored it. Most viceroys before Curzon – we might say all save Lytton – would have subjected such a report to scrutiny. Curzon fabricated a case with it, but this differed more in degree than in kind from the acts of his predecessors.

The report chimed with others which were accumulating of Russian activities in Tibet. Most of these concern Dorjieff, who flits through their pages, now 'dressed like a monk [while in Lhasa] in a long coat of red-ochre-coloured Tibetan woollen cloth', now sallying forth 'in the Mongolian fashion, i.e. in a yellow long coat, a short-sleeved petticoat, and a yellow cap'. One's incredulity at the seriousness with which Curzon eventually received these reports – he had earlier treated them with reserve – must be tempered by the realisation that when, at the end of 1902, he decided to concern himself with Tibet, he was quite bereft of rational motive for intervention. Further, by then Curzon had realised that Dorjieff and his accomplices had skipped to and fro across India, attracting attention indeed from the Special Branch and, on at least one occasion, occupying the mind of that renowned native agent, S. C. Das – the Hurree Babu of *Kim* – yet moving across the Viceroy's domains with complete freedom nonetheless.[35]

Dorjieff came to occupy a prominent place in Curzon's – and Younghusband's – demonology, not least because, by 1902, there was good circumstantial evidence that he was regularly on the move between Lhasa and St Petersburg, enjoying the confidence not only of the Dalai Lama but another potentate equally receptive to mystery men – Nicholas II himself. Curzon was outside this charmed circle. Dorjieff and his principal accomplice Norzanoff – a man much given, it seemed, to travelling between Odessa, Marseilles and Bombay, but scarcely disguised one would have thought by 'Mongolian features, slight moustache twisted down in Chinese fashion, medium complexion' – were, however, only parts of the whole.[36] The two agents – for such they certainly were – clinched a story which had been accumulating for some time. In October 1899, Colonel McSwiney of the Intelligence Branch, an experienced officer with no phobias, noted after an open mission to Tashkent: 'Not satisfied with scheming for a Port in the Persian Gulf, Russia is bent on being before us in Tibet. Lieutenant Kozlov's objective is *Lhasa*, by the Emperor's special command.'[37]

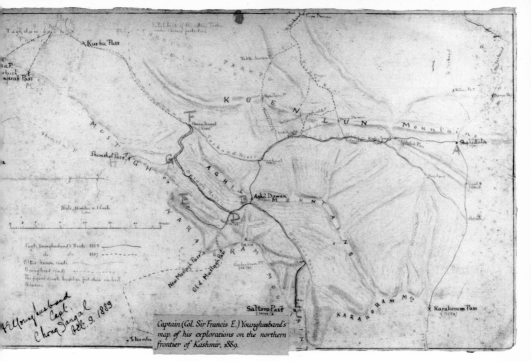

11 Shahzad Mir's map of the area traversed by Younghusband during his
'mission to the Northern frontiers of Kashmir'

12 Younghusband in Kashgar, October 1890,
seeking to bend the Chinese to his will

13 'The most superior person': Lord Curzon as Viceroy

14 Younghusband at forty, about to embark on his Tibetan adventure

15 The stand-by of mountain warfare – dismantled screw guns on the march

16 Brigadier-General Macdonald inspects Tibetan posts on the Karo La

17 Crossing the Tang La during the advance to Tuna, March 1904

18 Shelling a Tibetan village, 26 June 1904, during the advance on Gyantse

19 'Whatever happens we have got
The Maxim gun and they have not'

By the spring of 1902, the Russian interest in Tibet was known to be real – and rationalised as dangerous. Dorjieff now came to Lhasa bearing gifts. British officials were still perforce relying on second-hand intelligence, but they saw no reason to doubt that conveyed by 'Kawaguchi, the Japanese devotee [of Buddhism]. . . He declares that of five hundred camels which arrived carrying presents, one half were laden with small arms and ammunition.' A further report stated that '9,000 breach loading rifles of European make have been imported into the country'. When a rumour reached Calcutta that Dorjieff had boasted there would 'soon be Cossacks in the streets of Lhasa', few men and certainly not the Viceroy stopped to consider that, after many years, there were still no Cossacks in the streets of Kashgar – save for the Russian Agent's escort. Few men reflected that the very reports which told of rifles and 'other presents of more sinister import' also mentioned that the Tibetans let the rifles rust, and that 'such a thing as a Tibetan army in the ordinary sense of the word does not exist . . .[it is] an ill-armed and ill-organised rabble, incapable of a real defence, ignorant of the rudiments of warfare, and relying far more on bluster and numbers than on their own fighting qualities, which indeed may be said under such circumstances to be *nil*.'[38]

It would be interesting to know whether Curzon ever read this assessment, and if so, whether it affected a decision to achieve a viceregal *coup* which would be strategically brilliant yet militarily cheap. The Viceroy had a poor opinion of soldiers – his monumental clash with Kitchener was over personalities and the principle of who should be master, not the issue of Indian defence as such – and no love of punitive operations for their own sake. What we do know is that Curzon, as he sat down to write that hurried yet lucid dispatch of 8 January 1903, was ruled by several conflicting emotions and objectives. It has been generally supposed that Curzon in recommending action to Hamilton – a mission to Lhasa to settle outstanding issues, and the stationing there of a British agent to see they didn't crop up again – was governed by the factor which we have so far ignored: that Russia had concluded, or might conclude a treaty with China, which would give the former virtual control of Tibet. Such a rumour had been current for much of 1902, and although caution might have suggested that as its source was none other than Lessar – at the time Russian Minister in Peking – it could perhaps be a skilful *canard*, nerves in London were sufficiently frayed to react with some apprehension. Of course Curzon took advantage of this reaction – perhaps understandably so. Equally, in suggesting in his 8 January dispatch that negotiations between Calcutta and Lhasa should bypass Peking, he was doing no more than echo Lansdowne's conviction that China was of no account.

The wording of the dispatch was restrained enough, but it is impossible to escape the conviction that Curzon was bent on intervention of some sort whatever the Cabinet's reaction might be. The elements which combined to make up his case have been described at some length because few of them figured in the dispatch – but all were subsequently produced by Curzon to justify his actions. Moreover, although Lansdowne and Hamilton did react positively to the rumour of a virtual Russian protectorate over Tibet, their comments were not of the kind likely to satisfy the mind of a man determined to justify his actions, yet anxious, as always, to have others see them as eminently necessary and wise.

Indeed, not only in 1902, but subsequently, the Treaty issue was consistently played down in London, partly because the Cabinet was loath to risk any specific clash with Russia, and partly because the members of it who had dealings with Curzon were determined to contain him as much as possible. He had no real friends left; hence his ideas were unpopular. The War Office alone in England saw the mission to Lhasa as an acceptable solution to the problem of Russia in Tibet.[39] To Curzon this would have been cold comfort, and he would not have subscribed to the proposition that the main weight of the British counter-attack to Russia's advances in Tibet was to be borne by Lansdowne, in discussions with the Russian Ambassador in London.[40]

Here we come to the factor which was to dominate the Tibet expedition and its aftermath. Already, by the end of 1902, Balfour and Hamilton had had about as much as they could stomach of George Nathaniel Curzon. That they bore with his habitual rudeness and hyperegoism at all is a revealing comment on human relations; that they countenanced the Tibet mission – as it was originally known – is equally revelatory of the degree to which India remained the most crucial strategic factor in the cold war so far as Britain was concerned.

There is no point in dwelling here on Curzon's attitude to the Cabinet on the eve of his Tibetan adventure. The full hand will be shown later; moreover, Dr Mehra has meticulously documented the more telling examples of the Viceroy's letters to men whose responsibilities were equal to his, and who were answerable, as he was not, to a Parliament and a public. Like Lytton, Curzon had succeeded in ignoring his Council; as Younghusband subsequently noted, with some satisfaction, the Viceroy 'jumped' on any member who dared to disagree with him, and such was the mystique surrounding the Viceroy – as viceroy – that he got away with it. When Hamilton proved indifferent to this treatment, Curzon became hysterical. His constant pain and an ailing wife explain much, but the fact remains that the job had got on top of him.

There were always dangers in sustaining the role of viceroy. Egoists were particularly vulnerable. For Curzon, determined to brook no obstacles, the dangers progressively increased. The sense of isolation increased as a result. Curzon wrote to Arthur Godley, the Permanent Under-Secretary of State at the India Office, in June 1902: 'You send me out to India as an expert and you treat my advice as though it were of an impertinent schoolboy.'[41] Over the durbar Curzon went beyond all reasonable grounds of self control. He wished to associate this piece of imperial showmanship with a more solid gesture. Tax remission came to mind. Hamilton was cool to the idea. Curzon threatened resignation, not only to Hamilton, but to the King. In November 1902, Brodrick issued the first of several warnings: 'In this instance there has been unanimity of opinion in the India Office and the Cabinet and that they were all determined that if you elected to go on such an issue we must face it.'[42]

Curzon did not elect to go on this – or any other – issue. He had plans which transcended even Tibet's in importance; he wanted to be re-appointed for a further term; this had not been done since John Company's day, but Curzon believed he could do it. He was already preparing an approach to Balfour; some political caution came to hand. In writing to Balfour over the durbar issue in December, Curzon switched from threats to appeals: 'You have never served your country in foreign parts. For your sake, I hope you never may. English Governments have always had the reputation of breaking the hearts of their proconsuls from Warren Hastings to Bartle Frere. Do you wish to repeat the performance?'[43] Most unfortunately for all concerned, this tear-jerker had its effect. Despite broken hearts, other than Lytton's, being rather hard to recall – never was there a happier man than Lansdowne, and Dufferin's *savoir vivre* was a byword – the Cabinet decided to feel sorry for the man on the spot. The Viceroy sulked after his outburst – 'for three months Curzon stopped his weekly letter to Brodrick which he had written to him regularly for two years'[44] – but Hamilton decided to forgive. He chose an inopportune moment to do so.

12

Younghusband Digs
his Grave

The course of events in 1903, up to the telegram from Brodrick of 6 November, led inexorably to those of 1904. The year 1903 is interesting for the use which Curzon made of Hamilton's generosity, and the skill with which in October, he foisted on Younghusband the final responsibility for turning the Tibet mission from a frontier exercise into a major political operation. It would be an exaggeration to say that Curzon lost interest in Tibet once the mission was under way, but the evidence is clear that Younghusband took the bit between the teeth from the moment of his appointment. The result was that, in Brodrick's mind, Younghusband, not Curzon, became the man on the spot – in more senses than one.

Curzon failed to restrain his subordinate; indeed, he made no effort to do so. The Viceroy was cautious after his durbar outburst. He had secured agreement for the attainment of his objective; let his agent be the means of attainment. This strategy can now be seen as deliberate up to, and beyond, the moment – 11 October – when Younghusband was summoned to Simla after his fruitless three months at Khamba Jong. On that October day in Simla, Curzon specifically put the onus of an extended operation on his subordinate's shoulders. Thereafter, Curzon concentrated on his own affairs specifically, his reappointment as Viceroy. Younghusband, in urging more forceful action, said to himself that he knew his master's ways. If only he had known them.

Between 8 January and Younghusband's selection as Commissioner for the Tibetan mission on 5 May, Curzon and Hamilton conducted a careful correspondence by letter and telegram. The Cabinet refused to accept Curzon's 8 January proposals until the Russian situation had been clarified. On 20 February the Viceroy

179

was told to wait; on 24 February he was informed roads could be built through Sikkim to the Tibetan frontier; on 29 April Hamilton said that negotiations on that frontier, or a short distance inside Tibetan territory could be set in train. The Secretary of State still refused to consider a mission to Lhasa. But two points should be noted here – apart from the fact that Lhasa remained Curzon's goal. The correspondence in February did not reflect the views of the Cabinet as a whole; that body, was 'opposed to any action which "would raise in other parts of the world international complications and embarrassments or lead to Russia retaliating in other parts of Asia where her influence and material forces are stronger than our own"'.[1] Hamilton said this in writing to Curzon on 20 February. The words were clear and unambiguous, summarising what the Cabinet – as a whole – thought about the international situation; but by no stretch of the imagination could the words be construed as a total inhibition on the very idea of a Tibet mission.

Nor did the statement conflict with Hamilton's view that some move to counter Russian activity in Tibet should be permitted the Viceroy. There was no essential difference between Lansdowne and Hamilton on the priorities of Anglo-Russian relations; they were, after all, in daily personal communication. There was, by February 1903, a serious yet unacknowledged difference opening up between Lansdowne and Curzon. The Foreign Secretary was determined to keep the Russians in play, however much he might have engaged in occasional verbal remonstrance; the Viceroy was equally determined to teach them a lesson. Hamilton failed to come down decisively on one side or the other. Indeed, by April he was telling Curzon that Lansdowne and Benckendorff had reached a good understanding on the need to settle outstanding issues. As in the previous December, Hamilton was attempting to give Curzon a wider view of the international horizon; as on that earlier occasion the gesture boomeranged.

This potentially dangerous lack of a clear understanding between the Cabinet and Curzon as to what was both feasible and permissible was made worse by the 24 February accession to the request to build roads. Roads meant troops, to make and guard them. Troops meant either a flag march or a punitive operation; both implied raising the Tibetan stakes considerably. It was too much to expect that Balfour, lacking that experience of India of which Curzon had so carefully

reminded him, should see the implications of a road-making programme through a territory which had not hitherto enjoyed such an
essential ingredient to movement and communications. The Prime
Minister might be Chairman of the Committee of Imperial Defence,
but he never displayed much interest in details. Hamilton, however,
after eight years at the India Office, let alone a lifetime's involvement
in Indian affairs, should have known what roads meant. Either he
did not, or he was sufficiently responsive to the idea of a mission for
caution to be overcome. The Cabinet had refused an expedition to
Lhasa, but two clear rounds had already gone to the Viceroy by the
end of April; he had a mission in being; he had the means to back it
by force.

Thus, when Curzon and Younghusband met in Simla a week
later, the stage had already been set for something more dramatic
than that process which Younghusband had detested since his
expulsion from the Pamirs twelve months before: mere 'talkee
talkee' between civilians. The scene under the deodars at Anandale –
the Viceroy's summer residence in 'that curiously suburban eyrie'[2] –
has often been described. With Kitchener in attendance – loomingly
silent, broodingly averse to the whole business, yet oddly acquies-
cent in its already multifarious complications – the Viceroy poured
into Younghusband's receptive ear his ideas about Tibet. With the
world of Mrs Hauksbee before him – in truth the Guardians from
the Indian civil service taking their unaccustomed ease – Younghusband bent to an older theme, of frontiers and individual endeavour.
In his own words, 'Lord Curzon was now Viceroy, and he had
remembered David'.[3] The David in question was to be ill-rewarded
but he never complained about Curzon, nor regretted the decision
to embark on a mission which even he could see was essentially the
result of a viceregal whim.

Younghusband was so receptive to Curzon having selected him –
despite the assertion that 'I had never seen a Tibetan, or served on
the North-Eastern Frontier'[4] – that he swallowed the entire draught
of eloquence. Younghusband had already, earlier in 1903, been
subjected to the Curzon approach. He and his wife enjoyed an
unusual honour for a man in his position – guests of the Viceroy and
his Vicerene. Younghusband was quite indifferent to social success,
but Curzon urged his agent 'not to look upon him as Viceroy, but
as an old friend and fellow-traveller'; this was strong magic.[5] At
their next meeting, Younghusband was told a tale somewhat more

selective in its arguments and details than that which had been furnished to the Cabinet. This version of events, as related by Curzon to Younghusband, bears a striking resemblance to Lytton's seduction of Cavagnari twenty-six years before:

> The Tibetans had for some time past been troublesome as neighbours; they had broken the treaty which the Chinese had made with us on their behalf; they had blocked the trade between India and Tibet, and they had knocked down the boundary pillars; we had grave grounds for grievance against them. Still, we might have put up with these annoyances for a long time yet if it had not been that while they were being so unfriendly to us, and even refusing to receive letters from the Viceroy, they were sending agents to the Russians and receiving emissaries from them.
>
> This communication with the Russians, while repelling communication with us, was the real cause of the offence. If Russia were able to establish a position in Tibet, and we had no means of counteracting her activities, she might cause anxiety for us all along the North-Eastern frontier, as she had along the North-Western and Northern frontiers, and we might have to increase our garrisons on that border. To counteract the growing influence of the Russians in Tibet was the real object of my Mission.[6]

In one sense Curzon caught his fish before he played him. On the way to Simla Younghusband had written home: 'I am to go to Tibet in charge of a very important mission. Very strictly in confidence Lord Curzon had intended to send me to Lhasa with an armed force capable of putting down all resistance.' The official instructions which Younghusband received on 3 June, however, took the gilt off this particular piece of gingerbread. Younghusband was made Joint Commissioner with White; he was to seek negotiations with both Chinese and Tibetan officials, and he was to discuss grazing rights; he was allowed an escort of 200 men with a further 300 held in reserve inside Sikkim, but it was made clear that the role of this force was only to accompany the Commissioners to Khamba Jong. The possibility of boundary demarcation was to engage the Commissioners' attention, but the subject to which they should most earnestly address themselves was the chances of a trade centre being established at Gyantse, some 200 miles inside Tibet and well on the road to Lhasa, with a view, moreover, 'to having an alternative emporium' well beyond the Chumbi Valley.

These instructions also made clear that 'His Majesty's Government have decided that we should not press for the appointment of a Political Agent at Lhasa or Gyantse' but the Commissioners were urged to point out to their opposite numbers that a trade centre at the latter predicated the dispatch of representatives of the Indian government to see how commerce could be developed. Indeed the 1890 treaty provided for this development. Finally the Commissioners were requested to 'keep the Government of India fully informed of the progress of your negotiations, and I am to warn you that you should be careful to abstain from using any language or taking any action, which would bind the Government to any definite course hereafter, without first obtaining the sanction of the Government of India.'[7]

Official instructions were one thing: the Great Game quite another. 'This is really a magnificent business I have dropped in for' wrote Younghusband to his father on 21 May.[8] Few statements show more clearly how his ideas differed from others on what that business should be. The Cabinet, so far as it had a collective opinion on Tibet, was opposed to action: Lansdowne wanted to probe St Petersburg's diplomatic initiatives; Hamilton sought a cautious riposte to Russian operations; Brodrick was inert, even if the War Office was verbally active; Curzon was determined to shine; the government of India, in its official, bureaucratic personality, wanted to talk. Younghusband the agent, however, the man appointed by the Viceroy to represent Ius Britannicum, desired, indeed compulsively needed, action and the lone hand.

Younghusband may or may not have known that the Russian reaction to the mission remained quite detached, almost indifferent. With his tongue in his cheek, Lamsdorff suggested that perhaps the British wanted to build a railway to Lhasa. All that was quite beside the point. The Game would not be worth the candle to Younghusband if he was to be a mere tradesman, and the servant of bureaucrats to boot. He had not – on 1 June – asked for the escort to 'take their full dress uniform for ceremonial purposes' in order to talk about emporia. Requesting the services of Shahzad Mir meant little in itself – the Bengal Lancer was in any case engaged elsewhere – but there is no doubt that Younghusband's idea of the mission's objectives was about as far removed from those of the British government as anything could well be. Curzon, the one man capable of resolving these contradictions, was concerned only that his agent would fulfil his wishes, and take the consequences.

Younghusband's telegrams and letters to the Indian government's Foreign Department during the next three months show beyond any reasonable doubt that he had convinced himself that Curzon's mission was his, to be run as he wished.[9] Dane, the Secretary of the Foreign and Political Department in Calcutta, did nothing to disabuse him of this notion. The Blue Books on Tibet which were published in 1904 and 1905 are so much a record designed to exculpate the Balfour government that little space was found for documents incriminating Curzon or Younghusband. More private methods were used for the former; public accusation dealt with the latter. As a result, Younghusband's activities in the summer of 1903 were ignored; even Dr Mehra has not dealt with this period in detail. For him, as for other historians, 1904 is the most interesting year, as concerns this mission.

1904 for Younghusband was a year of fighting and marching, culminating in a triumphal entry into Lhasa, although followed by the darkness of condemnation and rejection but, those months of 1903 when he endured the frustrations of Khamba Jong tell us more about his inner motives and singular methods. On 3 June Younghusband wrote to Dane 'submitting a note on Russian attempts to reach Lhasa'. As, on his own admission, he had not yet read the Tibet dossier – this was to be done while experiencing the *longeurs* of Khamba Jong – the note can only be construed as a mixture of special pleading and wish fulfilment. On 22 June Younghusband said that the Chinese government representative objected to the British escort marching to Khamba Jong; this was not true; the representative mentioned, Captain Parr of the Chinese Customs, was British, like most of his colleagues in the senior ranks of that service. Parr was a loyal – and intelligent – servant of the Chinese government, but his conduct in 1903 shows that he was genuinely anxious to help Younghusband and White.

On 2 July Dane signalled to Younghusband that he was to use his discretion as to the date when he should march from Sikkim to Khamba Jong. The following day Younghusband took advantage of this discretion. He replied that he was delayed (at Tangu) by indisposition; this was a pretext for sending on White and the escort ahead of him, and doing so in order that they should arrive at Khamba Jong with all the appearance of a force whose leader, following more leisurely behind, would dictate terms when he arrived. Younghusband strengthened this procedure – which flouted both the letter and the spirit of his written instructions – by informing Dane that the Tibetans were making defensive preparations.

Curzon was remote from these details – or chose to be; Dane fully supported Younghusband. The escort marched ahead, arriving at Khamba Jong on 6 July. Younghusband did not arrive there until the 18th. In the interim he let White and O'Connor (the mission's secretary and Intelligence Officer) make the critical exchanges with worried and irritated Tibetans; the exchanges were angry and fruitless, indeed Younghusband said on 14 July that the Tibetan officials 'are stunned and bitter'. This was hardly surprising; Younghusband had used the same technique of forcing a quarrel which Cavagnari had employed in September 1878. By sending on a two hundred-strong force to Khamba Jong Younghusband had obtained a lodgement in Tibet, but it was one which was to prove costly in the end.

Not only that, but Younghusband was rapidly allowing events to get on top of him. He was fundamentally modest and self-effacing, but Curzon's flattery had worked on him nonetheless. White was necessary as a precipitant; his function otherwise was to act as a subordinate. At this time Younghusband made 'repeated references to the [Indian] Foreign Office having "a good wholesome respect of me"'; he insisted that all at Khamba Jong should recognise his rank – acting full Colonel – as that of the senior officer or official. 'When it was suggested that Ho [the principal Chinese representative] and Parr were equal in rank to him and White – he asked in pained surprise: "Did you ever hear of such impudence? And it will make the Viceroy's hair stand on end."' Recording such incidents would be pointless, were it not for the fact that they illustrate Younghusband's frame of mind, and the two dangerous notions which he harboured. The first was that he could goad his opposite numbers into making the kind of move which would justify a further advance. Ho and the Tibetans would talk, but that was all. Their refusal to negotiate was not, in July, sufficient justification for more drastic action.

Younghusband's second notion – illusion, rather – was that Curzon remained interested in Tibet. The Viceroy was still determined to send his agent to Lhasa; but that objective, sustained as Younghusband indulged in an uncharacteristic display of 'face', was just about the extent of his interest. There were more pressing matters to attend to once the agent of his whim had been despatched. A series of letters on the tricky question of a second term were being sent to Balfour. There was an even more immediately enticing prospect – a tour of the Persian Gulf, the scene of undoubted triumph, all the sweeter for it carrying no stigma of interference or alteration from London. Indeed on 5 May Lansdowne had stated that 'we should regard the establishment of a Naval base or of a fortified port in the Persian Gulf by any other Power as a very grave menace to British interests, and we should certainly resist it with all the means at our disposal'.[10] This sort of thing was somewhat removed from the view of the Cabinet – as a whole – and had little relevance to Lansdowne's earlier view of the Gulf. Since the 'means at our disposal' meant Indian troops, Lansdowne played straight into Curzon's hands.

During the summer months at Khamba Jong Younghusband dug his own grave; Curzon was indifferent to this process; Hamilton unaware of it. Throughout the remainder of July Younghusband worked at raising the stakes from a frontier mission to a march on Lhasa. He even wrote to the Amban in Lhasa, requesting a meeting with the Dalai Lama. What is more surprising, Dane approved. Next, Younghusband told the complaisant Foreign Secretary in Calcutta that Ho and Parr lacked sufficient status for negotiations to be fruitful. Here was another attempt to make Lhasa the scene of confrontation. When Dane commented on the status issue, Younghusband decided that he was the sole arbiter of affairs at Khamba Jong and would take his orders, as, in his words, 'personal to myself'. White was left in the dark. Younghusband's last act in July was to tell Dane that the Amban – by name Yen – had ordered the Commissioners to decamp from Khamba Jong. This was an unintentionally useful move by the Amban, since it suggested an intransigent attitude. Obstinacy alone, however, would not suffice.

On 1 August Younghusband signalled that a Russian party had been reported as moving towards Lhasa; on the 4th Dane was told that the Tibetans by the British camp were meditating attack, and that their delegates were 'very bumptious'. After that, Younghusband's flow stopped; a different technique was tried; O'Connor's intelligence diaries were utilised to show how badly the Commission's local agents – low grade spies, as Peter Fleming rightly calls them – were being ill-treated. But Younghusband and O'Connor –

who spoke Tibetan with rare fluency and, what was still more unusual, enjoyed the company of the country's recalcitrant inhabitants – were too well-trained and scrupulous to say that any Russians were actually and definitely engaged against the British mission. At no time in 1903 and 1904 was it possible to produce evidence on this rather fundamental point.

At last a positive reaction came from Calcutta. Sooner or later Curzon was bound to return to the subject of Tibet. He was not to know that since he last gave his mind to the matter, his agent had not only become determined to march to Lhasa, but had, to his own satisfaction, found justification for doing so. The subtle but crucial difference between a descent on Lhasa and, if necessary, a fighting march to it, escaped Curzon's mind. He was, however, responsible for Younghusband; if he had taken the trouble to read the latter's telegrams and letters for the preceding three months he must have known that his agent had acquired a fixation. On 16 September Curzon wrote to Hamilton in terms which indirectly only strengthened that expensive emotion.

The Secretary of State was told that the Tibetans 'had . . . definitely decided upon war', and that 'the Lhasa Government were "determined not to negotiate"'.[11] Curzon added that Tibetan troops were being collected – a situation which had led to the British Commissioners reinforcing their escort. To this fable, the fate of the two spies was thrown in as ballast, and the telegram concluded by urging penetration into Tibet proper, to Gyantse. Other dispatches and telegrams at this time spoke of Russian moves and the increasing frustrations endured by Younghusband. Reference was also made to a scheme of the latter's for acquiring the Chumbi Valley – technically in Tibet, physically, in being south of the Himalayas, within the British sphere – if all else failed.

Little notice was taken of this idea at the time, although 'the temporary occupation' of the valley was noted as a possible compromise. Hamilton had only learned of Younghusband's appointment as Joint Commissioner in July, and may have been cool to any ideas from that source. Nor were hints by Curzon of Russian activity particularly welcome in the India Office, especially as they took an increasingly dramatic form. Talking to Russians, quarrelling with them, and fighting them had by this time become three quite distinctive things in London. On 20 September, the India Office replied to Curzon's telegram of the 16th; an advance beyond

187

Khamba Jong was ruled out. It is at this time, however, that Curzon and Younghusband, in their different ways, got what they wanted.

The telegram which reached Curzon on 20 September was not signed by Hamilton; he had resigned on the 18th, and in the period which elapsed before Brodrick succeeded him at the beginning of October, Curzon's request of the 16th was discussed by Lansdowne and Balfour. Only in April 1904 did Brodrick, doubtless anxious to cover his tracks as the Tibet expedition plunged deeper into trouble, reveal the decision about Curzon's request of the preceding September. Reflecting not only Brodrick's caution but Balfour's indecision, the former's summary of events of April 1904 is a bewildering document. It is a revealing one, and perhaps the only absolutely vital piece of evidence in the whole business, since it expresses in every line the way the Game was played in London, how absolutely the acts of agents at 'a distant point' had become substitutes for policy – yet doubly useful as being capable of repudiation if need arose.

Balfour's reaction to Curzon's telegram of 16 September 1903 was summarised by Lansdowne thus, sometime between the 19th and the end of the month:

> He is incredulous as to the importance of Tibetan trade, and dislikes the idea of allowing ourselves to be permanently entangled in Tibet, and he is apprehensive of the risk of locking up a British Mission and escort in the heart of that country.

> But he realises that the course of events has been such as to make it inevitable that some measure of coercion should be applied in the event of such a rupture of negotiations as the Viceroy apprehends.

> He would, therefore, be prepared to sanction the occupation of the Chumbi Valley and the advance of the Mission to Gyantse, assuming that the Indian Government have satisfied themselves that this measure can be safely taken.[12]

Lansdowne supported Balfour's decision – if decision it can be called – and indeed sent the summary just quoted from the Foreign Office to the India Office on 30 September. The summary therefore bore the imprimatur of the Prime Minister and the Foreign Secretary. On the 30th 'India Office' – presumably the Permanent Under-Secretary, Godley, in the absence of the Secretary of State – 'then drafted a telegram', which read as follows:

In continuation of my telegram of the 20th September about Tibet. In view of the unsatisfactory nature of the Chinese reply to Satow's [the British Minister in Peking] representation, His Majesty's Government have again considered the position. They are now prepared, in the event of a complete rupture of negotiations proving inevitable, to authorise the advance of the Mission to Gyantse, provided you are satisfied that this measure can be safely taken, as well as the occupation of Chumbi Valley. Please report your plans for carrying out these measures, and especially for securing the safety of the Mission at Gyantse.[13]

Lansdowne approved this draft, which was then sent on 1 October – under Brodrick's authority. Lansdowne was careful to point out – in April 1904 – that 'the telegram did not contain a final and unconditional approval of the advance to Gyantse, but sanctioned this step only (1) "in the event of a complete rupture of negotiations proving inevitable", and (2) "provided the Viceroy was satisfied that the measure could be safely taken"'. But Lansdowne – and, what is more important, Balfour – missed in September 1903 and April 1904 the really central point. No Cabinet sanction had been sought or obtained for a mission which, however much ostensibly concerned with the Tibetan refusal to negotiate, was assuming the character of a punitive operation directed, moreover, against a people whose leader was widely said to be a Russian pawn.

The Cabinet had been reconstituted on 18 September, and Balfour had more pressing problems than Tibet to which to attend – or did he? 'These changes [in the Cabinet] had no immediate effect upon French and Russian negotiations, which were dictated by the needs of the moment and became more, not less, necessary in the following months.'[14] At the time in question Anglo-French relations – and by extension, Anglo-Russian – were in that stage described by diplomats as delicate. For once the euphemism was apt. Lansdowne and Cambon were getting very close to a deal on Morocco and Egypt; indeed on 1 October the Foreign Secretary made an offer of a *quid pro quo*. Benckendorff and Lansdowne were discussing Afghanistan (over Curzon's head, to his fury), and the Ambassador was making the point, one rather difficult to resist, that any settlement of Anglo-Russian differences should give the Russian government some definable rights in Kabul.

The Cabinet ignored Tibet between 18 September and 1 October;

this remains a mystery; in the next year it was to prove an expensive error. Brodrick's telegram of 6 November 1903, finally sanctioning the advance to Gyantse has usually been given as the date when things began to move, but it should now be clear that at least seven weeks before that date Curzon and Younghusband were given what they saw as the green light to march to Gyantse. Balfour and Lansdowne did not know that their muddled and ambiguous messages would be seized on by the Viceroy and his agent, although they might have shown more caution, and not merely more clarity of intention. Provisos and reservations about 'rupture of negotiations' and 'safety of the Mission' could easily be set aside by a Viceroy ambitious of fame, and an agent determined on action.

On 11 October, when Curzon and Younghusband again met in Simla, little time was spent in defending an assertion that negotiations had broken down. Instead, it was agreed that, in moving to Gyantse, the mission would be both secure from attack and in a stronger position for bargaining. In order to satisfy Brodrick's qualms, Tibetan perfidy was elaborately narrated. A full-blown mission escort, including a British element with Maxim guns, was carefully described as a guaraantee of safety; that this might provoke a Tibetan resistance was understood. Whatever else was to happen, the mission escort had the Maxim gun – and the Tibetans had not. A dispatch on the breakdown of negotiations was sent by Curzon to Brodrick on 26 October. In his telegram of 6 November the new Secretary of State replied as follows:

In view of the recent conduct of the Tibetans, His Majesty's Government feel that it would be impossible not to take action, and they accordingly sanction the advance of the Mission to Gyantse. They are, however, clearly of opinion that this step should not be allowed to lead to occupation or to permanent intervention in Tibetan affairs in any form. The advance should be made for the sole purpose of obtaining satisfaction, and as soon as reparation is obtained a withdrawal should be effected. While his Majesty's Government consider the proposed action to be necessary, they are not prepared to establish a permanent mission in Tibet, and the question of enforcing trade facilities in tl.at country must be considered in the light of the decision conveyed in this telegram.[15]

This telegram has usually been considered as a missive rivalling in ambiguity anything which Gladstone might have devised on a comparable occasion. Younghusband – in 1909 – called it a 'curious telegram'. It is difficult to see why. If anything, Brodrick had pulled together most of the woolly wording of the 1 October telegram. Doubtless the Secretary of State could have been more categorical; a really wise man would have thought twice before allowing any advance, to Gyantse or elsewhere. A specific objective, and the method of attaining it, had been outlined nonetheless. This was all by the by. It was too late for second thoughts. Curzon and Younghusband were on their way. They were not checked until, almost a year later, Balfour decided that Tibet was not worth an agent.

13

Verdict and Vindication

Events in 1904 moved to their appointed climax; the Cabinet in London, or those few members of it concerned, strove to see Tibet in the wider context of Anglo-Russian relations, yet, by August, wanted some easy pickings from Younghusband's journey into the interior of that perplexing land; Curzon, also in England between May and October, concerned himself with a second term; Younghusband, at the end of a very long and extremely tenuous line of communications, disappeared, literally and figuratively in the clouds, indifferent to the wider issues, convinced, as he said to his father on 19 August that 'we have a good hand'.[1]

The two questions at issue – whether it was strategically sensible to march a sizeable force, whose fighting element alone totalled 3,000 men by July 1904, into the unknown; and whether Britain, through its representative in India, had the right to do so – were virtually ignored. Perhaps only two men fully grasped the first point; Lansdowne had a sensible awareness of Britain's power and limitations; Kitchener, as Commander-in-Chief in India, knew that providing even the Tibet mission escort and ensuring its logistic support imposed a disproportionate strain on the country's strategic capacities. Being Kitchener, this point was exaggerated to embarrass the civil administration, but it was valid nonetheless.

As it was, the escort, operating at 15,000 feet for six months on end, lived on half rations, and survived largely by courtesy of the Tibetans and, in Lhasa, the Chinese. Between Lansdowne and Kitchener there was no channel of communication; between London and Younghusband there was, except on one occasion, no rational discussion at all on the problems to be faced and the rewards to be gained; Curzon virtually ignored his agent; the latter was able, in his mind, to score off the politicians at last. The Tibetan point of view had never been considered with much sense or objectivity; in 1904 it was ignored altogether. Supposed Russian machinations in Tibet were occasionally revived by Younghusband, but this factor in affairs rapidly decreased in importance; the Game was now something to be played for its own sake, and its dramatic elements were to be provided by the clash between authority in London and the man on the spot. The final irony was, however, an extreme and cruel example of that fate which, throughout the playing of the Game, struck down the agents in their moment of triumph.

On 11 December 1903 the mission and its escort entered Tibet, and by 4 January had reached Tuna. No opposition had been encountered, and the only problem vexing Younghusband was the attitude of the Escort Commander, Brigadier-General Macdonald. He was an undistinguished sapper, with an exaggerated sense of his own importance, but he was not the poltroon whom Younghusband, at the time and others subsequently, have made him out to be. In retrospect it can be said that he was the wrong man for a testing operation, although in fairness it must be added that he appreciated more clearly than Younghusband that it was hazardous in the extreme to march a force with an unavoidably large administrative and support element across a completely unfamiliar terrain. One officer in the escort put the military view succinctly: 'No one liked using our trained, disciplined and well-armed troops against a brave, ignorant and poorly-armed enemy. Our chief difficulties were supply and transport.'[2] A warrant officer of the Royal Fusiliers, whose simple diary of the expedition tells us more of its realities than pages of official print, refers repeatedly to hunger and fatigue.[3] British soldiers are great grumblers, but they rarely invent. Casualties in action were trivial; those from terrain and climate came to nearly one sixth of the numbers engaged.

Macdonald was a pessimist, and that was a pity, although his sole relevance to the story is that he was an irritant; with Younghusband nerved for the final gallop, anybody who disagreed with him was condemned. Macdonald had his problems, and they got him down; Younghusband was playing to win, against an opposition in London and Calcutta whose methods he considered more underhand than the unfortunate Tibetans with whom he was supposed to negotiate. The challenge strung him up to a new pitch of absolute determination.

The mission and elements of the escort spent three dreary months at Tuna. Macdonald refused to march straight for Gyantse, and Younghusband had no option but to wait until the former had strengthened, to his own satisfaction the base camp in the Chumbi Valley. A dash to Gyantse might have solved all problems: it might have seen disaster. Macdonald was excessively cautious, yet even a thruster would have winced at the condition of the baggage animals when they arrived at the base camp. Moreover, although there was no single occasion during the march to Lhasa and back when Tibetan troops delivered a successful attack or accomplished a sustained defence, there were many which went in favour of the escort contingents only through their being the professionals and their unfortunate opponents mere tyros.

What the Tibetans lacked in tactical skill they certainly made up in courage. Kitchener could have been generous with line-of-communication support, but the Commander-in-Chief thought that punitive operations – in effect, if not name – were a waste of time, and a check to his scheme for providing a three corps field army from India's own resources. In completing Roberts' work for such an army, Kitchener may have ruined the man who was the former's most ardent disciple. The delay at Tuna was to have a marked effect on the expedition's fortunes; paradoxically, Macdonald's determination to stay in Lhasa no longer than was absolutely necessary, was to affect Younghusband to an even more unfortunate degree.

Younghusband endured much at Tuna. The cold was intense, the altitude one where every act, the mental even more than the physical, drained strength and frayed temper. The Indian Foreign Department – Younghusband's sole contact with the outside world and the official arbiter of his mission's movements – seemed totally unsympathetic. He was told that Macdonald was the Commander of the entire force until Gyantse was reached. That Macdonald was senior to him in rank and that he had urged a large escort on Curzon in those summer days of 1903, was no comfort now. The consolation of a faith deeper than personal fulfilment was unconsciously growing within Younghusband but, on that frozen, empty, silent plateau, it was hidden, as elusive as the Tibetans to be bent to his will.

Nature briefly consoled, in the mountains which shielded this distant place from more than stumbling intrusion despite the coming spring, by the sight of 'a little vole . . . seen basking in the sun at the mouth of his hole'.[4] Such Franciscan moments, though, were rare. Nor was philosophical reflection – 'I studied Buddhism. And I finally rid myself of Herbert Spencer' – a subject to be pursued without peace and quiet.[5] The Tibetans prowled round the mission camp in a manner both timid and threatening; their presence, felt rather than seen, provoked Younghusband to rashness. 'At last I could stand it no longer, and taking only Captain O'Connor and Captain Sawyer with me, I rode over without any escort, and without giving them warning, straight into the Tibetan camp about fourteen miles away. I had wakened in the night with the strong conviction that this was what I ought to do, and I . . . proceeded to carry my conviction into effect the first thing next morning.'[6]

In fact, by riding to Guru after only a week at Tuna, Younghusband put his head in a potential noose. He did so because no Tibetan representative had been to see him – as he expected. The result was predictable; the Tibetans encountered at Guru were first friendly and polite; when Younghusband tried to force an embryonic negotiation on them they turned nasty. Younghusband was a brave man, with an undoubted presence; one officer, who rode by his side for many of the mission's remaining months recalled that he had 'a sharp steely gaze that looked you straight in the eye'.[7] On this occasion, the Tibetans were not impressed; Younghusband's references to malign Russian influence were not only repudiated, but his involuntary hosts sought to detain him when he rose to go. The representative of the King-Emperor was forced to climb down, and adopt the manner of a plain man doing his duty, who would, moreover, be punished if he failed in the attempt. This device worked; affability – doubtless specious, undeniably welcome, to the Tibetans – returned; the three British officers were allowed to leave.

In reporting the incident to Dane, Younghusband gave no hint that it rankled but, it cannot have improved his temper; by the end of March this had become an uncertain quantity. When the main body of the escort reached Tuna on the 30th, the Tibetans had made defensive preparations of a sort at Guru. The escort marched on the 31st; a motley Tibetan force was encountered at Guru, blocking the route by a kind of passive resistance less familiar in those days than ours. They were ordered to disperse; military aid to civil power was a technique well established by the British in India, but it was based on the premise that Indian lives were a credit in the imperial bank; if taken carelessly the credit diminished.

No such consideration obtained with Tibetans; to the men of 1904 they were sometimes amenable and sometimes threatening; which-ever was the case, they were not granted a political personality. When dispersal proved slow and the Tibetan attitude became hyster-ical and dangerous, an ostensibly peaceful mission metamorphosed into a punitive expedition. A shot rang out. 'There was a general scuffle, and Candler, the 'Daily Mail' correspondent was sitting down a little way off writing a telegram when some Tibetans went up to him, and cut one hand off, and badly damaged the other, and cut him badly over the head and very badly on one leg.'

The inevitable had happened; the escort's Maxim guns introduced the Tibetans to modern warfare; in a few minutes the ground was thick with their dead and dying – some 700 bodies were later counted. Those who possessed such short cuts to end arguments were shaken – 'sickened', as the officer commanding the Maxim gun detachment wrote to his mother. Belated compassion appeared. 'They left everything just as it was; in one tent I found a game of dominoes unfinished, and in another they had been playing with dice and apricot stones.'[8] Younghusband admitted that the whole thing had been a 'massacre', but blamed it on 'the stupidity and childishness of the Tibetan General. They will not believe in our power.'[9] Younghusband explained it all to Curzon, perhaps not expecting, and certainly receiving no reply.

At home the incident at Guru provoked a faint mutter of disquiet. This passed almost inaudibly through the House of Commons, but Benckendorff 'at once made enquiries, and Lansdowne privately acknowledged that Russian anxiety was reasonable. "I wonder what we should have said if it had been a Russian instead of a British 'political mission'!" '[10] Cambon however appeared as a mediator, suggesting that Britain should give Russia assurances on Tibet in exchange for the latter, in effect, supporting the Anglo-French deal over Morocco and Egypt. Lansdowne seized this ingenious formula; on 10 May he promised that Britain would keep clear of Tibet (after the mission had gained some measure of reparation) if other Powers did likewise.

Younghusband's name was brought into this interesting pledge – which also concerned itself with the Anglo-French-Russian three-way deal. Unfortunately Lansdowne omitted to tell Calcutta about these indications that improved Anglo-Russian relations were once again an important element in British foreign and imperial policy. Neither did Lansdowne do more than refer to the 6 November 1903 telegram as indicating the limits of Britain's interest in Tibet – and the limitations of Younghusband's authority. On 13 May Bencken-dorff declared his government's support for Lansdowne's proposal. In the Foreign Secretary's eyes at least, Egypt had become of greater importance than Tibet. Curzon, when he arrived home, was told of these developments; opposing them as he did – in that Indian affairs were subordinated to wider issues – it is perhaps not surprising that he made no effort to tell Younghusband of their significance until it was too late, and even then he wrote in no restraining tone.

Perhaps unaware of the sea-change occurring within him, and certainly ignorant of the compromises being hatched in London, the subject of these diplomatic exchanges pressed on for Gyantse. On 8 April, two hundred odd Tibetans were killed at Kala Tso, defending their position with matchlocks, and that euphoniously named but obsolete weapon the jingal. By 11 April Gyantse was reached. It could not be occupied or besieged without Macdonald's support. This was lacking but, by now Younghusband was determined to keep pushing, demonstrating that the Tibetans were militant as well as obdurate. The route from Gyantse to Lhasa (Younghusband's goal) was marked by natural defensive positions, which the Tibetans were known to be occupying. In Younghusband's eyes, they were now the enemy, and were to be defeated whenever and wherever possible. It was obvious, however, that fighting, least of all with these people, would produce nothing. The idea of negotiations had still to be entertained. In any case, until Macdonald brought up the bulk of the escort, an advance on Lhasa was ruled out.

Throughout April and May Younghusband ordered local oper-ations against a stiffening resistance, and urged stronger action on Calcutta and London. There was a further move. Ampthill, the acting Viceroy, saw among his tasks the continuation of what he imagined to be Curzon's Tibet policy: by the end of June, with Younghusband still checked outside Gyantse, and further talks with assorted Tibetan dignatories having proved abortive, Ampthill assented to an advance on Lhasa; on 6 July, and in subsequent telegrams, Brodrick finally agreed to this development, although he stipulated that there should be no British agent left at Lhasa after the conclusion of any negotiations.

Further messages in July and August, which were sent to Young-husband via Calcutta without comment, drew a clear distinction between political agents, who were categorically ruled out, and trade agents outside Lhasa, who were to be permitted. These twin concessions to Russian susceptibilities – a deal between Lansdowne and Lamsdorff was finally in train over Afghanistan, whereby the Russians were to be allowed commercial representation in Kabul – were not passed on to Younghusband. Brodrick later claimed – disingenuously – that his channel of communication had to be via Ampthill. The latter had no wish to usurp Curzon's role; the Viceroy did not write at all to Younghusband from England until 13 July; the following day, while that curious missive was on its way, Younghusband marched from Gyantse, on the last lap to Lhasa.

The events between Younghusband reaching Gyantse on 11 April and Lhasa on 3 August are significant as an example in missing, broken or ambiguous communications, occuring at a time when Younghusband more than ever felt himself to be playing a lone hand. He was virtually besieged at Gyantse, and there were moments when the contingent defending the mission headquarters was lucky to execute its forays without serious loss. The mission's dangerously exposed position did, however, work to Younghusband's advantage. After an attack on his headquarters on 5 May had been repelled with heavy loss to the Tibetans (it was as well that those Russian agents conjured up so easily by Curzon never taught their new allies the rudiments of infantry tactics), Younghusband urged on Dane the advance to Lhasa; the following day Ampthill gave his conditional assent; on the 12th Brodrick agreed that 'recent events make it inevitable that the mission must advance to Lhasa unless the Tibetans consent to open negotiations at Gyantse'.[11] He did, however, add the proviso that the Tibetans were to be given a month in which to mend their ways and agree to serious negotiations.

Younghusband, however, was no longer interested in negotiation, if indeed he ever had been. In the month following Broderick's conditional assent he went through the motions, but he drew on his strength and energies yet again to convince higher authority of the need for advancing on Lhasa, dictating terms, and establishing a British presence. To Younghusband's credit it must be said that he believed in arguing a case as well as establishing one by acting first and communicating the result afterwards. He was, however, by this time subject to strains which few men could have borne with equanimity. In the circumstances, his dispatch of 24 May, pressing once more for resolute action in the face of 'the lamas and that Siberian Buriat Dorjieff',[12] is a remarkable exercise in marshalling an argument. Yet, there can be little doubt that after Brodrick had circulated this dispatch to the Cabinet on 27 June, Younghusband was marked down for sacrifice if the Tibetan gamble failed. Three days earlier Brodrick had also provided the Cabinet with Curzon's case for strong action in Tibet; the combination, as it turned out – or as seen by Brodrick – was to prove irresistible; irresistibly damaging to Younghusband four months later, scarcely less so to Curzon when, in 1905, the Cabinet decided to dispense with his services.

Curzon's minute is a predictable document, and is chiefly memorable for containing some typical examples of his mock Gibbonian prose: 'I hope His Majesty's Government will never lose sight of the central fact that British interest in Lhasa is positive, legitimate and inevitable, and that Russian interest is factitious, ulterior, and pursued with unfriendly designs.'[13] Since the government had decided for the time being to see Anglo-Russian relations in a less lurid – if not less dangerous – light, Curzon's rhetoric was sadly misplaced. The interest of his minute, however, lies essentially in the fact that it urges above all things 'a permanent [British] agent in Tibet'.

Younghusband's dispatch urged this also; indeed the agent of Curzonian imperialism, besieged in a battered headquarters beyond the Himalayas, went much further. Younghusband not only argued that negotiations followed by withdrawal would simply invite a Russian riposte, but declared that Tibet must become virtually a British protectorate. Younghusband then argued, in great detail, for stationing a British Agent in Lhasa, backed by 'a considerable garrison'. More, he proposed that Britain should 'as an indemnity for the past misdeeds of the Tibetans, permanently occupy the Chumbi Valley'.[14]

Curzon was much more cautious – and much more careful in his language. Younghusband not only pitched his case just about as far as it would go – specifically in relation to a British Agent and the Chumbi Valley – but used phrases reflecting the outlook of a principal rather than an agent. Dorjieff was referred to as one 'who has taught the Tibetans to rely as trustingly on Russian support as Dr Leyds induced President Kruger to rely upon the Germans'.[15] This was not only nonsense but a doubly unfortunate analogy; the Cabinet had no wish to be reminded of the Jameson Raid and its consequence, the Second South African War. Finally, Younghusband must have completed the work of his own destruction when he stated flatly that the telegram of 6 November 1903 should no longer form the basis of British policy. Curzon felt just as strongly about Tibet as Younghusband – although for wholly different reasons – but, by June/July 1904 was no longer prepared to challenge the Cabinet on it.

On 8 July, two days after Brodrick's agreement to an advance on Lhasa, Curzon returned to the subject of what Britain should seek from Tibet. The tone is noticeably milder. The case for a British agent in Tibet is reiterated, but Curzon does not expect this to be accepted. Indeed, he says – surprisingly perhaps, sensibly without a doubt – that if the government do not want a political agent in Tibet but do want a trade one 'it seems a pity that it is not more explicitly stated, and I think that a private telegram to Lord Ampthill indicating that this provision is on no account to be omitted would be useful'. To this extent Curzon did seek to warn Younghusband, but he did so by throwing away his own case, in a document which was intended for the Cabinet alone.

In the sad story of the Tibet expedition Brodrick emerges with as little credit as Balfour. It is an exaggeration to say that he behaved vindictively to either Curzon or Younghusband – he bore much from the former and was concerned with the latter only as an agent who must not embarrass the government – but he emerges from the story in no very attractive light. Brodrick was too anxious to appear in the right, too quick to put others in the wrong. He was, in short, an average politician. He could be direct enough in summarising objectives, but rarely presented a coherent and detailed exposition of them for subordinates to work on. His telegram of 6 July was followed by others which, although sticking to the point that 'No Resident [was] to be demanded at Lhasa or elsewhere', required 'the Tibetans and Chinese to undertake that no portion of Tibetan territory shall be ceded to a Foreign Power without previous British consent'.[16]

This 'Most favoured nation' provision could reasonably have been interpreted by Younghusband as giving him some latitude in deciding how it was to be made effective, especially as it implicitly denied China's suzereignty over Tibet; arguably the provision could be made to stick only by stationing a British agent in Lhasa. A cautious agent, or one who derived stimulus from interpreting the Mandarin-like prose of Britain's imperial bureaucracy, would have clung to the letter of his instructions. We are not, however, dealing with a cautious or cunning man, nor one who was worldly-wise enough to grasp that the government in London would like to have the palm of Tibet without any irritating dust. Younghusband was a man of deep imperial convictions but, by July 1904, he was a seriously overtaxed agent of the Empire.

Brodrick could not be expected to know this. As he said six months later 'Younghusband is merely a name to me'.[17] Curzon, however, knew better. There is no point in dwelling on the fact that he chose to virtually abandon Younghusband at the very moment when the latter was about to set forth to Lhasa; it is enough to establish it as a clinching example of the fate which befalls agents who trust their superiors. Brodrick believed that once Curzon was in London 'Younghusband would not want for friends'. In fact, between leaving India at the end of April and returning five months later, Curzon wrote *once* to Younghusband: the latter wrote repeatedly, explaining and justifying his acts; yet, which is more revealing, Younghusband never asked Curzon to intercede for him. Curzon could have done much, just because Younghusband did trust him. Curzon's solitary letter of 13 July was not only too late to help, but gave Younghusband a brisk shove downhill. It presented a picture, false in outline and inaccurate in detail, of how the British government had thrown away all the advantages to be gained from the Tibet expedition in order to do a deal with Russia over France and Egypt.

Curzon portrayed himself to his faithful, weary agent as a man struggling with might and main to reverse so disastrous a policy, one concocted moreover by 'an administration never strong and now tottering to its fall'.[18] This was improper enough as written from one subordinate of that government to another, but Curzon then told Younghusband that 'I am now working to secure a modification or rather expansion of the orders of the telegram of July 6, which was sent off without ever being shown to me'.[19]

As we have seen, Curzon's efforts were directed to putting himself in the clear, but further, in his 13 July letter he told Younghusband that 'I have also got them to agree tentatively to the necessity of retaining the Chumbi Valley'. This was largely invention. The final instructions sent to Younghusband stated that the maximum period for which the Chumbi Valley was to be occupied would be three years. Ampthill, it is true, had suggested annexation but had been curtly rebuffed. The effect nevertheless of Curzon's statement on Younghusband can be gauged. Curzon completed his exercise in the transfer of responsibility by warning – or flattering – its recipient: 'I need hardly tell you that this letter is written in the strictest confidence.'

Allowance must be made for the fact that Curzon and his wife were ill for much of their stay in London. The conclusion seems inescapable nevertheless that he had washed his hands of the Tibet business. Curzon was not the first Viceroy to abandon an agent, nor was he the last proconsul to be, in due time, abandoned by a British government. But, by the summer of 1904, 'the pieces on a chess-board upon which is being played out a game for the domination of the world' – as Curzon put it so eloquently in *Persia and the Persian Question* – were, on the British side, at the disposal of a government apparently on its last legs. Curzon wanted above all things to be reappointed as Viceroy. His first biographer, Lord Ronaldshay, has said that it was others who demanded this. The facts are that Curzon specifically asked Balfour for another term in March 1903. Balfour pointed out the drawbacks, but gave a conditional assent. He added, however, that as 'the future of the government cannot be regarded as in all respects assured', Curzon had better discuss the matter face to face. In June 1903 Balfour repeated this decision in a letter to Curzon and, since the latter was trying to avoid the appearance of importunity, said 'Why of course it was your plan and your suggestion'.[20]

When Curzon arrived home in May 1904 he quickly saw that he would have to watch his step. His tour of the Gulf had been a glittering success – the rulers of Bahrain and Kuwait had proved far more tractable than those unruly fellows in Lhasa – and it must also have been clear to him within weeks of his arrival in London that the supreme importance of Indian affairs was securely lodged within the Committee of Imperial Defence. As Curzon wrestled with pain and ambition during those months when Younghusband struggled to reach his goal, the CID reaffirmed in several weighty papers all that the War Office had written the year before. Although Lansdowne's exchanges with Benckendorff at this time kept Anglo-Russian relations alive, the CID concerned itself primarily with 'advising on the training, equipping and paying of 100,000 men for no other object than to supply reinforcements for India'.[21]

Ironically, this CID emphasis on India was just where the catch lay. Balfour and Brodrick made it clear to Curzon that he could get another term if he did as he was told. Tibet was not mentioned specifically in this connection, but Afghanistan and Kitchener were. The Viceroy would arbitrate neither Afghan nor army affairs. Balfour did not spell these terms out in so many words until November 1904 – when he added that the Russian threat to India was as serious as it ever had been – but the price of a second term had been put to Curzon the previous July. Then, Tibet was mentioned. If Curzon did not accept the Cabinet's ruling on Tibet, 'it would be unwise for [him] to be reappointed to the Government of India after his leave expired'.[22] Curzon did accept these terms.

Of this twist to life lived by the will, Francis Younghusband, marching to Lhasa, was of course quite ignorant. Nor, when he arrived at his goal at last did he have much time for reflection. We can say it was fate which gravelled this true yet wayward player of the Game, although it was the mundane figure of General Macdonald who dogged him at the critical moment. Having reached Lhasa, Macdonald wanted to leave at once. He advanced some terribly weak reasons for doing so at the time when his own patient exercise in logistic forethought had paid off so well; at one point Younghusband was dragged from negotiations of lip-biting complexity with the Amban in order to tell Macdonald just how easily the seamstresses of Lhasa could provide the escort with warm winter clothing. Over this issue, Younghusband 'fairly let drive', as he reported to those loving companions, his only true confidantes – his father and sister, faithful recipients of hopes and fears for so many years.[23]

It is difficult to believe that good relations between Younghusband and Macdonald would have given the former that margin of detachment which he needed if he was to relate his objectives to those of the British government. Nor is it likely that prolonging the mission's stay in Lhasa beyond 15 October – a compromise date fixed by Kitchener and Ampthill – would have affected the outcome. Younghusband had reached Lhasa determined to impose his will on the Tibetans; once there he found the 'bumptious young Dalai Lama' fled, and no alternative individual or group which could be consulted or coerced.[24] There was, however, the Amban, Yu-tai, Yen's successor, a Mandarin who was shrewd enough to realise that Younghusband's determination to punish the Tibetans might work to China's advantage. There were also those instructions from Brodrick which appeared not only to endow Younghusband with plenipotentiary powers, but a wide measure of discretion in interpreting then. The fortuitous combination of these factors, acting on a mind and will which had striven unceasingly to accomplish some great thing for over a year, resulted on 7 September in what a learned and just analyst of these events has called 'one of the oddest treaties in the history of British diplomacy'.[25]

In the inner fastnesses of the Potola itself, and in an atmosphere combining formality and farce in about equal proportions, Tibetans, adroitly assisted by the joint efforts of the Amban, the Nepalese representative in Lhasa and a self-appointed emissary from Bhutan, consented to 'permitting the British Trade Agent at Gyantse to visit Lhasa if and when he saw fit', and swallowed an indemnity for unspecified misdeeds, the security for which was that the British should occupy the Chumbi Valley until the money had been paid.[26] The provision for an agent with quasi-political functions – for that is what permission to visit Lhasa inevitably implied – was a distinct contravention of the British government's communications of 6 November 1903 and 6 July 1904. To compound his diplomatic felony, Younghusband imposed his conditions on the Tibetans in a separate article, outside the main body of an agreement which technically he had no right to raise to the status of a Convention in the first place. As to the indemnity, the Tibetans had said categorically during the negotiations so obligingly arranged by Yu-tai that they could not afford to pay in the three years which had been laid down by Brodrick as the maximum period for which the Chumbi Valley was to be occupied. Younghusband therefore arranged for payment by instalments; the Chumbi would be occupied for 75 years.

Younghusband had reached his goal and imposed his will. That Yu-tai (who carefully did not sign the treaty), Captain Jit Bahadur from Nepal, and U-gyen Wangchuk from Bhutan had been midwives to this offspring of a shotgun diplomatic marriage, could not allay Younghusband's moment of triumph. Inevitably he relaxed; understandably he basked. 'The Tibetans, who, without being humiliated in a way which could cause resentment, had now learnt to accord us the respect which was our due. At the conclusion of the

Durbar I had the Lamas of the Potola presented with 1,000 Rupees. It was the first present, except to the poor, which I had given since my arrival in Lhasa. My motto had been: The "mailed fist" first and the sugar plums afterwards. The contrary procedure so often leads to trouble.'[27]

This mood did not last, despite the race meetings which the mission escort arranged and the entertainments – and provisions – which Younghusband's new-found subjects so readily provided. Younghusband was sublimely unaware of the storm that was about to burst over his head; yet he knew full well that he had done what he had been explicitly enjoined not to do. Anti-climax had set in and a degree of realism had come with it. This always chilling process led Younghusband to make a tactical mistake which was more damaging to him than any of his previous acts.

He at once reported that the Convention had been signed, and did so to Brodrick direct. Younghusband also told Ampthill that the indemnity terms had been fixed at the Tibetans' request. This was literally true but really disingenuous, since Younghusband had paid not the slightest attention to any Tibetan request – and did believe that the Chumbi Valley should be occupied for as long as possible. That, however, was not all. He made no mention in his signal of the separate provision for an agent, and only on 9 September did he dispatch a message about it. He sent this explosive information in a letter, which he knew therefore would take ten days to a fortnight before reaching Dane. Not only that, but Younghusband phrased this letter so as to make it appear that a British Agent would visit Lhasa only to discuss 'important commercial matters'.[28] This word-play was all right for Dane, who backed Younghusband to the hilt; it had no effect on Ampthill. Its effect on Balfour and Brodrick can best be described in the former's words – words whose purport the latter thoughtfully inserted in the subsequent Blue Book in order to show that the British government was no party to such acts.

Balfour wrote to Lansdowne on 4 October that Younghusband 'has not merely been disobedient but by his disobedience has touched the honour of his country'.[29] This was bunkum, but the Prime Minister came nearer the truth when he added that any attempt to defend Younghusband 'will only end in our sharing the discredit which must attach to his conduct'. To make sure that Younghusband did not gain the support of the King – there was a rather tortuous channel of communication, had the former chosen to use it – Balfour wrote to his Private Secretary on October 6 saying that 'the only chance of a permanent arrangement with Russia in Central Asia depended upon a mutual confidence that engagements would be kept; and this confidence Younghusband had now undermined'.[30] This was not exactly bunkum, but coming from a man sceptical of permanent arrangements between Britain and Russia, the assertion rang – and rings – with the unmistakable sound of a political half-truth.

Oddly and irrationally, it was the Chumbi Valley provisions which brought Younghusband down, not the scheme for an agent, against which Brodrick had been most insistent. When news of the Convention reached London not only was there initially praise for Younghusband, but no mutter of disapproval at another bit of tricky British business was heard from St Petersburg or other capitals. The explanation for the subsequent disproportionate reaction in London was threefold – possibly fourfold: the Cabinet as a whole came into the act at the last moment, and disliking what it found decided to punish Younghusband; the latter completed a prolonged course of independent action by refusing to renegotiate the Chumbi Valley provisions, leaving Lhasa without doing so on 23 September; by early October the congratulations of the Powers had been replaced by criticism of the one element in the Convention which directly concerned them – paradoxically one of the few where Younghusband had complied with his instructions.

The 'Most Favoured Nation Clause' aroused misgivings in Germany, France, Italy – and the United States, where Britain's cavalier attitude to China's suzereign power had on previous occasions resulted in pained and high-tone protests. Finally, Balfour and Brodrick saw Younghusband as Curzon's agent – which he was – and determined to punish him as his creature – which he most certainly was not. Younghusband sought for a leader but, perhaps to his credit, certainly to his cost, called no man master. Whether 'The Imperial Government had at last asserted its authority over the Indian' is highly debatable; but beyond doubt the former had again punished an imperial agent for excess of zeal.

What is clear, strange and yet revealing is that Younghusband was not made a scapegoat and his Convention repudiated because Britain feared repercussions from Russia. By October Russia and Japan had been at war for nine months and the initial Russian optimism had been replaced by a sullen awareness that the consolidation of their

20 Macdonald rides through the dead at Guru

21 Embarking mules at Chaksam ferry, 24 July 1904

22 Troops of the mission escort arriving outside Lhasa, 2 August 1904

23 Lhasa: the Tibetan delegation arrives at the mission headquarters

24 Younghusband's apotheosis: the Chinese delegation arrives in his headquarters at his bidding

25 Lhasa: the mission escort advance party marches in to the city

26 The light of experience:
Younghusband in his later years

Asian Empire had brought a new and frightful peril. The British government remained convinced that Russia would eventually win – so did the British defence establishment – but this belief, by October, had made for a mood of nervous truculence, not one of conciliation or compromise. On 23 October, indeed, this mood reverted to the old phobia; the Russian Baltic Fleet, on its way through the North Sea to its fatal rendezvous of Tsushima, fired on Hull trawlers, killing innocent British fishermen. This incident, exemplifying with cruel precision the blundering nature of that colossus which many British strategists had feared or chosen to fear for so long, destroyed any chance of an Anglo-Russian *entente* in 1904. It may be seen in some sense as a curtain raiser to the next round of the Game, one to be played on the British side by Younghusband's heirs and successors.

By the time Younghusband reached England on 3 December, he was already a name for the files rather than a subject for furore. Like Arthur Conolly, whom he so closely resembles, Younghusband had been a brave but unlucky player of the Game. He did not repine, however. Whitehall's bureaucratic malice, rather than any vendetta from Brodrick, pursued him with the diligence which he had hated and feared for many years. Godley, a patient and a just man, sought to defend him, but the system which had broken other agents in its time could not be checked by charity.

Even Godley was unable or unwilling to point out the contradictions and ambiguities in the instructions which Younghusband had received – and from so many different sources – nor, despite his unrivalled experience and high reputation could he remind his political masters that there had been moments in the preceding months when a desire to teach the Tibetans a lesson had been very strong in ministerial circles. Indeed, as late as 18 August Brodrick had given Younghusband 'a free hand'[31] over the indemnity but, as on so many occasions in the past months, had declined to explain just what this meant, except to say that 'the sum demanded should not exceed an amount which, it is believed, will be within the powers of the Tibetans to pay, by instalments if necessary, spread over three years. Colonel Younghusband will be guided by circumstances in this matter.'[32]

All this was somehow to be expected, as was the Cabinet hostility which greeted Younghusband's statement of 18 October – certainly a very impenitent document, in which all the advantages of Britain establishing a presence in Tibet are repeated with particular vigour and force. Ampthill tried to defend Younghusband's statement. This merely hardened Whitehall hearts, and led to a labyrinthine correspondence, worthy of an empire unconsciously in decline, on the exact degree of punishment – in the form of a lesser order of knighthood – which should be meted out to the erring agent. This too was unimportant. There were rewards which set criticism aside. On 19 December Younghusband had an interview with the King. 'I saw him quite alone. He placed me in a chair by his desk, and then in some indefinable way made it possible for me to speak to him as I would have spoken to my own father.'[33] The mission's Union Flag ('the flag known as a "Viceroy's flag" – a Union Jack with a star in the middle and the motto "Heaven's light our Guide" – flown by political officers in India') now flies in the Central Hall at Windsor Castle, over the statue of Queen Victoria.

Sentiments inspired by such actions sustained the British who played the Great Game. Few agents had, to the same degree as Younghusband, a sense of personal compulsion, but all shared a conviction that what they did was right, inevitable, sanctioned. Such a belief is beyond our judgement; it reflects something quite gone from our lives. What remains is the almost desolating gulf between the agents and those they served, and the great divide between simple believers and the manipulators of power. Let Godley, an impartial witness have the last word. 'Everyone who speaks to me about Tibet (not a very large number I must admit) seems to assume as a matter of course that the Government have come very well out of this business, and, not to put it too high, a great deal better than might have been expected.'[34]

Postscript

Sir Arthur Godley's dismissive and revealing remark at once prompts the question: why was Younghusband so swiftly shunted into a bureaucratic siding, thence into relative obscurity? His Presidency of the Royal Geographical Society was notable also for a vigorous assertion of authority. His work with the World Council of Faiths, although disliked by the British establishment in the 1930s, largely because Younghusband openly attacked Hitler and Mussolini as evil and godless men, was admired and produced many disciples. Still the fact remains that Younghusband was never consulted by higher authority on Indian or related affairs once 'the bright day was done'. His services were rejected on the outbreak of war in 1914 – a slight which he bore magnanimously but must have felt. From time to time he fired off waspish letters on assorted aspects of public affairs to the Editor of *The Times* and others, often written from the Travellers' Club, of which Younghusband was an habitué and honoured member. Many of these survive among Dame Eileen's papers and those in the Royal Geographical Society but few seem to have found their way into print.

A partial explanation for neglect may be seen in the manner adopted by Lady Younghusband. She was quick to take offence, on one occasion delivering an unkind and unnecessary philippic to the Secretary of the Royal Geographical Society for failing to notice that Younghusband had been elevated from Knight Commander of the Indian Empire to Knight Commander of the Star of India. Such a woman can delay or prevent her husband's rehabilitation, but Younghusband was not the man either to fight from behind his wife's skirts or disown what she said and did.

A more credible explanation for Younghusband's treatment is, quite simply, that as an agent who in authority's eyes caused trouble, he was punished with undue severity. One can think of other such instances, not least Eric Bailey, who marched with Younghusband to Lhasa. He became a notable explorer of the most distant parts of Tibet thereafter, and carried out with skill and verve an extraordinarily difficult and demanding intelligence operation in Russian Turkestan after the 1917 revolutions, but on returning to India via Meshed he was reprimanded for 'overstaying leave'. Bailey also was shunted aside, becoming later a somewhat idiosyncratic King's Messenger. Playing the Great Game was dangerous in various ways.

It was not as if Younghusband's world disappeared between 1904 and his death in 1942. Although India moved gradually towards self-government and independence, the process was bitterly contested by conservative politicians in Britain – by none more vehemently and consistently than Winston Churchill – and throughout this prolonged struggle the sub-continent's priority role in all policies of and plans for imperial defence was never seriously contested. The Committee of Imperial Defence remained an element in 'the permanent government' which dominated – it did not merely influence – strategic decisions in Whitehall and the Cabinet. Throughout the inter-war period, and indeed much of the Second World War, imperial factors weighed far more heavily with British governments and the Chiefs of Staff than Continental commitments. The CID's early prescription for a pre-emptive war against Russia remained doctrine until 1927 and did not receive its quietus until 1934, on the eve of belated rearmament against a threat from Germany which could no longer be ignored.

Yet despite the survival of strongly held convictions about the defence of India, and more deeply felt (if rarely expressed) emotion about British India as such, Younghusband did not become one of the men to whom those in authority turned for the informed view, the perceptive comment. To use John Buchan's word, Younghusband did not acquire the 'totem', the mark of esteem accorded – in fiction – to Sandy Arbuthnot and Richard Hannay by worried men in Whitehall and Downing Street. Although Younghusband's life in the wilds was far more dangerous and adventurous than Buchan's heroes', he remained, oddly, outside the charmed circle. In his later years Younghusband spoke not infrequently on the BBC, but any strong expression of opinion or feeling was quickly discouraged. An internal minute of infinite chill suggests that he should be allowed to speak only when nobody was listening, 'say at four p.m. on Sunday afternoon'.

If Younghusband did feel excluded from the affairs of men, he displayed little concern, drawing upon his own inner world for something more than mere consolation in adversity. A man of the world would have fought his way back, possibly come back with some sort of public recognition. Younghusband was not quite of this world, and worldly men of power may have had some dim recognition of the fact.

Notes

1   *An Introduction to Sir Francis Younghusband*

1 Francis Younghusband, *The Light of Experience*, Constable, 1927, p. 79.
2 Ibid.
3 George Seaver, *Francis Younghusband*, John Murray, 1952, p. 100.
4 Ibid., p. 377.
5 Younghusband, *Light of Experience*, p. 115.
6 Younghusband's projection of himself as a man apart led him to falsify the picture of his schooldays. Clifton was unusual amongst Victorian public schools in allowing boys plenty of free time, alone if they wished. The record shows that Younghusband participated fully in school activities, when it suited him.
7 Younghusband, *Light of Experience*, p. 141.
8 Letter written en route to India: 'Sunday evening July 16, 1882; on board the *Weston Hall*'.
9 Seaver, *Francis Younghusband*, p. 9.
10 Younghusband, *Light of Experience*, p. 115.
11 'This is the first and most essential thing to learn about India – that there is not, and never was an India . . . no Indian nation, no "people of India", of which we hear so much.' Sir John Strachey, *India, Its Administration and Progress*, Macmillan, 1903, p. 12.
    Strachey, as Finance Member of the Viceroy's Council in the 1870s, witnessed the first stirring of Indian nationalism: he chose to dismiss it.
12 Peter Fleming, *Bayonets to Lhasa*, Hart Davis, 1961, p. 91.

2   *Key Issues*

1 H. W. C. Davis, *The Great Game in Asia*, Raleigh Lecture, 1926, p. 5.
2 For a valuable discussion of Russophobia, and the degree to which it

distorted British foreign and imperial policies until at least the later years of the nineteenth century, see J. H. Gleason, *The Genesis of Russophobia in Great Britain*, Harvard, 1950. As late as *1927*, however, the Chiefs of Staff argued that 'The most probable war of the near future in which the British Empire might be engaged is against Russia in Central Asia'.

3 Colonels W. S. A. Lockhart and R. G. Woodthorpe, *Confidential Report of the Gilgit Mission*, 1889.

4 The First Afghan War, 1878–1880

1 Sir John Kaye, *Lives of Indian Officers*, Strahan, 1867, vol. II, pp. 1–66.

2 J. A. Norris, *The First Afghan War*, Cambridge, 1967, pp. 90, 167, 170, 202, 209.

3 Ibid., p. 90.

4 Ibid.

5 Ibid., p. xiv.

6 Kaye, *Indian Officers*, pp. 1–66.

7 Ibid.

8 Ibid.

9 Ibid.

10 Ibid.

11 Malcolm's views are expressed in a memorandum prepared in November for Bentinck in an endeavour to convince the Home government that British authority in India should be clearly defined both politically and geographically.

12 Kaye, *Indian Officers*, pp. 1–66.

13 Ibid.

14 Ibid. Burnes's Service Record in The Bombay Army List states that Auckland was not prepared to listen to other peoples' assessments of the Afghan situation. A full account of the Vitkievitch mission is in Samson 'An Indian Officer', *Russia's March Towards India*, Low, 1894, vol. I.

5 The Cold War, the 1860s and 1870s

1 F. H. Skrine and E. D. Ross, *Heart of Asia*, Methuen, 1899, Appendix I.

2 The Circular is discussed in A. P. Thornton, *For the File on Empire*, Macmillan, 1968, p. 143. The British Ambassador in St Petersburg, Sir Andrew Buchanan, was neither deceived nor alarmed by the Circular, in which respect he set a pattern for his successors regarding Russia's Central Asian policies.

3 G. A. Alder, *British India's Northern Frontier 1865–95*, Longmans, 1963, p. 17.

4 Alder, *Northern Frontier*, pp. 36–7.

5 R. B. Shaw, *Visits to High Tartory, Yarkand and Kashgar*, John Murray, 1871, p. 257.

6 Alder, *Northern Frontier*, p. 37. 'The Progress of Russia in Central Asia' reveals that the War Office never thought much of Kashgaria as an invasion route.

7 *Journal of the Royal Geographical Society*, vol. XI, p. 118.

8 'Proceedings of the Royal Geographical Society', vol. XIV, p. 73.

9 The fullest account of native agents' operations is to be found in Records of the Survey of India, vol. VIII, 1915. See also Montgomerie's account in *Journal of the Royal Geographical Society*, vol. XLI, pp. 132–93, and vol. XLII, p. 180.

10 Lockhart and Woodthorpe, *Gilgit Mission*.

11 Hayward's account of his travels was read to a meeting of the Royal Geographical Society on 13 December 1869: 'Proceedings', vol. XIV.

12 The mystery of Hayward's death has never been solved, although various explanations have been given of its cause, and of who actually struck him down. It is clear, however, from manuscript material in the Royal Geographical Society, that Hayward managed to do a good deal of exploring north of the Hindu Kush and the Karakoram, as well as making a detailed survey south of the mountains. Hayward's comments on the cruelty and oppression of Ranbir Singh, of his designs on Yasin, and of his desire to have some sway *north* of the Karakoram, were not the kind of information which the authorities in Jammu – or Peshawar – would have liked disclosed. In fact, in a letter written to Murchison from Srinagar on 11 May 1870 Hayward, after referring to the progress of the 'Pamir Expedition up to the Middle of March', and stating that he had seen Mayo at Murree, went on to say: 'You will see at once why the Kashmir authorities were so anxious to dissuade me from any attempt to penetrate beyond Gilgit.' Even more awkward must have been the next comment. 'I might have allowed myself to more than hint at the presence of Russian agents who are now in Kashmir, of the spies and agents of the Maharajah who are now in Central Asia, and with a system of communication kept up with Tashkent and the Court of Bokhara by this route of Gilgit, Yassin & Kilat.' In an earlier letter to another correspondent, Hayward had said: 'I had a very satisfactory interview with Lord Mayo, and am anxiously awaiting the result of the arrangements with the Maharajah at Sialkot.' It is fairly clear therefore that Hayward became a man who knew, or suspicioned, too much, and became more of a liability than an asset to the authorities in Peshawar once he started to spot the weakness of using Ranbir Singh as a satellite.

13 Others in the party included Tara Sing, 'A Rawalpindi Merchant, who had previously visited Yarkand, and who on this occasion acted as Treasurer'; and Corporal Rhind, 92nd Highlanders, 'as Camp Sergeant

and piper', whose wearing of the kilt on at least one occasion caused much consternation. 'The locals fancied that he had forgotten his breeks in the hurry of preparing for the visit', Biddulph Diary, Hereford County Record Office.

14 The second Forsyth mission was well reported in various accounts. In addition to the official reports, and addresses to the Royal Geographical society, members of the mission kept diaries and wrote books. The quotations and sources to the end of this chapter are cited collectively as Forsyth Reports. In particular, Biddulph's Diary is valuable in describing the alternations between stimulus and *ennui* so characteristic of intelligence operations. The diary records the frustrations of a situation where, having marched to Kashgar, across the Kuen Luen and through Yarkand – 'a solid, compact, prosperous town' – Biddulph was forced to kick his heels in Kashgar. He watched Yaqub Beg's army drilling – 'in that well known military formation of sixes and sevens' – and, for a few days managed to travel north of Kashgar, where he saw an eagle flown at a wolf. He witnessed the treaty ceremony between Forsyth and Yaqub Beg and was told by the former that he was to gain 'a complete knowledge of the Russian Frontiers'. But Yaqub Beg kept so close a watch on the party that Biddulph brought back from Kashgaria accounts of misfortune rather than Russian operations. 'At Yangi Hissar Gordon was sketching and, as usual, a lot of men came round him, among them one who, to Gordon's surprise began to read out the names written under one of the sketches, apparently forgetting himself. Gordon at once turned round and said: "You are an Englishman", at which the man put his hands to his face and ran away. Gordon came in to breakfast, and when he came out, the man had gone. There is little doubt he is an Englishman. I fancy his history is that he deserted during the Crimean War, was sent into Central Asia to get him out of the way, deserted again from the Russians, and is now living in misery, ashamed to acknowledge himself to us.'

15 In June 1875 Bellew, in London, wrote an official appreciation: 'A Consideration of the Present Anglo-Russian Position in Central Asia'. This appreciation is a classic example of agents' inability to be consistently objective. Bellew wrote very sensibly about the effectiveness of Russian rule in the Khanates – largely because it consisted of 'a civilised government and a disciplined army' – but could not see that the lack of these elements weakened the British position on the Northern Frontier, above all in relation to Ranbir Singh and Sher Ali. Biddulph and other members of the second Forsyth mission had made it clear in their reports that Russian rule was effective and that Yaqub Beg had no wish to quarrel with his powerful neighbours. Further, the experiences of Forsyth's agents in 1874 had shown that Sher Ali did not want them in Wakhan, however much he – and they – believed it to be Afghan territory. Sher

Ali in fact refused to let the agents return to India via Kabul. Even Forsyth reported that the Russians regarded Wakhan as 'independent', and it was the ruler of that state who saw himself as feudatory to Bokhara. Biddulph's diary also makes it clear that Russian intrigue in Kashgaria and in the ill-defined territories to the west, was something with which local rulers were well acquainted. Despite all this, Bellew argued that Ranbir Singh should stabilise the situation for the British in India by annexing all the territory up to the Hindu Kush. What Bellew quite overlooked or ignored in making this recommendation was that Ranbir Singh could not annex on this scale without coming into conflict with Sher Ali. Hayward had noted this difficulty in 1870 – not only his fate but his appreciations seem, however, to have been ignored by the agents of the mid-1870s.

6   The Cold War, 1860s and 1870s

1 Robert Blake, *Disraeli*, Eyre & Spottiswoode, 1966, p. 658.
2 The correspondence relating to Lytton's appointment is to be found in the original among the Lytton Papers now in the Hertford County Record Office (a collection supplemented by material still at Knebworth), and in Lady Betty Balfour's edition of her father's letters. This material is perhaps the most revealing indication of Disraeli's intensely subjective approach to imperial affairs which has so far come to light. The correspondence is revelatory not only of Lytton's self-confessed neurasthenia, but also of his complete unwillingness and entire unfitness for the position of Viceroy. It is Lytton throughout, writing from Lisbon in November 1875 with its 'irregular work and light responsibility', who stresses to his implacable patron not only his 'absolute ignorance of every fact and question concerning India, as well as [his] *total want* of experience in every kind of *administrative* business', but also the fact that his illness, 'extremely painful, enfeebling and depressing', is 'liable to be acutely aggravated by any great anxiety', so much so that 'occasionally, indeed, it incapacitates me altogether for the most ordinary mental labour' (author's italics). To all of this Disraeli replied the following month 'We have carefully considered your letter, and have not changed our opinion'. As Lord Blake says of Disraeli in his biography (p. 766): 'To him, more than to most politics avowedly was "the great game" '. Lytton's neurotic introspection – the remark about his personality will be found in a letter to his daughter, in vol. II, p. 424, of the letters – should arouse pity. In Disraeli it apparently aroused hopes of a pliant agent.
3 Alder, *Northern Frontier*, p. 109 expands on this point.
4 Letter to Spencer Wilkinson of 18 November 1896, Roberts Papers in the possession of the Ogilby Trust.

5 Lytton Papers, Hertford County Record Office.

6 The original dispatches between the British and Russian governments for the period in question are to be found in various sources, principally the Public Record Office (in the Foreign Office Series No. 65 – Russia), and in the several series of 'Correspondence Respecting Central Asia, presented to both Houses of Parliament by Command of Her Majesty'. It is in the latter (C-2164; No. 62) that we find a letter from Gorchakov to Schuvalov (once again 'gracing London drawing-rooms') which reads as follows (the 'double date' of the Old Russian and Western calendars does not affect the points at issue).

St Petersburgh, February 3/15 1876
His Majesty the Emperor has learned with much interest the contents of the Memorandum accompanying a despatch from Lord Derby, which Lord A. Loftus read, in my absence, to the Acting Minister for Foreign Affairs.

I enclose herewith a copy of this document, which is a reply to the Memorandum dated the 11th May 1875, which your Excellency was instructed to communicate to the Principal Secretary of State of Her Britannic Majesty regarding the relations of the two Governments in Central Asia.

Our august Master has learnt with satisfaction the friendly desire, therein expressed, to prevent, by frank explanations, any cause of misunderstanding between the two Cabinets. His Majesty appreciates likewise the breadth of view with which Lord Derby puts on one side discussions of detail and restrictions which are inapplicable in view of the ill-defined conditions of the countries over which the two Governments have to exercise their influence.

Have the goodness to inform his Excellency, by order of our august Master, that we entirely agree in the conclusion that, while maintaining, on either side, the arrangement come to as regards the limits of Afghanistan, which is to remain outside the sphere of Russian action, the two Cabinets should regard as terminated the discussions relative to the intermediate zone, which have been recognized as unpractical; that, while retaining entire freedom of action, they should be guided by a mutual desire to pay due regard to their respective interests and necessities, by avoiding, as far as possible, any immediate contact with each other, and any collisions between the Asiatic States placed within the circle of their influence.

We are convinced that by keeping to this principle, and cultivating feelings of equity and reciprocal goodwill, the two Cabinets will succeed in consolidating the friendly relations so happily established between them, for the advantage of the general peace in Europe and Asia.

Your Excellency can renew to Lord Derby the assurance that he may reckon on our frank co-operation for this purpose.

Accept, &c.

The letter has been given in full because it illustrates the extreme difficulty of deciding what the participants knew, let alone believed, or chose to believe, or communicated to each other and to their rivals. Setting aside the diplomatically ambiguous – and indeed almost contradictory – wording of the letter as a whole, it is reasonable to assume that Gorchakov and Schuvalov, and certainly Kaufmann and his colleagues, felt that they had some justification in regarding a mission to Kabul as in no way in breach of the stipulation that Afghanistan 'is to remain outside the sphere of Russian action'. Derby's memorandum of 25 October 1875 to which Gorchakov refers (C–2164: No. 54) had made it clear that the British government based its policy on the Russian government's pledge 'not to extend the frontiers of Russia beyond their present limits in Central Asia, either on the side of Bokhara or on that of Krasnovodsk and the Attrek'. Derby then played, unwittingly or not, into Gorchakov's hands. In his memorandum, Derby turned the 1873 Agreement about a neutral zone – made on the basis that the Oxus should not necessarily be taken as defining Afghanistan's northern limits, the formula for which was 'the territories in the actual possession of Sher Ali should be considered as forming the limits of Afghanistan' – into a quite different set of ambiguities. Derby declared that in 1873, the British government abandoned the idea of a neutral zone and 'insisted on including Badakshan and Wakhan within the limits of Afghanistan, because such delimitation was, in their view, strictly in accordance with historical facts, and, therefore necessary in order to satisfy the legitimate claims of the Ameer'. To assert this was to go far beyond the claims actually made in 1873; the hand of the India Office had been at work on Derby – or his draftsman. Assertions about 'historical facts' and 'legitimate claims' therefore led Derby to conclude by stating 'Her Majesty's Government have always deprecated the further extension of Russian territory towards the Afghan borders . . . They have now received with the most sincere satisfaction the assurances conveyed in Prince Gortchakow's despatch as to the enlightened conviction of His Imperial Majesty that such extension, either on the side of Bokhara, of Krasnovodsk, or of the Attrek, is contrary to Russian interests, and that formal orders have been given that all future action in those regions is to be strictly confined to the defence of existing limits and the protection of property and commerce from pillage and brigandage'.

By February 1876 the British and Russian governments were therefore thoroughly at cross purposes. Setting duplicity aside, the Russians probably did believe they could push on to the Oxus (as the southern limit of 'Bokhara'); extend their sway among the Turcomans (since references to the area east of the Caspian had been left so vague); and have some relations with Kabul. The British, especially the Anglo-Indians, believed this gave Sher Ali territory north of the Oxus; all, save Salisbury perhaps, believed Russia had no right to any relations with Kabul. None of this confusion might have mattered so much if Derby, Salisbury and Lytton had been properly in touch at the critical times, and if there had been any acceptance on the British side that the documents in question were capable of more than interpretation. Thus these documents are not only crucial for the period in question, but are important for understanding the 1880s. At the time of the 1885 Penjdeh incident, several British officials not only believed that the 1873 Agreement remained in force, but that Afghan territory lay on the right bank of the Oxus.

7 Lytton Papers.
8 Royal Archives, B. 57.22.
9 Kelly Prosons Day, *Life of Sir Louis Cavagnari*, 1881.
10 Lady Betty Balfour, *Personal and Literary Letters of Robert, First Earl Lytton*, 1906, vol. II, p. 120.
11 'British Academy Proceedings', vol. XXVIII, p. 61.
12 George Douglas Campbell, 8th Duke of Argyll, *The Eastern Question*, Strahan, 1879, vol. II, p. 196.
13 G. D. H. Howard, *Splendid Isolation*, Macmillan, 1967, p. XIII.
14 Figures cited are to be found in the 1877 volume of 'The Progress of Russia in Central Asia'. It has been persuasively argued that the idea of large-scale offensive operations (from India) against a major European military power (Russia) dated from the 1860s when Sir Charles Mac-Gregor, in the Quartermaster-General's Intelligence Branch in Simla, wrote schemes about a four corps field army which bear a close resemblance to the strategy which was actually formulated in the 1880s (*Historical Journal*, vol. XII, no. 1). But apart from the fact that Mac-Gregor, as a strategist, was a Russophobe of the first degree, this is not even circumstantial evidence of plans, concerted or otherwise, to mount a major pre-emptive campaign against Russia. A four corps army meant something in the region of 100,000 men. A campaign based on Afghanistan was, however, another possibility, and Maurice Cowling has said that Lytton was sent to India for this purpose ('Lytton, the Cabinet, and the Russians', *English Historical Review*, 1961, p. 61). It seems apparent from the Lytton Papers – and indeed the published *Letters* – that Lytton, in his view, was sent to India by Disraeli not only to cause a noise and splash, but to checkmate Kaufmann, by making Sher Ali come to heel.
15 Cavagnari's sources of intelligence were so poor that he was forced

either to drop, or to fabricate, a case. Nor was he a beneficiary of intelligence from the one source which for long had tried to discover what was going on in Afghanistan. This was the native agent in Meshed: he came under Thomson in Tehran, and the latter's reports to the Foreign Office throughout 1878 give a good indication of the level at which native agents were forced to operate. The Meshed Agent had to rely on a 'Kandahar Pedlar who is on intimate terms with me'. The Meshed Agent made an accurate assessment of what actually took place in Kabul during the time of Stolietev's visit, but it was an assessment which Lytton refused to consider.

16 Loftus had provided Salisbury with news of Abramov's column by 16 July. Moreover, the 'Intelligence Branch of the Quartermaster-General's Department, Horse Guards, War Office' regularly received and translated accounts published by the Imperial Russian Geographical Society of reconaissance operations by Kaufmann's subordinates.

17 Chamberlain to Lord Lawrence, 26 January 1878.

18 Cowling, 'Lytton, the Cabinet, and the Russians'.

19 Royal Archives.

20 Blake, *Disraeli*, p. 662.

21 G. W. Forest, *Life of Sir Neville Chamberlain*, Blackwood, 1909, p. 477.

22 Ibid., p. 478.

23 Ibid., p. 494.

24 Ibid., p. 479.

25 Ibid., p. 480.

26 Cowling, 'Lytton, the Cabinet and the Russians', p. 72. Salisbury was very unhappy at this decision, but did not fight it. The 19 October Cabinet is in fact a classic instance of government in London – and specifically Salisbury at the Foreign Office – denying the man on the spot his freedom to act – until the last moment, when he regains it.

27 India Office Records.

28 Lord Roberts, *Forty-One Years in India*, Macmillan, 1914, pp. 395–6.

7   The Cold War, the 1880s

1 A. J. P. Taylor, *Bismarck*, Hamish Hamilton, 1955 edition, p. 210.

2 Sir Henry Rawlinson, *England and Russia in the East*, John Murray, 1875, p. 322.

3 M. S. Rajan, *Journal of Contemporary History*, vol. 4, no. 1, p. 94.

4 'Précis on Afghan Affairs, 1879–1893', p. 130 (a collection in the Foreign Office Library).

5 Ibid.

6 Memorandum of 20 July 1878.

7 Sir Thomas Holdich, *Indian Borderland*, Methuen, 1909, pp. 96–105.

8 Ibid.
9 Gladstone to the Queen, 12 March 1885 (Royal Archives).
10 Taylor, *Bismarck*.
11 This is a curious message. So far as can be seen, Dufferin put this question to Ponsonby, for immediate transmission to the Queen. It was Kimberley nevertheless who replied the same day (Royal Archives).
12 Royal Archives.
13 Holdich, *Indian Borderland*, p. 129.
14 Holdich, *Indian Borderland*, p. 131.
15 Taylor, *Bismarck*.
16 Holdich, *Indian Borderland*, p. 135.
17 Sir West Ridgeway, *The New Afghan Frontier The Nineteenth Century*, October 1887.
18 Ibid.
19 Holdich, *Indian Borderland*, p. 153.
20 C. E. Yate, *Northern Afghanistan; Letters from the Boundary Commission*, Blackwood, 1888.
21 Ibid.
22 'Proceedings of the Royal Geographical Society', January 1884, pp. 17–18.
23 Lockhart and Woodthorpe, *Gilgit Mission*.
24 Ibid.
25 Ibid.
26 Ibid.
27 Ibid.
28 Ibid.
29 H. A. Lamb, *China-India Border*, Oxford, 1964, p. 42.
30 India Office Records.

8   *Novitiate*

1 Letter to Emily Younghusband, 7 January 1883.
2 Seaver, *Francis Younghusband*, p. 93.
3 Francis Younghusband, *The Heart of A Continent*, John Murray, 1896, p. 211.
4 Ibid., p. 213.
5 Seaver, *Francis Younghusband*, p. 55.
6 Younghusband, *Heart of A Continent*, pp. 35–8.
7 H. A. Lamb, *Britain and Chinese Central Asia: The Road to Lhasa 1767 to 1905*, 1960.
8 A good sample of the level of intelligence about Afghanistan can be found in the Peshawar confidential Diary for June 1888 (FO/65/1352). Although Colonel Waterfield, the Commissioner, was half Afghan, his

sources were no better than that of 'an intelligent man in the Native Army', or 'Abdul Rahman, formerly an Hospital Assistant in Peshawar, and now the physician and surgeon of the Amir's household'. The result, despite much intelligent surmise based on instinct and experience, is inevitably a hotchpotch of rumour and guesswork.

9 Memoir, *The Times*, 1 December 1888.
10 Royal Archives (N.44.5).
11 There is a copy of the instructions, together with Younghusband's maps, in the Royal Geographical Society. His manuscript diaries of the mission (also in the R.G.S.) are, however, a more revealing source of information.
12 Diary, Younghusband, 14 September 1889.
13 Younghusband, *Heart of A Continent*, p. 263.
14 Diary, Younghusband, 16 September 1889.
15 Younghusband, *Heart of A Continent*, p. 250.
16 Seaver, *Francis Younghusband*, p. 113.
17 Younghusband, *Heart of A Continent*, p. 251.
18 Seaver, *Francis Younghusband*, p. 123.
19 Younghusband's first encounter with Safdar Ali (Diary, 14 October 1889) demanded the steadiest nerves. 'After a time we saw a tower at the top of a cliff and as we came closer saw that this whole line of cliff where it was accessible was covered by a loop holed wall at the upper end of which was a second tower . . . This was the den of the Kanjuti robbers'. With his Gurkhas piqueting the cliff, Younghusband sought admission. 'Experience has shown me that it does not do to appear to be in a hurry on these occasions.' A sentry made as if to seize him. 'But the man sprang aside again with a laugh & seeing it was intended for a joke I laughed too. It might have cost the gentleman dear though if he had kept it up longer, for he would certainly have had a bullet through his head from my Goorkhas who were just behind me, if not from my revolver.'
20 Younghusband, *Heart of A Continent*, p. 272.
21 Alder, *Northern Frontier*, p. 211.
22 Seaver, *Francis Younghusband*, p. 137.
23 Younghusband *Heart of A Continent*, p. 277.

9   Crisis on the Pamirs

1 The manuscript report is dated 30 December 1889. The printed copy is in the India Office Library.
2 Nisbet's praise is contained in a covering letter to Mortimer Durand.
3 'Mission Report', p. 66.
4 Younghusband, *Light of Experience*, p. 53.

5 Ibid., pp. 50–1.

6 Alder, *Northern Frontier*, p. 207.

7 Ibid., p. 153, citing R. Mitchell. 'The Regions of the Upper Oxus', 'Proceedings of the Royal Geographical Society', June 1884, p. 489.

8 'Royal Geographical Society Supplementary Papers', vol. I, part I, 1884, p. 243.

9 Alder, *Northern Frontier*, p. 201, citing Ridgeway to Durand, 23 October 1885.

10 'The Progress of Russia in Central Asia: 1886 Report'; p. 17.

11 Morier [St Petersburg] to Foreign Office, 29 September 1886.

12 Dufferin to Cross [Secretary of State], 8 September 1887.

13 'Mission Report'.

14 'W. J. Cunningham Esq., Offtg. Secretary to the Government of India, Foreign Department to Captain F. E. Younghusband, on Special Duty', Simla, 23 June 1890 (India Office Records).

15 To Emily Younghusband, from Kashgar, 26 May 1891.

16 Younghusband, *Light of Experience*, p. 56.

17 Younghusband's address, 'Proceedings of the Royal Geographical Society', April 1892, p. 229.

18 Younghusband's report to the Foreign Department, 18 November 1891, summarising his activities in 1890 and the early part of 1891 (India Office Records).

19 Ibid.

20 Lansdowne to Cross, 11 March 1891.

21 Alder, *Northern Frontier*, pp. 224–5.

22 Foreign Office memorandum of 30 January 1892 (Foreign Office Library). The otherwise trivial reference to Davison is given because it sufficiently conveys, for the period, the collective Foreign Office, and indeed India Office, dislike of agents, accredited or otherwise, attempting to bind the Indian and Home governments to policies and decisions based on guesswork and prejudice.

23 Younghusband, *Heart of A Continent*, pp. 325–31. The account has been compressed, but the text is entirely Younghusband's. There are many official papers on the arrest, but this account fairly represents what took place.

24 Letters to Younghusband's father and sister Emily, 4, 11, 21 and 27 August 1891.

25 FO 65/1417 is the main source for Salisbury and Morier acting in tandem to defuse the Pamirs crisis. Salisbury's views on the necessity of a working relationship if not a *rapprochement* with Russia have already been made clear. Morier, who had been Ambassador since November 1885, had long been Russophil, governed by the belief that European security depended on something more than a *rapprochement*, one which

nevertheless would be wrecked if disputes about India were allowed to distort the British foreign policy. See, in this connection: Agath Rahm, *Sir Robert Morier: Envoy and Ambassador in the Age of Imperialism 1876–1893*, Oxford, 1973.

26 *Letters of Queen Victoria*, third series, vol. I, pp. 193–4.

27 Younghusband, *Light of Experience*, p. 62.

28 Partly because of the relative freedom which members of the St Petersburg embassy enjoyed in their contact with the Russian government at various levels, and in their travels. The War Office in London, despite the forward strategies which were concocted in Simla, continued to analyse objectively Russian movements towards and on the Pamirs.

29 The summary of events which follows is taken from FO 65/1413–1435. This collection includes material from all the interested parties.

30 A. J. P. Taylor, *The Struggle for Mastery in Europe*, Oxford, 1954, p. 339.

31 Cab. 37/33. A summary of events dated 30 January 1893.

32 Morier to Salisbury, 27 January 1892.

33 C. J. Lowe, *Reluctant Imperialists*, Routledge, 1967, vol. II, p. 95.

34 Rosebery to Howard, 13 November 1893.

35 Lansdowne note to Foreign Office, 29 June 1894.

10   The End of the Affair?

1 We may read, thanks to Peter Fleming, a curious document in the India Office Records, namely a memorandum by Lord Midleton (the former St John Brodrick) entitled: 'Relations of Lord Curzon as Viceroy of India with the British Government 1902–5'. It is marked 'secret' and, the most important factor, further marked: 'Seen and approved by the Earl of Balfour [A. J. Balfour] June 1926'. This memorandum is a sustained attack on a man who had lately died (20 March 1925), and its timing and contents are alike indicative of long-pent rancour bursting forth. The details, however, are not seriously in dispute, and although it is just possible, if one is a pedant, to say that Curzon resigned in 1905, there is no doubt that his refusal to accept the Cabinet's rulings then on various issues reflected Balfour's determination to get rid of him. The account in the 1926 Memorandum of Curzon's behaviour in 1904 regarding Tibet is a sustained example of double-think, an attempt to make Curzon the scapegoat – twenty-two years after the event.

2 Younghusband, *Light of Experience*, pp. 70–1.

3 The memorandum in question (India Office Records) forms a classic demonstration of the agent's alienation from the bureaucrat. Lyall, Stewart and their kind were not bureaucrats in fact but, in the India

Office of the mid-1890s, they had grown cautious at last. Stewart was the most critical of Younghusband's strategic notions. In his memorandum of 26 March 1895, Stewart wrote 'Lord Roberts's remarks on Captain Younghusband's lecture to the Geographical Society last night form the text of *The Times*' article. These remarks will be telegraphed all over the world and to India, and the Russian Foreign Office will see that the Pamir settlement has done nothing to lessen the Russophobia which exists in India and to some extent in this country, or to mitigate the craze of the people who think that the only way to defend India is to lock up an army in the regions of the Hindoo Koosh, where the advantage of our organization and arms must practically be nullified and lost.'

What principally seems to have irritated the India Office about Younghusband was his conviction that Russia still threatened India, not his desire to strengthen Chitral. Certainly Younghusband's annotated copy of the official papers relating to the campaigns which followed the siege of Chitral reveal an outlook which did tend to see a Russian under every rock.

4 *The Geographical Journal*, vol. vi, 1895, p. 422.
5 Younghusband, *Light of Experience*, pp. 69–70.
6 Seaver, *Francis Younghusband*, p. 70.
7 Younghusband, *Light of Experience*, p. 72.
8 Seaver, *Francis Younghusband*, p. 167.

11   Tibet: The Curtain-Raiser

1 Fleming, *Bayonets to Lhasa*, p. 90.
2 Salisbury to the Queen, 27 February 1897.
3 For Curzon's views on the Gulf and British relations with the Powers see B. C. Busch, *Britain and the Persian Gulf, 1894–1914*, University of California Press, 1967.
4 Sir Thomas Raleigh (ed.), *Lord Curzon in India*, 1906, p. 587.
5 The letters to Roberts are amongst the papers held by the Ogilby Trust.
6 George Monger, *The End of Isolation*, Nelson, 1963, pp. 97–9.
7 Taylor, *Struggle for Mastery in Europe*, pp. 346 & 370–1.
8 For Balfour's overseas policies as a whole – such as they were – see Denis Judd, *Balfour and the British Empire*, Macmillan, 1968.
9 Dame Eileen Younghusband provided this comment.
10 Fleming, *Bayonets to Lhasa*, p. 293.
11 Monger, *Isolation*, p. 108.
12 A. P. Thornton, *The Imperial Idea and its Enemies*, p. 125.
13 WO/106/48.

14 Ibid.
15 Cab. 37/64.
16 B. H. Sumner, 'Tsardom and Imperialism in the Far East and Middle East, 1880–1914', Raleigh Lecture on History, 1940, p. 27.
17 See for example, Lessar's 'Military Routes to the Indo-Afghan Frontier', from 'Russian Official Records of Geographical, Topographical and Statistical Materials on Asia' (FO 65/1413).
18 Cited in Sumner, 'Tsardom and Imperialism', pp. 42–3.
19 P. Mehra, *The Younghusband Expedition*, Asia Publishing, 1969, p. 156.
20 Ibid., p. 158.
21 Sir Louis Dane, 'Record and Reactions: A Footnote to History', *Journal of the Royal Central Asian Society*.
22 Lamb, *Britain and Chinese Central Asia*, p. 266.
23 Fleming, *Bayonets to Lhasa*, p. 30.
24 Chapman correspondence in WO 106/16.
25 'Norzanoff, Dorjieff and Missions Between Russia and Tibet.' This imaginative piece of work (India Office Records) was concocted by the Indian Government Foreign Department in April 1902.
26 Lamb, *Britain and Chinese Central Asia*, p. 266.
27 April 1902 compilation as given above.
28 Kintup would have ended his days in poverty had not F. M. Bailey, who served in the mission to Tibet, found and succoured him. The Great Game was hard on all. (Information kindly provided by the late the Hon. Mrs Irma Bailey.)
29 H. R. Bower, *Across Tibet*, Rivington Percival, 1894, p. 97.
30 April 1902 Compilation.
31 Ibid.
32 Bower, *Across Tibet*, p. 94.
33 April 1902 Compilation.
34 Ibid.
35 Das, treated by Kipling as a joke Indian, was a very considerable scholar of the Tibetan language, and knew the country well from clandestine visits, as his journals in the Royal Geographical Society clearly reveal.
36 April 1902 Compilation.
37 McSwiney's report is in the India Office Library.
38 'Military Report on Sikkim and the Chumbi Valley', 1903 (India Office Library).
39 D. Dilks, *Lord Curzon in India*, Hart Davis, vol. 11, 1970, pp. 78–96.
40 Monger, *Isolation*, pp. 115–6.
41 Mehra, *Younghusband Expedition*, p. 107.
42 Ibid., p. 109.
43 Ibid., p. 111.
44 Ibid., p. 111 note 62.

12 *Tibet: Younghusband Digs his Grave*

1 Monger, *Isolation*, p. 115.
2 Fleming, *Bayonets to Lhasa*, p. 71.
3 Younghusband, *Light of Experience*, p. 80.
4 Ibid., p. 81.
5 Mehra, *Younghusband Expedition*, p. 183.
6 Ibid., p. 184.
7 The Instructuions are to be found in 'Papers Relating to Tibet', ed. 1920, pp. 198–200.
8 Cited in Fleming, *Bayonets to Lhasa*, p. 71.
9 Younghusband's telegrams and letters for this period are in the Curzon Papers (India Office Records).
10 Monger, *Isolation*, p. 123.
11 Mehra, *Younghusband Expedition*, p. 198.
12 Cab 37/70.
13 Ibid.
14 Monger, *Isolation*, pp 135–6.
15 Cited in Fleming *Bayonets to Lhasa*, p. 95.

13 *Tibet: Verdict and Vindication*

1 Cited in Fleming, *Bayonets to Lhasa*, p. 216.
2 Diary of Lieutenant F. M. Bailey, 32nd Sikh Pioneers.
3 Diary of Regimental Sergeant-Major P. A. Coath (courtesy of the Royal Fusiliers Regimental Museum).
4 Fleming, *Bayonets to Lhasa*, p. 141.
5 Younghusband *Light of Experience*, p. 206.
6 Ibid., p. 89.
7 Bailey, Diary.
8 Ibid.
9 Cited in Mehra, *Younghusband Expedition*, p. 223.
10 Monger, *Isolation*, pp. 160–1.
11 Cited in Fleming *Bayonets to Lhasa*, p. 174.
12 Cab 37/70.
13 Curzon Papers
14 Cab 37/71.
15 Ibid.
16 Ibid.
17 Brodrick to Curzon, 8 December 1904 (India Office Records).
18 Mehra, *Younghusband Expedition*, p. 229.
19 Ibid., p. 394.
20 The correspondence is among the Curzon Papers.
21 There is another large batch of material on the Russian threat to India

and the measures which should be taken to meet it for the period in question. In May 1904, for example, the CID had printed for the Cabinet the record of a 'War Game played at Simla in 1903'. The Russians, committing up to 300,000 men, defeated the British outright in a series of engagements designed by GHQ in Simla to show that neither Afghanistan nor the Northern Frontier states could be relied on, and that a British and Indian force of approximately 190,000 could only gain a decisive advantage over the Russians if it invested Afghanistan well in advance of any Russian move. The War Game was also an elaborate if clumsy argument for the rapid reinforcement from the Empire as a whole of the Continental Army in India.

22 Broderick (Lord Midleton) memorandum of June 1926.
23 Cited in Fleming, *Bayonets to Lhasa*, p. 244.
24 Cited in Mehra, *Younghusband Expedition*, p. 229.
24 Lamb, *Britain and Chinese Central Asia*, p. 302.
26 Ibid.
27 Francis Younghusband, *India and Tibet*, John Murray, 1910, p. 306.
28 Younghusband's letter is in the Curzon Papers.
29 Monger, *Isolation*, pp. 170–1.
30 Ibid., p. 171.
31 Cited in Mehra, *Younghusband Expedition*, p. 255.
32 Cab 37/72.
33 Younghusband's *India and Tibet*, p. 333.
34 Godley to Curzon, 16 December 1904 (India Office Records).

Index

Godley, Arthur, 177, 188–9, 207, 208
Godwin-Austin (K2), 36–7, 107
Gorchakov, Prince, 25, 47, 48, 49–50, 68, 75
Gordon, Major T. E., 41–2, 43, 44, 56, 118, 145
Grant, Charles, 19
Granville, George Leveson-Gower, 2nd Earl, 47, 48, 72, 80, 119, 120
Great Pamirs, 32, 40, 43
Great Trigonometrical Survey of India, 28
Grey, Charles, 2nd Earl, 19
Griffin, Lepel, 58, 70
Gromchevsky, Captain, 110, 111–13, 116, 117, 123, 125
Gulab Singh, Rajah of Jammu, 26, 27
Guru, incident at, 195–6
Gyantse, Younghusband's march to, 190, 191, 194, 197

Habibullah, Amir for Afghanistan, 146, 157–8
Haines, General, 57, 58, 61
Hamilton, Lord George, 156, 159, 160, 162, 167, 175, 176, 177, 178; and the Tibet mission, 179, 180, 181, 183, 187, 188
Harcourt, Sir William, 139
Hartington, Lord, 55
Hastings, Warren, 8
Hatzfeldt (German Ambassador), 134
Havildar, the: missions beyond Northern Frontier, 39–40
Hayward, George, 28, 29–32, 38, 39, 40, 74, 90, 97; traverse of Kashgaria, 37
Hedin, Sven, 124
Helmand desert, 18
Herat: secured by Afghanistan, 22–3

Hicks-Beach, Sir Michael, 154
Hindu Kush, 36, 54, 58, 127
Holdich, Sir Thomas, 78–80, 83, 86, 130
Holland, Henry Richard Fox, 3rd Baron, 19
Hume, Joseph, 19
Hunza, 92, 102, 103, 106, 111, 112, 135

Ianov, Colonel, 113, 126–8, 130, 131, 132, 133, 137, 138
Ibrahim Khan, 41
India: Curzon as Viceroy of, 154–5; field army in, 11–12; internal security, and Afghanistan, 22, 23
Ishkoman Pass, 42–3

Jameson, Dr Starr, 147–8
Jameson Raid, 4, 199–200
Jammu, 27, 30, 36, 44, 116; journey to Yarkand from, 34–5
Japan: and Russia, 161, 166, 206–7
Jenkins, Colonel, 66–7

K2 (Godwin-Austin), 36–7, 107
Kabul Residency, attack on: in the Second Afghan War, 69–70
Karakoram mountains, 36–7; Younghusband's exploration of, 106–8, 117
Karakoram Pass, 37, 100, 101, 106, 107
Kashgar, 31, 33, 38, 41, 42, 104–5; Forsyth missions to, 30, 32, 36, 38, 39, 41–2, 44, 75; trade with, 26; Younghusband in, 123–6; see also Singkiang.
Kashgaria, 35, 39, 41, 118; Shaw and Hayward's travels in, 28–30
Kashmir, 18, 23, 26, 43, 104, 148; Younghusband's mission to, 102